I0881546

WIDOW CITY

The Early Modern Exchange

SELECTED TITLES

The Age of Subtlety: Nature and Rhetorical Conceits in Early Modern Europe, Javier Patiño Loira

Redreaming the Renaissance: Essays on History and Literature in Honor of Guido Ruggiero, edited by Mary Lindemann and Deanna Shemek

Ordering Customs: Ethnographic Thought in Early Modern Venice, Kathryn Taylor

The Waxing of the Middle Ages: Revisiting Late Medieval France, edited by Tracy Adams and Charles-Louis Morand-Métivier

Gendering the Renaissance: Text and Context in Early Modern Italy, edited by Meredith K. Ray and Lynn Lara Westwater

Storytelling in Sixteenth-Century France: Negotiating Shifting Forms, edited by Emily E. Thompson

England's Asian Renaissance, edited by Su Fang Ng and Carmen Nocentelli

Performative Polemic: Anti-Absolutist Pamphlets and Their Readers in Late Seventeenth-Century France, Kathrina Ann LaPorta

Widow City

Gender, Emotion, and Community
in the Italian Renaissance

Anna Wainwright

UNIVERSITY OF DELAWARE | UNIVERSITY OF DELAWARE PRESS

Newark

Library of Congress Cataloging-in-Publication Data

Names: Wainwright, Anna, author.
Title: Widow city : gender, emotion, and community in the Italian Renaissance / Anna Wainwright.
Description: Newark, DE : University of Delaware Press, [2025] | Series: The early modern exchange | Includes bibliographical references and index.
Identifiers: LCCN 2024043280 | ISBN 9781644533604 (cloth) | ISBN 9781644533598 (paperback) | ISBN 9781644533611 (epub) | ISBN 9781644533628 (pdf)
Subjects: LCSH: Widows in literature. | Widows' writings, Italian—History and criticism. | Italian literature—History and criticism.
Classification: LCC PQ4055.W53 W35 2025 | DDC 850.92—dc23/eng/20250115
LC record available at https://lccn.loc.gov/2024043280

A British Cataloging-in-Publication record for this book is available from the British Library.

∞ The paper used in this publication meets the requirements of the American National Standard for Information Sciences—Permanence of Paper for Printed Library Materials, ANSI Z39.48-1992.

udpress.udel.edu

Distributed worldwide by Rutgers University Press

To Martha Fay, vedovetta feroce

Contents

Acknowledgments

After many years spent considering the various communities I examine in this book—emotional, social, literary—I feel very lucky to have myself been welcomed into a community of scholars and friends both kind and extraordinary from my first days as a student of Italian literature. I owe the greatest debt to Virginia Cox, who has answered every question, email, and random query over the past decade and a half on the topic of widowhood and a million others with thoughtful, productive answers and infinite patience. She continues to be a most inspiring interlocutor, guide, and collaborator. I also owe deeply felt thanks to Jane Tylus for our conversations on literature, religion, and gender and her generous and frank guidance over the years, on this and other subjects. Gerry Milligan has always been a generous and incisive reader of my work and has helped to shape how I think about masculinity, dissimulation, and appearance in the Renaissance (along with many other things). Lina Bolzoni inspired and challenged me in both New York and Pisa and made me a bolder scholar.

For more than twenty years of council and friendship, I am most grateful to Elissa Weaver, my undergraduate advisor at the University of Chicago, and to Justin Steinberg, who has been a valued mentor and friend since then as well. I was a very lucky undergraduate to land in classes with you both. I am thankful to Shannon McHugh, whose mentorship and friendship know no bounds and with whom I look forward to collaborating for many years to come. My deep thanks also go to Jessica Goethals for her sage counsel, kindness, and friendship. Melissa Swain has read every word of this book and kept a loving-yet-sharp eye on my work; I will be forever grateful for her brilliance and friendship. Joseph Perna and Danielle Callegari have sustained me with advice, fellowship, brilliance, and fun throughout. Unn Falkeid introduced me to a new way of understanding the Italian Middle Ages, and our collaborations continue to make me think differently.

Many scholars in the field have proved crucial mentors and interlocutors. My heartfelt thanks to Teodolinda Barolini for her incisive comments on my chapters on Dante, Petrarch, and Boccaccio and the warm welcome she and her students have given me into their own intellectual community; to Grace Delmolino for talking Boccaccio with me; to Allison Levy for her counsel on studying widows and her remarkable and pathbreaking scholarship on the subject; to Sarah Gwyneth Ross for always offering an interesting and revelatory take; and to Lisa Sampson for opening up my understanding of how to read a Renaissance text. I am grateful for the intellectual (and emotional) community I have found at the University of New Hampshire, above all the remarkable and inspiring Amy Boylan. This book would not have been possible without the support of so many at UNH: Lisa Hartford, Nicole Gercke, Ann Zimo, Nora Draper, Paula Salvio, Elke Nash, Claudia Sbuttoni, Kristen Swann, Dennis Britton, Harriet Fertik, Michael Leese, Stephen and Kathy Brunet, Will Smiley, Madhavi Devasher, Cristina Faiver-Serna, Stephen Trzaskoma, and Scott Smith. Special thanks to Dean Michele Dillon, who has been an enthusiastic sponsor of this research, and to Katie Umans at the UNH Center for the Humanities. I am grateful to the community at the Norwegian Institute in Rome, who sustained me during my fellowship year there in 2019–2020. Generous support from the Research Council of Norway, the Mainzer Fellowship in Gender and Sexuality, the American Order of the Savoy Foundation, the Friends of FAI, the Di Croce Fellowship, the Gladys Krieble Delmas Foundation, and the Renaissance Society of America allowed me to pursue my research in the United States, France, Italy, and England. At the University of Delaware Press, I am deeply indebted to Julia Oestreich for her support, grace, and generosity and to Meredith Ray for her encouragement and belief in this project from the outset. I thank the anonymous readers for their wise and constructive feedback.

I am also profoundly grateful for the community of fierce women who have shaped who I am and what I like to think about: Martha Fay, Sara Dais, Lucy Wainwright Roche, Carol Fahey, Sloan Wainwright, Suzzy Roche, Marie Gamboa, Molly Greenberg, Marina Cummins, Bridget Early, Katy Early, Siân Evans, Roberta Inserra, Cecilia Amaducci, Liz Tunick Cedar, and Nina Braddock. And every day I thank my lucky stars for my smart, funny, and patient husband Jim; my beloved and wild children, Clara and Sylvie; and even little loving Pepper, whom we miss terribly. Without all of you, as the old saying goes, this would have been done a lot sooner.

Introduction

In her universal history *Le livre de la mutacion de la fortune* (The Book of the Mutability of Fortune), Christine de Pizan (1364–1430) offers her readers an elaborate description of her transformation by Fortune into a man following the death of her beloved husband: "Then my mistress, who diminishes the joy of many, came to me and touched me all over my body. . . . I awoke, and things were such that I felt immediately and without a doubt that I was entirely transformed. My limbs felt stronger than before and the sadness and weeping which had previously afflicted me, were gone. . . . I had become a true man."[1] This remarkable, evocative description of the author's transformation is often cited in scholarship on widowhood, and understandably so. It is a particularly generative point of entry into thinking through the view of widows as a discrete category of person in medieval and early modern Europe: a gendered category certainly, but one to which conventional rules of binary gender did not necessarily apply. As Leah DeVun has argued, "Our ideas about sex and anatomy are never just about a physical act or about our physical bodies; instead, they are always ideas about what it means to be human and what it means to be a self in relation to other selves and to the world."[2]

Though it is cloaked in the dreamy, allegorical imagery characteristic of de Pizan's writing, the sex change the author describes in these lines is also presented as a rather literal one. Blake Gutt observes that Christine suggests very clearly in the work that the categories "metaphor" and "truth" do not necessarily cancel each other out but can instead exist alongside each other: we thus do not necessarily have to assume that the writer is describing an exclusively metaphorical transformation, as we might once have.[3] The author's physical body, as well as spirit, is being described as no longer that of a woman but that of a man. This new, "male" Christine now possesses a deeper voice, a stronger, more muscular body, and a bolder heart.[4] This physical and spiritual change has been enabled by the death of the narrator's husband, an event so cataclysmic that it has provoked a profound cellular transformation in the widow left behind.[5]

Christine became a widow when she was only twenty-five years old.[6] Born in the Republic of Venice in 1364, she moved as a young child to Paris when her father Tommaso di Benvenuto da Pizzano, or Thomas de Pizan, accepted an appointment as astrologer at the court of King Charles V (1338–1380). She married another member of the court, the notary Etienne du Castel, when she was still a teenager in 1379; he died a decade later. Left to support her three children and her own recently widowed mother, she turned to writing for the court. She is generally considered the first woman writer in Europe to make a living off her work, and her identity as an author is tightly tied to the different ways she played with gender in her various works.[7] Following Gutt's analysis, I would suggest we take at face value de Pizan's description of true transformation for the narrator of the *Mutacion*, at once a metaphorical *and* realistic description of how the author conceptualized her own sex and gender identity, on both personal and universal levels, in the wake of her husband Etienne's death.

Christine's metamorphosis is illustrative of the extraordinary transformative possibilities for premodern women as they transitioned from the social category of "wife" to that of "widow." She was by no means the only writer to suggest that widows transformed into men following their husbands' deaths. Male authors before and after her, from San Bernardino da Siena (1380–1444) to Giangiorgio Trissino (1478–1550) to Giulio Cesare Cabei (1530–1622), toyed with the gender-fluid nature of widowhood, often arguing that widowed mothers should be both mother and father to their half-orphaned children. Indeed, in her important work on the intersection of masculinity and widowhood in Florentine portraiture, art historian Allison Levy has observed that "the widow, in her indeterminateness, might be read as hermaphroditic."[8] Writing in praise of the widowed poet Vittoria Colonna (1492–1547) in the sixteenth century, Michelangelo famously described her as "un uomo in una donna, anzi un dio" (a man in a woman, nay, a god), what Sara Adler calls an "androgynous über-woman."[9] Unlike the widows addressed by Bernardino, Trissino, and Cabei, Colonna herself did not have children; the perception of a gender-fluid nature of widowhood was not based solely on societal concerns over who might take up the paternal role after a man's death. The potential for a kind of rhetorical androgyny in widows was linked instead to something more abstract and even elevated, which Christine gets at in her description in *Mutacion*: a transformation of identity after the death of one's husband that is so radical it can push against the very boundaries of gender.

Widows and Meaning

The widow, by definition, is a figure associated with death and mourning. In the medieval and early modern periods, a woman's fundamental social identity changed when her husband died, as she became a symbol of his loss and a living, corporeal monument to his legacy—an ambassador between the living and the dead. The widow has also always been a profoundly *gendered* identity, inextricably linked in memory and psychology to women. As Irene Zanini-Cordi points out, "In social history and custom, as well as in literature, the widower is guaranteed a certain invisibility, while the widow, different from wives or nuns, acquires a stupefying visibility."[10] Widows in literature are identified as widows; widowers, on the other hand, are people who happen to have lost a spouse. This gendered distinction is evident in the extensive sociohistorical scholarship on medieval and early modern widows, which has demonstrated how women were affected by the circumstances of widowhood in significant economic and social ways. There is far less scholarship in the history of premodern widowers. In recent years, the powerful role of widows in Renaissance Italy has come to the fore, as social historians have called attention to the critical importance of widows' dowries within the social and economic networks of Renaissance city-states such as Florence and Venice and art historians have documented the ways in which noble widows negotiated their artistic agency as both patrons and subjects.[11] Important work on how widows were advised in Renaissance conduct literature has also emerged over the past decade, offering us a comprehensive overview of the ways male authors as diverse as Girolamo Savonarola (1452–1498), Juan Luis Vives (1493–1540), and Lodovico Dolce (1508–1568) instructed widows in their texts.[12] What has not been interrogated holistically is the similar dominance of widows and widowhood in the Italian literary tradition and how this connects to what we know of the historical situation of widows in Italy in the years from roughly 1300 to 1600.

Widow City: Gender, Emotion, and Community in the Italian Renaissance is the first scholarly work to investigate the evolving role of the widow from allegorical subject to author in medieval and early modern Italian literature. Through an analysis that cuts across genres, my study establishes the cultural and political significance of widowhood in Italy, from the works of canonical authors such as Dante, Petrarch, and Boccaccio, who constructed a rich poetic vocabulary around widowhood, to those of the numerous widowed writers who rose to prominence in the sixteenth century and radically changed the conversation on public mourning, offering an entirely new perspective on widowed identity. Engaging with broader intellectual discussions around the performance of gender, the history of emotions, the politics of mourning, and the construction of community, I argue that widows served as central models in a literature of exemplarity, demonstrating the proper way to grieve and mourn as a citizen. They had also long been figures provoking great anxiety: their status as unattached women and even the way they performed their grief after the death of their husbands could be viewed as very real threats to the stability of the social order. Widows are thus key to broader intellectual understandings not just of literature but also of community and civic life in late medieval and early modern Italy.

In the remaining pages of this introduction, I establish the historical and theoretical framework for this book's exploration of widowhood in the Italian Renaissance. I first discuss the presence of and prescriptions for widows in biblical and patristic sources and then offer a review of the significant sociohistorical research that has been conducted on Italian widows in the medieval and early modern periods, including on remarriage, widows' dowries, the interactions between rich and poor widows, and the prominent role played by noble widows as agents of charity and artistic patronage. Finally, I address sociocultural concerns over how widows performed grief and conducted themselves following the deaths of their husbands, alongside the rise in prominence of widowed writers in the sixteenth century, thereby establishing the stakes of the project for broader understandings of gendered emotional expression.

Widows in the Christian Tradition

Women have always played a central role in a community's civic management of mourning.[13] We might think of Andromache's public speech upon seeing her husband Hector's lifeless body in *Iliad* 22, of the women around her joining in her weeping, or of how she leads the women in the mourning ritual in the final lines of the poem in *Iliad* 24:

> Andromache of the white arms led the lamentation
> of the women, and held in her arms the head of manslaughtering Hektor:
> "My husband, you were lost young from life, and have left me
> a widow in your house, and the boy is only a baby
> who was born to you and me, the unhappy." (*Iliad* 24, 723–727)

As we will see, Dido and other famous widows from the classical tradition were central to texts of exemplarity and conduct from Boccaccio onward. The primary rules by which late medieval and Renaissance widows were governed, however, which were evident across literature and the visual and material culture of the period, were those articulated by the Fathers of the Church and that had roots in the Hebrew Bible and the Gospels.

A few overarching themes, both ethical and practical, emerge from the innumerable representations of widows in the Old and New Testaments. Widows, alongside strangers and orphans, are viewed as vulnerable figures of otherness in the community who are to be pitied and protected. Isaiah 1:17 reads, "Learn to do well; seek judgment, relieve the oppressed, judge for the fatherless, plead for the widow."[14] The widows of the Bible are also models for how to be strong and valuable contributors to one's city or community, from the Old Testament's Judith to Luke's Anna of Phanuel. In the story of the widow's mite, recounted in both Luke and Mark, a poor widow contributes all she has to the temple treasury and is praised by Christ for her generosity:

> And Jesus sat over against the treasury, and beheld how the people cast money into the treasury, and many that were rich cast in much. And there came a certain poor widow, and she threw in two mites, which make a farthing. And He called unto him his disciples, and saith unto them, "Verily I say unto you, That this poor widow hath cast more in, than all they which have cast into the treasury: For all they did cast in of their abundance; but she of her want did cast in all that she had, even all her living." (Mark 12:38–44)

This story reveals the ideals of modesty and humility of widows as well as their perceived responsibility to their community. Throwing in what money she has, the widow contributes to the communal pot, much as she is expected to do through prayer on behalf of not just her husband but all those around her.

The Christian expectation that widows would pray on behalf of and for the entire community was tightly linked to the central tenet that a "widow indeed" or *vere vidua* should not remarry. For Saint Paul and those who followed, chastity was the ideal recourse after a husband's death; remarriage was undesirable, but it was far better than succumbing to the temptation to engage in extramarital sex. In 1 Corinthians, Paul states, "I say to the unmarried, and to the widows: It is good for them if they so continue, even as I. But if they do not contain themselves, let them marry. For it is better to marry than to be burnt" (1 Corinthians 7:8–9). In his epistle to Timothy, Paul elaborates this point further, dividing widows into two camps: the vere vidua and those younger widows who should remarry rather than leave themselves vulnerable to temptation and, perhaps even worse, ill repute:

> Honour widows, that are widows indeed . . . she that is a widow indeed, and desolate, let her trust in God, and continue in supplications and prayers night and day. For she that liveth in pleasures, is dead while she is living. . . . Let a widow be chosen of no less than threescore of age, who hath been the wife of one husband. . . . But the younger widows avoid: for when they have grown wanton in Christ, they will marry; Having damnation, because they have made void their first faith. And withal being idle they learn to go about from house to house; and not only idle, but tattlers also, and busybodies, speaking things which they ought not. I will therefore that the younger should marry, bear children, be mistresses of families, give no occasion to the adversary to speak evil. (1 Timothy 5:3–17)

Paul's vere vidua, then, is a woman past the age of sixty who devotes herself to God and her community after her husband's death, able to avoid the temptations from which her marriage originally rescued her. Anna of Phanuel is generally considered the model for the ideal widow as we see her in Paul's instructions: "And there was one Anna, a prophetess, the daughter of Phanuel, of the tribe of Aser; she was of a great age, and had lived with an husband seven years from her virginity; And she was a widow of about fourscore and four years, which departed not from the temple, but served God with fasting and prayers night and day" (Luke 2:36–37). Younger widows—not a small group—were cast from Paul onward as suspicious, wanton, and altogether too risky a category of woman to remain unattached.

According to the influential prescription articulated by Jerome in *Against Jovinianus*, a widow was not as holy as a virgin, who would, it was believed, be blessed a hundredfold in Heaven. And yet she was considered holier than a woman with a living husband, who was still sexually active and who would receive only thirtyfold blessings upon her death as a result. Though not technically pure, a widow who did not remarry was considered chaste, and when she died she would be blessed sixtyfold as a reward.[15] Further to this prescription, Jerome worked to establish a common understanding of the ideal early Christian widow through the posthumous *vita* of his close friend and interlocutor, the widow Paula. In her, we already see a departure from the strict sorting of widows into young and old by Paul. According to Jerome, Paula, a wealthy mother of five who was widowed as a young woman at the age of thirty-two, turned to God after her pagan husband's death and devoted the remainder of her days to giving away her wealth and engaging in spiritual discussion with Jerome. He depicted Paula (now one of many patron saints of widows) as a model of virtue and charity who rejected the hedonism and wealth of early Rome, leaving behind her children other than her devoted daughter Eustochium, making a long pilgrimage to Jerusalem, and founding a hospice, monastery, and convent in Bethlehem, before dying there in 404. Though she was widowed at a fairly young age, she did not remarry but rather hewed closely to the Pauline model of the vere vidua.

Katherine Clark Walter has observed that in the early Middle Ages "Christian authors emphasized widowhood as a new opportunity for widows to establish themselves in a chaste way of life that effectively distanced themselves from secular concerns."[16] In Jerome's letter to Eustochium after Paula's death, he praises the widow both for the severity of her grief at the loss of her husband and for how well she was able to overcome it: "When [her husband] died, her grief was so great that she nearly died herself: yet so completely did she then give herself to the service of the Lord, that it might have seemed that she had desired his death."[17] While to modern ears (or even early modern ones) Jerome's assertion that she seemed to desire her husband's death might sound odd, it is also emblematic of an ideal continually propagated by the Church: however sad husbands' deaths were, they left widows, their worldly duties fulfilled, free to dedicate themselves to their faith while still on earth.

Augustine takes a similar tack in his "Letter to a Widow," in which he urges the wealthy widow Proba to model herself after Anna of Phanuel:

> For what could be more suitably the business of your widowhood than to continue in supplications night and day, according to [Paul's] admonition, "She that is a widow indeed, and desolate, trusteth in God, and continueth in supplications night and day"? It might, indeed, appear wonderful that solicitude about prayer should occupy your heart and claim the first place in it, when you are, so far as this world is concerned, noble and wealthy, and the mother of such an illustrious family, and, although a widow, not desolate, were it not that you wisely understand that in this world and in this life the soul has no sure portion. . . . Now what makes this work specially suitable to widows but their bereaved and desolate condition? Whosoever, then, understands that he is in this world bereaved and desolate as long as he is a pilgrim absent from his Lord, is careful to commit his widowhood, so to speak, to his God as his shield in continual and most fervent prayer. Pray, therefore, as a widow of Christ, not yet seeing Him whose help you implore.[18]

Here we see widowhood specifically identified as an office with duties both private and public. The widow's duty to pray is important not only for her husband but for the Christian community writ large. Even more striking, Augustine underlines the belief that widows are paradigmatic of the pilgrim soul, the condition of widowhood from which all humanity suffers.[19]

As we can see, despite the tremendous influence of Paul's writings on widows, subsequent thinkers did not always stick to his strict definition of the vere vidua as excluding younger women and, indeed, regularly viewed widows of all ages as a boon to the Christian community who should not remarry. Paula and Proba represent early examples in a long line of wealthy Christian widows who turned to religion and thus lived respectably outside the confines of remarriage, even engaging actively in intellectual and theological debates of the day with the most prominent male thinkers. While these widows refused to stay silent or isolated from society, their insistence on active engagement was undergirded by a spiritual authority unique to widowed women. Birgitta of Sweden (1303–1373), discussed at length in chapter 3, lived out a full "second career" as a high-profile visionary in her nearly three decades of widowhood, communicated with popes and princes, and founded a monastic order that still exists today.[20] Although she did not officially take vows, Vittoria Colonna, a central character in chapters 4 and 5, used the convent of San Silvestro in Rome as home base between 1538 and her death in 1547 and was heavily involved in the reform movements of the period.[21]

Widows in Late Medieval and Early Modern Italy

Over the past few decades, social and economic historians have demonstrated the critical importance of widows to Renaissance city-states such as Florence and Venice, from the fight to control their dowries to their roles as printers, merchants, and de facto rulers. Art historians have documented the ways in which noble widows influenced the Renaissance art market as both patrons and subjects, and literary historians have shed light on the poetic contributions of Italy's most famous widows. Taken together, these distinct fields of interrogation suggest just how important *real* widows—those known to the historical record—were to the ideological and material construction of Italy and *italianità*. It is therefore striking that the long-standing and central role of widows and of metaphorical "widowhood" (e.g., the widowed city, the widowed poem) within the Italian literary tradition has thus far escaped holistic assessment.

Though *Widow City* is the first to examine the importance of widows and widowhood to the Italian literary and intellectual tradition from Dante, Petrarch, and Boccaccio to the end of the Renaissance, it enters a rich conversation across disciplines on widowhood as well as the relationship between gender, emotion, and community in early modern Italy. These include the pathbreaking single-authored studies of widowhood in Italian art history by Levy, and in the religious context by Clark Walter,[22] as well Sharon Strocchia and Carol Lansing's work on mourning and gender in medieval and Renaissance Italy and Juliana Schiesari's on gender and emotion.[23] As the study of women's writing in Renaissance Italy has blossomed in the past three decades, scholars have demonstrated the significant cultural influence of numerous widowed writers, including Lucrezia Tornabuoni, Alessandra Macinghi Strozzi, Antonia Tanini Pulci, Vittoria Colonna, Veronica Gambara, Chiara Matraini, and Francesca Turina, weaving them into the standard Italian canon through literary analysis as well as important critical editions of their works.[24] *Widow City* builds upon a remarkable scholarly foundation, tracing literature's dialogue with broader societal discourses on widows across the peninsula while also analyzing how widows embodied and performed mourning as a gendered, public practice. I am also attentive throughout the study to Barbara Rosenwein's theory of "emotional communities" as "groups that share the same or very similar norms and values about emotional behavior and even about feelings themselves."[25] As will become evident to readers over the course of the book, it is productive to think about widows, especially widowed writers in the sixteenth and seventeenth centuries, as a kind of emotional community themselves.

As scholars have shown, Italian widows of the late medieval and early modern periods had to grapple with the socioeconomic concerns of their families, both natal and marital, and were often pressured or forced into remarriage soon after the deaths of their husbands.[26] While in theory the widow's dowry could offer wealthy women some financial and personal freedom in widowhood, it also represented significant capital that many fathers and brothers wanted either to have returned to them or to quickly invest in a second advantageous marriage.[27] In response to such family desires, the Florentine government enacted strict laws that made it difficult for widows to reclaim their dowries after their husbands' deaths, despite their legal right to the money.[28] Christiane Klapisch-Zuber, in her now-classic "The 'Cruel Mother,'" presents the typical Florentine widow in the early modern period as an oppressed figure, caught between the financial and political desires of her own family and those of her husband's. Here, Klapisch-Zuber coins the term "passing guests" for Renaissance Italian wives, asserting that women had no permanent security or true home in either their father's house or their husband's.[29] Her "cruel mothers" were young eligible widows forced to abandon their children after the death of a husband, then quickly married off to another man by their families in order to make good use of their dowry, which in many cities was returned to a widow upon her husband's death. Klapisch-Zuber argues that the typical Renaissance widow was considered a grave risk to her family and society due to her sexuality and a threat to her family's honor from the day she was widowed, incapable of controlling her own sexual desires.[30]

This was not viewed as a small problem, given the size of the widowed population: as David Herlihy and Klapisch-Zuber demonstrated in their landmark study of the Florence *catasto* of 1427, widows in that year made up an extraordinary 25 percent of the population in the city of Florence; the percentage was 13.6 in other Tuscan cities. Of women over the age of forty, 18 percent were widowed, as were 45 percent of women over the age of fifty. Widowers, on the other hand, were far fewer in number: according to the catasto, they accounted for less than 5 percent of the Florentine population in 1427.[31] This discrepancy was in part due to the substantial age gap between men and women that typified Florentine marriages.[32] Furthermore, property-owning men of all ages across Quattrocento Italy routinely remarried after the deaths of their wives. Women, on the other hand, generally remarried only if they were still relatively young when their husbands died.

While much of the work on Italian Renaissance widows has been on the Florentine case, as evident from the preceding pages, Venice proves an important counterpoint, especially given the material addressed in the last chapter of this study. Stanley Chojnacki has revealed what he describes as "a more unambiguously positive picture than the Florentine one" for Venetian wives and widows, arguing that women were central to the financial stability of Venice during the Renaissance and possessed great economic power and influence, especially after the deaths of their husbands. In contrast to Klapisch-Zuber's theory of women as "passing guests," Chojnacki demonstrates that Venetian widows connected their families of birth and marriage, belonging not to neither but to both. In Venice, remarriage was extremely uncommon. Young patrician widows with children remarried at a rate of 9 percent; documents from the period between 1589 and 1607 show that, as in fifteenth-century Florence, there were nearly five times as many widows as widowers within the city limits.[33] Chojnacki observes, "In Venice it was women, either acting personally as widows or by designating agents to act for them, who managed the outcome of a marriage already ended or whose end was being anticipated. In this they were supported by two powerful patriarchal structures, their families and government institutions."[34]

While upper-class widows in Venice operated within and influenced the economy of the very patriarchal systems that so often sought to control their movements, for poor women the effects of widowhood were more often than not economically devastating.[35] These widows tended to rely either on speedy remarriage or, failing that, on the kindness of civic charities—which were themselves often funded by wealthy widows or by wealthy men attentive to the civic and spiritual imperative of caring for vulnerable widows.[36] In a prominent Florentine example, the Orbatello home for widows was founded in the early 1370s by merchant Niccolò Jacopo degli Alberti (1327–1377), who was hopeful that the widowed residents would work together to pray him into Heaven.[37] Monica Chojnacka has shown that in Venice poor and working-class widows and their children might move in with neighbors after the deaths of their husbands and work as servants, while others discreetly moved in with men who paid their way in return for sexual favors.[38] Some widows moved to Venice from other parts of the north in order to live more economically and sometimes remained perpetually itinerant within the city limits.[39] Nicholas Terpstra highlights the trials of young, working widows in early modern Bologna, pointing out that women were more likely to outlive their husbands than the reverse; children to support made life all the more difficult.[40] Despite such day-to-day financial hardships, as Isabelle Chabot points out, poor Italian widows across the peninsula were generally viewed charitably by society, following the biblical model, as cases to be pitied, while many upper-class widows were viewed with deep suspicion because of their financial and thus personal freedom.[41]

The relationships between widows across class lines reveal the way that widowhood was an identity unto itself, connecting those of vastly different worlds. The letters of

Lorenzo de' Medici's widowed mother, the writer Lucrezia Tornabuoni (1427–1482), show numerous poor Florentine widows writing to her asking both for her financial help and for her to wield her political influence to advocate on their behalf, and her actually engaging in that advocacy.[42] In Bologna, widow Giulia Zambeccari Bianchini left money in her 1559 will for a house in which all widowed women in her family could live for generations, provided that they dedicate themselves to good works rather than remarry.[43] Rich widows were also highly attuned to their status as charitable patrons: Terpstra highlights the case of Pazienza Barbieri Bolognetti, a Bolognese widow who established a home for sex workers with her fortune.[44] As Carolyn Valone and Nicholas Eckstein have shown, rich widows were responsible for the commission and building of numerous churches and chapels that changed the face of their Renaissance cities.[45]

Widows and the City

As the title of this book suggests, I am attentive throughout the study to the link between widows and the "city." I use this term not only in the literal sense of the civic space in which so many widows lived but also in the sense of the common "organizing principle" of the allegorical city, as described from Lamentations to Augustine to Christine de Pizan.[46] Accordingly, a helpful and expansive definition for the city is, as Augustine states, a "multitude of people joined together by some communal bond."[47] As Marilynn Desmond points out, the city was a common protagonist in medieval historical narratives, a rhetorical paradigm of which Christine was keenly aware.[48] Sarah Kay observes that an important difference between Augustine's original conceit of two cities—one of God and one of Man—and Christine's city of ladies in her most famous text, *Le livre de la cité des dames* (*The Book of the City of Ladies*) is that Christine is interested both in "earthly honor," how people conduct themselves on earth or in the City of Man, as well as in the inclusion of women in the allegorical idealized city.[49] Like Dido, who built the city of Carthage after her husband's death in Phoenicia, Christine became, in her widowhood, a city builder. Through the construction of the city of ladies, Christine crafted a parallel world in which virtuous women—many among them widows—were civic leaders. She welcomed into her city not just Christian women but also the pagan exempla who would become de rigueur in florilegia and conduct literature aimed at instructing widows on the right way to behave. Through this construction project, she bolstered both her personal reputation and her economic security after her husband died.[50]

It is no mere coincidence that much of the sociohistorical and art historical work on widowhood has focused on cities. As Herlihy explains, it was the exaggerated age gap of Florentine marriages that made widows so much more plentiful in Florence than in the surrounding Tuscan countryside, where men tended to marry women closer to their own age.[51] In practical terms, it was often easier to remain a widow in the city than outside of it.[52] The unique relationship between the city itself and widows went beyond demographic and remarriage concerns, however, and hit at something deeper. As I discuss in chapter 1, Cristelle Baskins has elaborated the role of the personified widowed Rome in visual art of the Trecento, as has Falkeid in her study of the Avignon Papacy.[53] In Levy's masterful *Re-membering Masculinity in Early Modern Florence: Widowed Bodies, Mourning, and Portraiture*, she points to a complex relationship between city and widow in Renaissance Florence, which played out in portraiture, the positioning of statuary, and theater productions in the city's *piazze*. Levy's choice to focus on artistic representation in Florence specifically not only elucidates the particular situation of widows in Florentine cultural production but also demonstrates the broader symbiosis between widows and the urban spaces they inhabited and built and has been generative for the development of this book's broader framework.

There are at least two "widow cities" that we might identify in Italy in the early modern period. The first, more conventional one, which was built on Boccaccio's *De claris mulieribus* (*On Famous Women*) and Christine's *Book of the City of Ladies*, was populated by virtuous and devoted widows from the biblical and pagan traditions—Lucretia, Judith, Dido, Anna of Phanuel, Artemisia—as well as by contemporary famous widows such as Colonna and her peer Veronica Gambara (1485–1550), both of whom made their way into numerous conduct manuals and female biographies, as I discuss in part II of this study. This city was an imagined community of virtuous widows who behaved in the traditionally prescribed way. But there was also a second "widow city," an emotional community of widowed writers—including but not limited to Gambara and Colonna—who were conscious of the symbolic importance of their own identity, took hold of societal narratives around widows, and cultivated a "poetics of widowhood" to make their voices heard.

As I demonstrate throughout this study, widows played a central yet sometimes controversial role in how the community was conceptualized in medieval and Renaissance Italian literature. The figure of the widow often served as a symbol for a city's mourning, but could also speak to its resilience and the possibility of healing from collective trauma. The authority granted to the widow's voice in the Italian literary tradition owes a particular debt to the Book of Lamentations, which opens on a mournful Jerusalem, "widowed" of her people following the destruction wrought by the Babylonian army: "How doth the city sit solitary that was full of people! how is the mistress of the Gentiles become as a widow" (Lamentations 1:1). Jerusalem herself calls out to passersby, demanding witnesses to her misery: "Oh all ye that pass by the way, attend, and see if there be any sorrow like to my sorrow" (1:12). She is both an object of pity and a model of mournfulness, her performance of grief proffered as a barometer against which any and all affective experience can be measured.

The metaphorical widow of Lamentations has long served as a template for how to grieve loss as a collective as well as how to rally communal or even nationalistic fervor. Dante's famous invective in Canto VI of *Purgatorio* presents a pathetic widowed Rome—"la tua Roma che piagne / vedova e sola" (your Rome, who weeps, widowed and alone)—within an "enslaved" and "whorish" Italy, a conceit sustained by Italian writers from Petrarch to Leopardi.[54] The rhetorical tradition of Italy and her cities as grieving, defiled women was strengthened during the political crises of the fifteenth century, from laments mourning the Fall of Constantinople post-1453 to preachers in the 1480s and 1490s who capitalized on fears of the sexual violation of Christian women at the hands of the Muslim Ottomans by describing Italian cities as feminine victims of wartime violence to rally support for a new crusade.[55]

Despite the rhetorical utility offered by the figure of the openly grieving widow, a concern that further complicated the perception of widows in civic space, as well as their treatment, was how to manage female emotions, especially grief. As I discuss throughout this study, widows' grief was viewed warily in the late medieval and early modern period, and outward displays of mourning by women, once performed on the streets of the city, began to be forced indoors and into female-only spaces as early as the Trecento.[56] The question of how a widow should mourn—and how much and for how long—was a vexed one, addressed time and again by church and secular authorities. Vives devoted Book III of his *Education of a Christian Woman* to widows, writing, "The greatest proof of a shameless and cruel mind is not to weep over a husband who has died." And yet he warned against mourning to excess: "There are two types of women equally guilty, though in opposite ways, in the matter of mourning a lost husband: those who mourn too much, and those who mourn too little. . . . Let a widow mourn her dead husband with true affection, but not cry out or afflict herself by beating her hands together or with blows to her limbs or body. In her grief, she should observe modesty and moderation and not make such a show of distress that others will see it." Vives further insisted that widows should not remarry but rather "cultivate the memory of her husband, not as if he were dead, but absent, with more veneration and piety than weeping," advocating a more dignified, "clean" model of mourning.[57] We might recall here Jerome's friend Paula, who mourned her husband "so much that she almost died of grief," before switching tack, turning "so ardently to the service of God that she might have seemed to desire her husband's death."[58]

Renaissance conduct literature in general reflected the views propagated by Paul, Jerome, and Augustine, while also incorporating practical concerns, with widows featured as a group of great importance to the larger community. Vives, for instance, insisted that widows refrain from socializing and pray, as Paul instructed, both "day and night": "To make myself clear, the widow should pray more frequently and with greater devotion, fast longer, attend mass and sacred functions, read more diligently, and turn her thoughts to those things that improve life and morals."[59] In Girolamo Savonarola's *The Book of the Life of the Widow*, the firebrand preacher argued that widows ought to serve their cities and the Church following their husbands' deaths, while Lodovico Domenichi included Paul and Jerome's preaching in his section on widows in *La nobiltà delle donne* (The nobility of women, 1552).[60] In his *Epistola de la vita che dee tenere una donna vedova* (Letter on the life a widow should lead, 1524), Trissino went even further, insisting quite remarkably that widows should consider themselves men both "in spirit and in body" in the wake of their husbands' deaths—recalling Christine's description of her own body made newly male following her husband's death over a century before.[61] In the Counter-Reformation, Cardinal Agostino Valier (1531–1606) emphasized the importance of widows as both models for and cultivators of civic virtue who should work to improve their communities after the example of the Hebrew widow Judith. Cabei advocated that widows avoid remarriage, not only out of piety but also in order to protect the children from their first marriage. In short, early modern Italian widows were expected to stay chaste and true to their husbands' memories, devote their time to prayer, and avoid society, all while caring for their children, inspiring others through their acts, and protecting themselves from the constant threat of remarriage. They were to do all this while performing the appropriate level of grief—not too great, and not too small.

Widows and Writing

Widow City analyzes these varied societal understandings of and expectations for widows against the backdrop of an unprecedented cultural phenomenon in early modern Italy. While de Pizan's writings about her own widowhood were rare in her time, by the fifteenth and sixteenth centuries Italy was home to a now well-studied boom in women's writing, unmatched anywhere else in Europe. In the sixteenth century, there were more than two hundred published Italian women writers on record, compared with thirty in France and even fewer in other European countries.[62] If we consider these numbers in relation to the percentage of Italian women who were widowed, a striking picture emerges of widowed women with the space and economic opportunity to read and produce literature that was welcomed and celebrated by Italy's reading public. While the allegorical widow remained an active tool for male political writers in humanist Italy, women writers, many of them widowed themselves, emerged as a major intellectual and publishing force. By the sixteenth century, celebrated poets such as Colonna and Gambara as well as lesser-known but no less ambitious widowed writers like Chiara Matraini (1515–1604) and Francesca Turina (1553–1641) not only incorporated their experience as widowed women into their work but made it central to their authorial identities. We see this most clearly in the case of Colonna, who, happily, has been the subject of ample scholarly attention.[63] As is now well known, Colonna rose to special prominence in her widowhood and was praised by the leading male writers and cultural leaders of the period. Colonna radicalized the way in which Petrarchan poetry as established by Pietro Bembo could be used, writing about her dead husband not simply from the vantage point of a grieving widow but as a Petrarchan lover, thereby propelling both herself and her husband to immortal fame.[64]

This celebration of the widow-poet—a new voice in Italian intellectual culture—was nevertheless complicated by the tension between the rhetorical utility of the allegorical widowed city and the potential of real widows to instigate social crises. *Widow City* highlights the precarious authority of widows who publicized their grief in a society that tightly regulated women's emotional expression. Widowhood indicated a physical uncoupling from the patriarchy; while a widow's task was ostensibly to safeguard the well-being of her late husband's soul, her presumptive sexual experience, and sometimes even financial independence, posed an existential threat to the social structures she was meant to embody and protect. This is palpable throughout canonical literature, from Dante's condemnation of Dido to the Circle of Lust in *Inferno* V, to

Boccaccio's many "merry widows" who spend their mourning period satisfying their carnal desires, to numerous later works by seminal authors of the Renaissance, including those by Machiavelli and Castiglione. This clear cultural program was aimed not just at controlling widows' behavior but at fashioning public understandings of what made widows either "good" or "bad." Part III of *Widow City*, "The Widow's Voice," illuminates how women writers, both widowed and not, reconfigured public perceptions of widowhood through their texts. In so doing, this study probes the boundaries between literature and social practice, community and identity, and gender and genre in Italian Renaissance culture.

Organization of the Study

Widow City is organized into three parts, with six chapters in total. Part I, "Widowhood and the *tre corone*," addresses the widow's origins in the Italian canon through an analysis of works by the canonical authors Dante, Petrarch, and Boccaccio, commonly referred to as the *tre corone*, or "three crowns," of Italian literature. In chapter 1, I trace the long-standing metaphorical link between widows and the city from its origins in Lamentations to the appropriation of this model by Dante and Petrarch, as well as the connection to women as a community's designated mourners. From here, I consider a thorough line of widows and widowhood in Dante's *Commedia* as well as in Petrarch's lyric poetry. In chapter 2, I probe the archetype of the "merry widow" through an analysis of Boccaccio's *Decameron* and *Il corbaccio*. Throughout Part I, I argue that these early, defining works of Italian literature developed a foundational poetic vocabulary, as well as a clear and distinct ethics of widowhood, that would be engaged with by writers throughout the Renaissance.

Part II, "Context: Model Widows, Holy and Historical," is divided into two chapters offering historical context on the evolving role of widows in early modern Italian society. In chapter 3, "Sacred Role Models from Judith and Anna to Birgitta of Sweden," I train my focus on saintly widows in Rome, including Birgitta of Sweden, Francesca Romana (1384–1440), and Ludovica Albertoni (1473–1533). I argue that with these holy widows we see the development of a new brand of widowhood in which the prior focus on safeguarding the late husband's well-being in the afterlife is sublimated in favor of an expanded role in society. Although this kind of widow still derives her authority from the loss of her husband, she exploits that authority and directs her focus outward to benefit her fellow citizens. As I demonstrate, holy widows at the threshold of early modernity played a major role in the articulation of their own identities and legacies, through visions, letters, and the establishment of religious orders, acting as a hinge between earlier canonical, reductive perceptions of widows and a new kind of widow identity—and voice—forged by secular writers. The fourth chapter, "Dido, Death, and Exemplarity: Public Widowhood from Petrarch to Vittoria Colonna," turns from examples of holy widows to the many secular widows of influence in Renaissance Italy, from Caterina Cornaro and Caterina Sforza to Colonna and Gambara. A connecting thread in this chapter is the widowed Colonna, recognized in both her lifetime and contemporary scholarship as the "ur-widow" of the Renaissance and as a primary literary role model for other widowed women writers. I locate the traumatic half century of the Italian Wars (1494–1559) as the cultural moment when the social value of widowhood underwent a crucial transformation, as widows began to take ownership of the rhetorical potential of widowed identity that had been developed through Italian literature, serving as both models of mourning and symbols of hope and strength for the community.

Part III, "The Widow's Voice," turns first to writing by widows themselves and then to the widow's voice in dialogue. Chapter 5, "Widowed Verse: Christine de Pizan, Vittoria Colonna, and Francesca Turina," considers what Maria Serena Sapegno and Tatiana Crivelli have termed *rime vedovili*, or "widowed verse": *in morte* or commemorative poetry written by widows to honor their husbands.[65] While much scholarship has focused on Colonna's landmark *vedovili*, I contextualize her innovative voice within a broader galaxy of widowed poets, from de Pizan to later writers who strove to outdo her. I argue that many widowed poets exploited long-standing tropes of widowhood in poetry to forge their own identities as authors, while creating a space where female grief, long tightly regulated, could be celebrated rather than silenced. Chapter 6, "'Widowhood for Its Own Sake': Widows in Two Dialogues of the Counter-Reformation," shows that, at the end of the sixteenth century, there were examples in print of widows liberated from their marriages who argued in eloquent rhetorical language that there was an innate value to widowhood. I analyze the characters of Ippolita in Bernardo Trotto's little-studied *I dialoghi del matrimonio e vita vedovile* (Dialogues on marriage and widowed life, 1578) and Leonora in Moderata Fonte's more famous *Il merito delle donne* (*The Worth of Women*, 1600), two young, eloquent, and wealthy women who found their widowhoods to be not only liberating but downright fun. I put them into conversation with the conduct literature directed at widows in the same years, demonstrating that many writers in the Counter-Reformation had a far more nuanced understanding of female desires and agency than we might believe. The book concludes with a brief epilogue looking at the way eclectic widow lineages and communities continued to be forged in the seventeenth century, including by the widowed corulers of Florence, Christine of Lorraine (1565–1637) and Maria Maddalena of Austria (1589–1631), known as the *tutrici*.

Widows were everywhere in Renaissance Italy. Most married women were widowed in their lifetimes, and the figure of the widow appears regularly throughout the literature of the period, from the comic to the tragic, the devout to the heretical. There exists in Italian Renaissance literature a particular consciousness of the important and multiple contributions made by widows to how society is shaped, a discourse originating in both the biblical and classical traditions that changed considerably from touting the ideal of the pious, devoted widow we see in Dante to advancing a model of self-fashioned, remarkably independent widowhood "per se stessa" (for its own sake) that was promulgated not only by widowed poets themselves, but also across dialogue, poetry, and treatises published during the Counter-Reformation. The evolution of this particular discourse, this "poetics of widowhood," has much to tell us about the intersections of gender, emotion, and politics in Renaissance literary culture.

PART I

Widowhood and the *tre corone*

CHAPTER ONE

Dante, Petrarch, and the Ethics of Widowhood

In the formative years of Italian literary identity, the *tre corone* played continually with the idea of the widow, constructing a poetics—and an ethics—that would endure as both template and foundation for Renaissance literary representations of Italian widowhood. In the following pages, I examine Dante and Petrarch's experimentation with widowhood as metaphor—the widowed city, the widowed poem—in lyric poetry. I then consider Dante's incorporation of widows throughout the *Commedia*, arguing for their significance to how the poet constructs Purgatory and thus how widows themselves were viewed in relation to the afterlife. In the next chapter, I turn to the analysis of Boccaccio's own stable of widows—merry and otherwise—in the *Decameron* and *Il corbaccio*. While this is not intended to be an exhaustive survey of widows in Trecento literature, the selected texts offer us a framework for how to read widowhood in the Italian tradition after the tre corone, while underscoring the presence of widowhood in the development of the Italian "canon."

With this first chapter, I introduce several key themes critical to this study's overall consideration of the relationship between widowhood and civic life in Italian Renaissance literature. These include what I label Dante's ethics *and* his poetics of widowhood, the sociopolitical anxiety surrounding the sexual desire and general "unruliness" of widows, the relationship between widows' eloquence and their prayers, and the strategic performance of widowed grief. Examined together, these themes illuminate how widowhood functions as a key component of the social order as represented in Italian literature between the fourteenth and sixteenth centuries, from Dante until the Counter-Reformation.

Lamentations and the Widowed City

"How doth the city sit solitary that was full of people! how is the mistress of the Gentiles become as a widow. . . . The ways of Sion mourn, because there are none that come to the solemn feast: all her gates are broken down: her priests sigh: her virgins are in affliction, and she is oppressed with bitterness" (Lamentations 1:1, 1:4). Thus begins the biblical Book of Lamentations, with the city of Jerusalem described as "widowed" of her people following the destruction by the Babylonian ruler Nebuchadnezzar in 587 B.C.E. Jerusalem is given voice and cries out, bewailing her status as a sorrowful, aggrieved victim: "Oh all ye that pass by the way, attend, and see if there be any sorrow like to my sorrow. . . . From above he hath sent fire into my bones, and hath chastised me: he hath spread a net for my feet, he hath turned me back: he hath made me desolate, wasted with sorrow all the day long" (Lamentations 1:12–13). Across the five chapters of Lamentations, the widowed city of Jerusalem is continuously depicted, in her own words and those of others, as the female victim of war, sexually assaulted, her virgins captured—a blunt reminder of not only war's toll on cities but also the profound violation of a city's women.

Lamentations has long served as an affective template, a model for how to grieve loss.[1] The widowed city mourning her lost population in Lamentations is read in the Christian tradition as an allegory for the Christian people mourning the death of Christ, with Christ in the position of bridegroom and the Christian people that of the grieving, widowed Jerusalem: the faithful will be reunited with their savior through his return to earth; the widow will be reunited with her beloved husband through her own death. Outside the bounds of liturgy, the metaphor of the widowed city became a central rhetorical tool in Italian political discourse. Rome was cast as a widowed, disconsolate woman when the Church was ripped from its "rightful" place in Rome during the Avignon Papacy (1309–1377), often referred to as the second Babylonian Captivity.[2] We see one important appropriation of the Lamentations model in Dante's angry Epistle XI to the Italian cardinals in conclave at Carpentras after the death of Clement V. For Dante, Rome is now the widowed city, the cardinals corrupt priests like those in Jerusalem in the days before the destruction of the temple.[3] Dante returns to this theme in his angry apostrophe in *Purgatorio* VI, in which Italy is a female body degraded—"non donna di province, ma bordello" (not a ruler of provinces, but a whore!)—and Rome, a widow abandoned by the pope, cries out in anguish: "Vieni a veder la tua Roma che piagne / vedova e sola, e dì e notte chiama: 'Cesare mio, perché non m'accompagne?'" (Come and see your Rome, which weeps / widowed and alone, and day and night calls out: "My Caesar, why do you not keep me company?").[4]

The "city-as-widow," or as *almost* a widow, was a trope used by writers and visual artists throughout the Trecento, as Cristelle Baskins has demonstrated.[5] Of note, Convenevole da Prato depicted Rome as a widow in his *Panegyric to King Robert of Anjou* in 1335/1336; an illuminated version of the *Panegyric* presented to the king by the city of Prato shows Rome as a desperate widow pulling at her hair after having been abandoned by multiple popes.[6] In 1344, in the series of murals Cola di Rienzo (1313–1354) commissioned for public buildings in Rome, in the final image on the façade of the Senator's Palace on the Capitoline Hill, Rome is a disconsolate widow pulling at her hair while praying in an endangered ship, chiming with Dante's description of Italy in his digression as a "nave senza nocchiere in gran tempesta" (ship without pilot in a great storm; *Purg.* VI.77).[7] Cola ordered a second depiction of Rome as a widowed woman be painted on the façade of Sant'Angelo in Pescheria.[8] In Petrarch's Epystola II.5 to Clement VI of 1347, the poet writes from the perspective of the personified, widowed Rome, much as the widowed Jerusalem herself speaks in Lamentations 1:12–17. The widowed Birgitta of Sweden, a central character in chapter 3 of this study, also engaged with the imagery of Rome as "quasi vidua" like Jerusalem, endowing herself with authority to speak out on Rome's behalf as a "fellow widow."[9] The widow as an allegorical figure for the wounded city during this tumultuous period thus became a rhetorical touchstone, easily recognizable, a way to demonstrate the sense of grief, loss, and rage felt by her citizens.

While a widow could serve as a symbol of grief, and even as motivation toward political action, there was also an underlying anxiety regarding the widow's unruly expression of her emotions. This was part of a broader preoccupation with the societal effects of emotional excess dating from the thirteenth century; as Carol Lansing has described, theorists "concerned about stable political order turned to Stoic as well as Augustinian ideas about the restraint of the passions."[10] Emotional restraint was invariably gendered male, even when that was not necessarily reflective of practice; Lansing, for instance, points to numerous instances of men "caught" performing excessive grief in public.[11] Baskins has argued that in the visual art of the Trecento, the figure of the widow is just as much linked to the possible dangers associated with the wailing woman as to the image of the abandoned city.[12] This anxiety was a broader Trecento concern, which carried on throughout the Renaissance, and not just in Rome. "It was primarily the responsibility of women to learn, enact, and transmit to others the standard techniques of mourning," Sharon Strocchia explains, "which included physical gestures, loud laments, and often dramatic, self-inflicted injuries." The dramatic way in which women had mourned in public dating back to antiquity, however, was also considered dangerous and might lead to "violence, vendetta, or other breaches of civic order and decorum" if acted out in the streets.[13] This disquiet is most famously illustrated by Petrarch in a 1373 letter, in which he beseeches Francesco I da Carrara, Lord of Padua (1325–1393) to move any ostentatiously weeping women indoors in the northern city lest "someone who did not know what was happening could easily think that here was a madman on the loose or that the city was under enemy attack."[14] Petrarch points specifically to the public disturbance women cause and the risk that such a disturbance might make people fear that the city was being attacked, echoing deep concerns among civic leaders surrounding the disorderly way in which women grieved in public.

While Petrarch pitches his advice to the princely ruler of Padua and not the leaders of the Florentine republic, his letter nevertheless remains an important source for understanding how the humanist project worked to constrain female voices, especially those of widows. In Florence, leaders employed an assortment of methods of control in order to rein in widows and their public performances of grief, from barring women from public funerals to broader ideological shifts in what kinds of emotion were deemed socially acceptable at all.[15] In addition to increasingly stringent ideas around emotional expression, sumptuary statutes revealed a persistent mistrust of widows and the suspicion that their public performance of grief might not be sincere.[16] The traditional white *benda* the widow was required to wear around her head was, Diane Owen Hughes suggests, "deliberately poor or humiliating, a sign of her rejection of the world and of her loss of identity."[17] In Florence, women were seated separately from men and ordered during funeral services by preachers, including San Bernardino da Siena, to stay at home to grieve after the service; if they were allowed to take part in the procession at all, they were placed at the end of the cortege. In other cities, including Bologna in 1276 and Ascoli Piceno in 1377, sumptuary laws explicitly prohibiting women from attending funerals and the processions that followed were passed.[18] After these laws were instituted, widows who violated them and mourned for their husbands in public were sometimes fined for their improper demonstrations of widowed grief.[19] "The domestication of female lament," Hughes argues, "served to deprive women of a public voice of memorialization in the commune," what Juliana Schiesari has called the "defeminization of the public sphere."[20] It is worth considering, of course, just how firm the boundary was between statute and actual practice; as Lansing has observed, the archive offers numerous examples of complaints that suggest the laws against public mourning were not followed, by both men and women.[21]

This tension between the cultural ideal of a widow as a universally recognizable model of public grief and the social reality of grieving widows kept inside and away from view is evident in Dante's appropriation of the Lamentations model. His letter to the cardinals, mentioned above, is his second known use of the Lamentations incipit; he first employed the trope of the widowed city earlier, in a different and more personal context, and in that instance it was Florence who was cast as aggrieved widow. Halfway through his *Vita nuova*, he inserts the same opening lines from the Vulgate before describing his native city in vernacular as *quasi vedova* due to his beloved Beatrice's death: "Poi che fue partita da questo secolo, rimase tutta la sopradetta cittade quasi vedova dispogliata da ogni dignitade" (Because she had departed from this world, the entire above-named city was like a widow despoiled of all majesty; 30:1).[22] "Widowing" the city of his birth, he places Florence in an illustrious collective of mourning, widowed cities.[23]

Dante positions the two lines from Lamentations at the beginning of chapter 28, to announce his beloved Beatrice's death. The Lamentations incipit, quoted in Latin, is a disconcerting and confusing interjection into the vernacular text of the *Vita nuova*, a linguistic "interruption" that mirrors the disorienting rupture the poet has experienced through Beatrice's death itself.[24] In chapter 30, he repeats the same opening lines from Lamentations, now paraphrased in vernacular, clarifying that they refer to "la sopradetta cittade": Florence, *his* city (*Vita nuova* 30:1–2). Unlike the political widowings of Rome and Jerusalem, however—traumas inflicted on the entire population of those cities—Dante widows Florence because of the death of a single, beloved citizen, a private event Dante grants an astonishingly public import. Defending himself against potential criticisms over the presence of Latin in an otherwise-vernacular text, he explains that he is quoting from another letter (now lost, if it ever existed) in which he wrote to the "principi de la terra" (rulers of the land) lamenting that the city of Florence has been left "quasi vedova dispogliata da ogni dignitate" (like a widow despoiled of all majesty) after Beatrice's death (30:2–4).[25] These lines, inserted in the official, public language of Church and law into a text on private grief written in vernacular, also highlight Dante's perception of his beloved's death as a collective, public loss. The entire city has become like a grieving widow, stripped of its dignity, its very identity shaken and changed by the loss of a single citizen. Florence becomes the widowed city of Lamentations 1 and 2, Dante and his fellow citizens the widows and orphans of Book 5.

Dante's use of Lamentations to elevate both his own grief and that of Florence pushes against the boundaries of what widowhood can mean—and who can be one. Not only has Dante's city become "like a widow," but so has he: not just a bereft lover, or even a male widower, but a widow in the gender-specific sense of the word, tied to the grieving widowed city of Lamentations. He describes himself as "ancora lagrimando in questa desolata cittade" (still shedding tears in this desolate city; *Vita nuova* 30:2–3), his tears as abundant as those of the personified Jerusalem in Lamentations. Connecting his own grief to the universal meaning behind the cycle of grief depicted in Lamentations, Dante endows his private mourning with public import, thereby complicating the authority and symbolism behind widowed grief. The *Vita nuova* serves as monument to his love for Beatrice: a literary mausoleum made up of prose and poem that memorializes her loss.

Dante furthers the idea of metaphorical widowhood in chapter 31, casting the canzone "Li occhi dolenti" (My sorrowful eyes) itself as a "widow": "E acciò che questa canzone *paia rimanere più vedova* dopo lo suo fine, lo dividerò prima che io la scriva. . . . Io dico che questa *cattivella canzone* ha tre parti" (And in order that this canzone may seem to remain all the more widowed after it has come to an end, I shall divide it before I copy it. . . . Let me say that this sad little song has three parts; *Vita nuova* 31:1–3, emphasis mine). His overall description of the poem brims over with what I would describe as a widowed lexicon, most prominently through his use of the verb *disfogare*, perhaps best translated as to release or expiate one's emotions. Jelena Todorovic notes that the verb *disfogare* is used five times in the *libello*; it becomes *sfogar* in Petrarch's *Canzoniere*, where it is also used five times.[26] Nancy Vickers argues that Dante's "purpose [after Beatrice's death] is to convert all songs and sonnets '*in morte*' into 'widows,' to underline the loss of the earthly referent for his words of praise, to foreground rupture, emptiness, and vulnerability."[27] This is evident in the poet's meticulous explanation, described above, of how "Li occhi dolenti" seems to be left "widowed." Placing the commentary before the poem—the first time he does so in the *Vita nuova*, in a pattern that will continue for the rest of the text—Dante asserts that he makes the poem "seem more like a widow"; the chapter will end without the cushion of commentary to which the reader has been habituated through the first part of the book, instead left bare (31:1).

The diminutive he applies to the canzone, "cattivella," possesses a particularly gendered vulnerability and is consonant with "vedovella," which Dante also deployed in his later work, as we will see presently.[28] Importantly, however, just as how in chapter 30 the city is "quasi vedova," the poem here is not completely widowed but rather only *seems* to be widowed. Dante's metaphorical vision of widowhood is always a "quasi" or "near-widowhood": just as Jerusalem is *quasi vidua*, Florence is *quasi vedova*, and the poem itself should only appear to be *più vedova*.[29] His metaphorical widowhood, then, can be understood as asymptotic, always approaching, but never reaching, full widowhood, which is reserved for actual female widows alone. This originates from the Lamentations-read-as-Christian-allegory model, in which there is always hope for the return of the city's inhabitants, and the return of Christ.[30]

In Dante's case, "quasi-widowhood" might also be interpreted as the poet's own desire to find membership in the community of women kept away from public view, devoting themselves to unrestrained grief, while also acknowledging that he will never quite make it across that particular, gender-specific threshold. As Teodolinda Barolini observes in her analysis of "Voi che portate la sembianza umile" (You whose expressions are so meek and low), in Dante's sonnet we see evidence of the particulars of gendered Duecento mourning, in which a group of women are described as performing the appropriate affect for the act of mourning itself. Barolini argues that the Dante of the *Vita nuova* "is not comfortable with the social norms with which he lives, [and is] a poet who uses poetry to create occasions for dialogue and encounter that are not permitted by the world around him. His intense desire to participate in the female work of mourning . . . verges on impropriety. His is a desire that threatens to trespass the rigid social barrier placed between male and female and that also risks feminizing him."[31] The desire articulated by Barolini is amplified when the poet deploys the Lamentations incipit, as he brings together the allegorical widow of Scripture and the private women doing the work of mourning in Florence. His private grief pushes against boundaries, spilling over from public to private and inhabiting both spheres. His "little widow," the poem itself, does the work of expiating his grief for him, working in female-only spaces he cannot broach as a male poet.

Dante's grief in the *Vita nuova* is characterized by a persistent need for relief, and his use of the word *sfogar* will be continually echoed by Italian lyric poets, from Petrarch to later widowed women writers such as Vittoria Colonna. While, as Martinez observes, the *Vita nuova* is a book "saturated in tears," the outward evidence of internal grief, in "Li occhi dolenti," the poet insists tears are not enough.[32] Speech is necessary to relieve, or expiate, his grief:

> Ora, s'i' voglio sfogar lo dolore,
> che a poco a poco la morte mi mena,
> convenemi parlar traendo guai.
>
> (Now, if I want to let my sorrow vent, by which, a little at a time, death nears,
> I am constrained to speak in words and wails.) (31:4–6)[33]

Dante explains that he must address this discussion of grief to a female audience: only a female heart can understand the depths of sorrow the poet experiences upon his love's passing, allowing him to sfogar or "liberate" his heart from grief: "non voi parlare altrui, / se non a cor gentil che in donna sia" (I'll speak to no one new, save to the open heart that women give; 31:10–11).

The second section of the canzone is focused on the exaltation of his love object: not even the cathartic exercise of weeping can relieve the universal grief felt by her loss, and his soul, like the city "dispogliata di ogni dignitade" (despoiled of all majesty; 31:30), has been stripped "d'onne consolar" (of all consolation; 31:40), his heart "diviso" (split in two; 31:45).[34] Alone in his grief ("sol nel mio lamento"; 31:54), he speaks to Beatrice in what Barolini describes as his "signature move," direct discourse: "Or se' tu morta?" (Are you really dead? 31:55).[35] Speaking to his dead beloved is all that can comfort him ("mentre ch'io la chiamo, me conforta"; 31:56), for all those around him *seem* to have abandoned him ("ogn'om par che mi dica: 'Io t'abbandono'"; 31:67).[36] Whether his male friends and interlocutors have abandoned him or not, he still has his "pietosa canzone" (sad canzone), that widow of his own invention, and together they can forge a small community, two grieving widows who need not mourn alone. In the canzone's *congedo*, he addresses the poem directly, instructing it on its greater mission:

> Pietosa mia canzone, or va piangendo;
> e ritruova le donne e le donzelle
> a cui le tue sorelle
> erano usate di portar letizia;
> e tu, che se' figliuola di tristizia,
> vatten disconsolata a star con elle.
>
> (My sad canzone, go your way and weep:
> Search out those women and those girls again
> To whom your sister-kin
> Would once upon a time bring happiness:
> While you, who are the daughter of distress,
> Go off disconsolate to be with them.) (31:71–76)

It is here in this "widowed" poem that an Italian poetics of widowhood begins. It is a poetics in which the mourning voice searching to expiate their grief (sfogar) must always be gendered feminine—either by transforming the poem itself into a widow, as Dante does, or, later, through the voice of the widowed woman poet herself.

Dante's insistence that his poem must *continue* to weep feeds into a larger ethical argument of his libello, which is also evident in the *Commedia*: for him, there is no end to a "true" widow's mourning. For Dante, widowhood is necessarily a permanent state, as Beatrice reminds the Pilgrim in the Earthly Paradise when she chides him for having temporarily forgotten her; he has allowed himself to be consoled. As Barolini has recently argued, the sonnet "L'amaro lagrimar che voi faceste" "marks an important 'contractual' moment in Dante's itinerary," one with "enduring repercussions."[37] In the poem, he turns back to his own weeping eyes as the libello nears its end, and chastises them for not weeping enough; their "vanità" wounds him. He then submits to his eyes the ethical imperative to which he will also hold himself throughout the rest of his life's work: "Voi non dovreste mai, se non per morte, / la vostra donna, ch'è morta, obliare" (You mustn't ever, until death is here, / efface your lady, who is long since dead; 37:12–13). The lover's duty after the death of the beloved, then, is to mourn and memorialize her to the larger community after her death. Dante will transfer this ethical stance from his own "quasi-widowhood" in the *Vita nuova* to the widowhoods of numerous characters throughout the *Commedia*, who exist as a community of mourning widowed *women*, one that crosses over the boundaries between the world and the afterlife. As we will see, this also becomes a broader ethics in Italian literature, from the male writers who follow Dante to the widowed women writers who express their grief later in Petrarchan verse.

A first example is close at hand: we see a second widowed canzone in Petrarch's *Rerum vulgarium fragmenta* (hereafter *RVF*). Poem 268—the mournful "Che debb'io far? Che mi consigli, Amore?" ("What should I do? What do you advise me, my love?"), in which Petrarch announces his beloved Laura's death—concludes with a description of the poem as "vedova sconsolata in veste negra" (a disconsolate widow in black dress). As critics have long noted, the poem owes much to the *Vita nuova*'s "Li occhi dolenti"; Vickers observes, "in these two parallel *canzoni* . . . we can read the dynamics of . . . a father/son exchange. It is, moreover, the metaphor 'song is widow' that insists that we acknowledge that relationship."[38] Throughout *RVF* 268, the language of rupture, despair, and desire for death is readily apparent—"Madonna è morta et à seco il mio core, / et volendol seguire, / interromper conven quest'anni rei" (My lady is dead and has my heart with her, and if I wish to follow it I must break off these cruel years; ll. 4–6)[39]—as is the presence of a group of ladies he hopes will console him.

> Donne, voi che miraste sua beltate
> et l'angelica vita
> con quel celeste portamento in terra;
> di me vi doglia, et vincavi pietate;
> non di lei, ch'è salita
> a tante pace, et m'à lassato in guerra.
>
> (Ladies, you who wondered at her beauty and her angelic life and her bearing so heavenly on earth: Grieve for me, and let pity for me vanquish you, not for her, Who has risen to such peace and has left me in sad war.) (ll. 56–59)

He also resolves to continue spreading the fame of his beloved through his poetry, per Laura's own instructions:

> et sua fama, che spira
> in molte parti ancor per la tua lingua,
> prega che non estingua,
> anzi la voce

al suo nome rischiari,
se gli occhi suoi ti fur dolci né cari.

(and she begs you not to extinguish her fame, which sounds in many places still by your tongue, but rather to make bright your voice with her name, if her eyes were ever sweet or dear to you.) (ll. 73–78)

In the last stanza, Petrarch transforms the canzone into a widow itself, as Dante does in "Li occhi dolenti." In contrast to his predecessor, Petrarch labels the canzone itself within the body of the text, draping it in widow's weeds, the poem's last line a description of the poem as "vedova sconsolata in veste negra." In a further departure from *Vita nuova*, in which Dante urges his "widowed" canzone to find comfort with the group of likeminded female mourners he longs to join, Petrarch instructs his own widowed canzone to retreat from society. As Vickers observes, "Petrarch's widow is ultimately a widow in isolation; Dante's, by contrast, is to be inscribed in a community of mourning, in a city that laments"—to a degree, a preview of two different models for widows we will later see in Renaissance Italy.[40]

Fuggi 'l sereno e 'l verde,
non t'appressare ove sia riso o canto
canzon mia, no, ma pianto;
non fa per te di star fra gente allegra,
vedova sconsolata in veste negra.

(Flee the clear sky and greenery, do not approach where there is laughter and singing, my song, no, but where there is weeping; it is not fitting for you to be among cheerful people, disconsolate widow in black garments.) (ll. 78–82)

In Petrarch's version of the widowed canzone, then, we see a shift from that of Dante: it will not do for the widowed canzone to remain among the "gente allegra" or "happy people" out in the world. The poem is now an outsider, widowed, inconsolable, dressed in black. The decorous thing for the poem to do is to retreat from the world, away from people who can still experience joy, love, or sociability.[41]

The two poems of bereavement for the beloved discussed here may end differently, with one text being directed into a community of mourners and the other retreating to an isolated existence, but the two poets have committed themselves to the same ethical imperative through a distinctive poetics of widowhood, in which mourning is inscribed in poetry and made eternal. Dante's "se non per morte" stance, and Petrarch's imitation of it, is crucial to the representations of widowhood discussed in this chapter and in those that follow. Indeed, this ethical imperative is intimately connected to the affective performance, and emotional labor, of women, which was being consistently muffled by civic authorities in this period. Dante's establishment of the moral precedent to memorialize the beloved through speech, tears, and poetry plays as much into the development of the ideal Renaissance widow as does the patristic dictate that widows avoid remarriage in order to safeguard their chastity and serve God. As I demonstrate in the following section, Dante's depiction of widows in the *Commedia* marries the *Vita nuova*'s figurative "quasi-widowhood" grounded in emotion and grief with the way virtuous widows figured into the development of Purgatory as a third destination for the dead.

The Widows of the *Commedia*

Widows are plentiful and prominent players in Dante's *Commedia*. The widowed empress of Babylon, Semiramis, is the first sinner we meet in *Inferno*; the widowed queen of Carthage, Dido, the second.[42] Both are women who ruled cities—empires that served, respectively, as threats to Jerusalem and Rome—but in Dante's world they have been relegated to the Circle of Lust alongside Paolo and Francesca, punished for having succumbed to lust after the deaths of their husbands. When Dante asks his guide at the entrance to the Circle of Lust, "Maestro, chi son quelle / genti che l'aura nera sì gastiga?" ("Master, who are those / people whom the black wind so chastises?"; *Inferno* V.50–51),[43] Virgil points first to Semiramis; it is her personal failures as a widow and as a mother that have led to her placement in the second circle.[44] In addition to her faithlessness to her husband King Ninus after his death, she brought shame upon them both by falling in love with their son.[45] Dante's Virgil describes Semiramis as "rotta," or "broken," not only as a mother but as a protector of her dead husband's son, a defective, corrupt failure of a widow. Next appears Dido, the widowed Carthaginian queen who, as Virgil writes her, was defeated by her love for Aeneas. Her Trojan lover is not mentioned by name in Canto V, but her husband is; it is Dido's abandonment of Sychaeus's memory that has landed her in the second circle. Virgil, who dedicated all of *Aeneid* IV to the passion of the Queen, offers here but a brief two-line summation of her and her sin, tossed off with the dismissive "l'altra": "L'altra è colei che s'ancise amorosa, / e ruppe fede al cener di Sicheo" (The next is she who killed herself for love / and broke faith with the ashes of Sichaeus; *Inferno* V.61–62). These two short lines are weighted with significance, alluding to the tragic tale of Dido as told by Virgil in his own great epic. Yet the humanity granted Dido in the *Aeneid* is lacking in Dante's version; she is dealt with quickly and with little nuance. As with Semiramis, for Dante, Dido's sin is one of rupture: through her affair with Aeneas, she "broke faith" to Sychaeus's memory. Importantly, she is identified by name here not by Virgil but by Dante the poet, when Francesca da Rimini emerges from the *schiera*, or the "flock" of souls, to speak: "cotali uscir de la schiera ov'è Dido / a noi venendo per l'aere maligno" (so did they emerge from the flock where Dido is, coming to us through the cruel air; *Inferno* V.85–86); the entire group of sinners is identified by her name.[46] It has become a collective, shameful identity, her name shorthand for being felled by love. Dido herself does not speak, an echo of Book VI of the *Aeneid* when Aeneas sees her in the Underworld, her self-inflicted wound still fresh; once an eloquent speaker, she is rendered eternally speechless after her suicide in Virgil's poem.

These two widowed rulers in Hell foreshadow the examples of widowed loyalty in the second canticle of the *Commedia, Purgatorio,* in which widows play a central role as mediators skilled in the art of persuasion. A widow's mediating role in Purgatory was perhaps the most important assigned to widows in the Christian Middle Ages, ensuring a smooth transition for their husbands and others from the purgatorial mountain into Heaven. Purgatory itself is a space of mediation; the souls, hoping to be released from the penitential environment of the mountain into Heaven above them, must depend on the actions of their loved ones on earth, a delicate hostage negotiation performed through steady prayers, devotion, and tears.

Purgatory began to be viewed as a space that could be controlled by those on earth in the eleventh century, as Jacques Le Goff argued in his landmark *The Birth of Purgatory.* This new paradigm offered a novel and easily manipulated kind of power to the living over the dead, and benefited from Dante's devotion of a full canticle of the *Commedia* to Purgatory's inhabitants and geography.[47] The role Dante's text played in the development of Purgatory as a well-defined space should not be understated—nor can his attention to widows as a prominent part of the mountain's bureaucratic structure. Le Goff has been criticized for neglecting the pivotal role female spirituality played in Purgatory's development. Barbara Newman points out that visionary women "seem at the very least to have served as midwives at the birth of purgatory."[48] Clark Walter suggests specifically that Le Goff underemphasizes the fundamental role widows played in advancing the importance of Purgatory in the Middle Ages.[49] Indeed, in his analysis of the important role played by those still living on earth for Purgatory's inhabitants, Le Goff skates over the rather important connections between widows on earth and men's advancement up the mountain.[50] As Clark Walter and others have since demonstrated, a widow's daily life was effectively harnessed and organized by the Church through the importance placed on widows as central intercessors for the souls in Purgatory. Clark Walter argues that medieval widows were trapped in a "purgatorial" space on earth themselves, caught between a spiritual obligation to their dead husbands and the competing socioeconomic interests of their natal and husband's families. Responsible for praying their spouses out of Purgatory, they were inherently separated from the living and thereby controlled, their "disorderly" grief channeled into prayer rather than the disturbance of "the public thoroughfares," about which Petrarch complained.[51]

Dante's conception of good widowhood in Purgatory was crucial in concretizing society's view of widows as crucial, influential intercessors. Throughout *Purgatorio,* we hear talk of widows, who are depicted as alternately neglectful and skilled in their roles as terrestrial negotiators.[52] The heavy ethical responsibility assigned to the widow is seen as early as Canto V, when the nobleman Bonconte da Montefeltro, who died on the battlefield at Campaldino, complains to the pilgrim Dante that he is still stuck in Ante-Purgatory because his wife Giovanna has forgotten about him:

Io fui di Montefeltro, io son Bonconte.
Giovanna o altri non ha di me cura,
per ch'io vo tra costor con bassa fronte.

(I was from Montefeltro, I am Buonconte. Neither Giovanna nor any other takes care for me, so I go with lowered brow among these people.) (*Purg.* V.88–90)

Spared the horrors of Hell by uttering the Virgin's name at the moment of his death on the battlefield, Buonconte needs his wife to finish the job by praying him out of Purgatory and into Heaven. Who the "altri" (others) are is unclear, although we are soon given an indication of who might be expected to take on the task if a widow does not devote herself to it soon enough. In Canto VIII, Dante encounters the Pisan Nino Visconti, who begs the Pilgrim to remind his daughter Giovanna to pray for him because his wife, Beatrice d'Este, is abandoning her widowly duties by marrying the Ghibelline ruler of Milan Galeozzo Visconti (no relation to Nino):[53]

quando sarai di là da le larghe onde,
dì a Giovanna mia che per me chiami
là dove a li 'nnocenti si risponde.
Non credo che la sua madre più m'ami,
poscia che trasmutò le bianche bende,
le quai convien che, misera, ancora brami.
Per lei assai di lieve si comprende
quanto in femmina foco d'amor dura,
se l'occhio o 'l tatto spesso non l'accende.

(When you are back beyond the wide waves, tell my Giovanna to call out for me to the place where innocents are answered. I do not believe her mother loves me anymore, since she gave up the white fillets, which, wretched, she will yearn for again. Through her one readily understands how long the fire of love lasts in a female, if sight or touch do not frequently kindle it.) (*Purg.* VIII.70–78)

The name "Giovanna" recalls Buonconte's own derelict widow a few cantos back; Nino's daughter Giovanna, who would have been just nine years old in 1300, must take on her "disloyal" mother's unfulfilled obligations. He does not utter his wife's name here, but Beatrice d'Este's sorry fate would have been well-known to Dante's Trecento readers: forced into a second marriage in 1300, she has been defended by recent critics (as well as some contemporary commentators) for having little choice in her marriage to Galeazzo Sforza, which brought her financial disaster when he lost Milan in 1302.[54] Nino's mournful lament "non credo che la sua madre più m'ami" draws on the ethical groundwork laid out in the *Vita nuova*, with its emphasis on the permanence of love: it is the greatest betrayal, Nino believes, that his widow has turned to another man on earth. The case of Beatrice, her first husband, and her remarriage to the tyrant Galeozzo brings to the fore both the historical complications of remarriage for widows—they often were not able to remain devoted widows praying their husbands up the Mountain of Purgatory even if they wanted to—and Dante's insistence on absolute loyalty to the dead beloved, no matter how difficult that often was for women in practice.[55] Nino's bitter observation that Beatrice will regret having given up the "bianche bende" of widowhood for her new marriage suggests that the poet, if not the Pilgrim or Nino, is perhaps sympathetic to the difficulties Beatrice has had to manage on earth in her widowhood.[56]

As members of the living world, Giovanna and Beatrice are not given the opportunity to speak on their own behalf. Instead, we hear about them only through the resentful, even defamatory, words of their husbands: these wives had a specific job to do, we are told, and they did not do it.[57] These sequential reports of widows' neglect underline the remarkable power a widow was believed to wield over her husband's eternal fate and reputation through her words and prayers, and are a reminder of how grave an abuse of this power it is when women do not attend to their dead husbands' fate. This is reinforced by Giovanna and Beatrice's foil, Nella Donati, who appears in Canto XXIII. As Dante has nearly completed his journey up the Mountain of Purgatory, he is surprised to come across his friend and poetic rival, Forese Donati, who has not been dead five years but has already arrived at the Terrace of Gluttony, just two terraces down from the Earthly Paradise. Donati proudly explains that it is all thanks to his devoted wife, the "vedovella" or "little widow" Nella, who has tirelessly negotiated his journey toward Heaven with a persistent display of "pianger dirotto" and "sospiri," "broken weeping" and "sighs," an alchemic combination of prayerful speech and the nonstop public performance of her grief.[58]

> Sì tosto m'ha condotto
> a ber lo dolce assenzo d'i martìri,
> la Nella mia con suo pianger dirotto.
> Con suoi prieghi devoti e con sospiri
> tratto m'ha de la costa ove s'aspetta,
> e liberato m'ha de li altri giri.
> Tanto è a Dio più cara e più diletta
> la vedovella mia, che molto amai,
> quanto in bene operare è più soletta.

> (I have been so quickly brought to drink the sweet wormwood of our sufferings by my Nella and her broken weeping. With her devoted prayers and sighs she has drawn me from the shore of waiting, and she has freed me from the other circles. My little widow, whom I dearly loved, is the dearer to God and more beloved the more isolated she is in her good actions.) (*Purg.* XXIII.85–93)

Nella's prayers wield a considerable—and particular—power. There is a touch of humor in Forese's triumphant praise of his "vedovella," which is compounded by the existence of the famous *tenzone* between the real-life Forese and Dante, in which Nella is portrayed as a wife left sexually dissatisfied in the bedroom.[59] Although Forese may not have fulfilled his "conjugal debt" to Nella while alive, Nella has certainly fulfilled her widowly one to him with her ostentatiously dutiful prayers.[60] Forese's line "m'ha condotto . . . la Nella mia" conjures an image of the little widow pulling him up the mountain by the hand, entirely in control of her dead husband's physical and eternal destiny. Her "pianger dirotto" is also a pragmatic performance of mourning. Her histrionic displays of grief serve as a means of negotiating her husband's progression up the mountain, be they an expression of authentic grief or not. The language Dante uses to describe her performance recalls the affective theatrics commonly associated with women's mourning, but Forese's description of her is proud, not ashamed. Nella has negotiated a more lenient sentence for him through a carefully curated performance as inconsolable, a widow who, like the city of Florence, has been "dispogliata da ogni dignitade" (despoiled of all majesty); whether she actually *feels* that way is, perhaps, beside the point.

We will see this kind of affective performance again, from the widow in Boccaccio's *Il corbaccio* to poetic works by women writers of later centuries who perform their own grief through verse while using a markedly similar vocabulary centered around weeping and sighing. In Dante's poem, both Pilgrim and reader are separated from the widows Giovanna, Beatrice, and Nella through layers of hearsay: Giovanna and Beatrice's disregard for their husbands' fate, and about Nella's theatrical demonstration of grief, are all mediated through their husbands' words as well as through the Pilgrim's memory of his trip through the underworld. In Canto X of *Purgatorio*, the poet plays with a different mediation strategy, introducing the "vedovella" who appeals to the emperor Trajan to avenge her son's death through the extended ekphrasis on Purgatory's walls. Like Nella, it is through her affective demonstration of pain and suffering that the widow in Canto X proves an effective negotiator; it is also her petition to the emperor that leads him to his ultimate salvation by Pope Gregory, reminding us of the terrific potential of a widow's words.

While Canto X's "vedovella" is markedly different from Forese's little widow in many ways, both are positive examples of the persuasive rhetorical power of a widow's persistent prayers.[61] Whereas Nella's "pianger dirotto," "prieghi devoti," and "sospiri" move her dead husband up the mountain, Canto X's widow also expands the role of the ideal widow in the *Commedia* from one of simple devotion to one's own husband to that of an ambassador on behalf of the broader civic community. At the start of the canto, Virgil leads the Pilgrim along the rocky precipice of the Terrace of Pride; the images carved into the walls represent history's greatest examples of humility, artfully designed by God as instructive images for shades guilty of pride to observe and study. The first example is the Annunciation; in the second the great King David appears naked, dancing with joy before the ark as Michal glowers in the background. The third image is of the emperor Trajan and the widow, who pleads with him to avenge her murdered son (*Purg.* X.76–84). Dante's description focuses intently on the external signs of her persona as a grieving widow: she is identified in the first terzina as a "vedovella," suggesting she is dressed in widow's weeds, although we are told nothing of her own husband or the circumstances of his death. Her conspicuous display of grief contrasts starkly with the symbols of war surrounding Trajan, as the widow stands in all her pitiful humility before the pomp of the mighty emperor and boldly demands that he avenge her dead son before he departs for battle.[62] Trajan, not the widow, is the example of humility in this story. The "miserella" is instead audacious, asking that he put aside his universal, public responsibility as emperor and military commander to relieve her personal suffering. Unlike the two previous scenes on the walls of the mountain, a dialogue occurs between Trajan and the widow, providing us with insight into the grief the widow says she feels. She tells the emperor her heart is breaking; the emperor is at first impatient with her and tells her to wait until his return (X.85–86). But she responds with a question that signals her firsthand knowledge of death's utmost certainty: "'Segnor mio,' come persona in cui dolor s'affretta, 'se tu non torni?'" ("My lord," like one whose grief is urgent, "and if you don't return?"; X.86–88). Trajan's response, that his replacement will avenge her son if he dies in battle, is met with even greater skepticism from the persistent widow: "L'altrui bene a te che fia, se 'l tuo metti in oblio?" ("What will another's good be to you, if you forget your own?"; X.89–90). Moved by her emotion but also by her determination, Trajan finally relents (X.91–93).[63]

The story of Trajan and the widow provides the shade readers in Purgatory and the living readers of Dante's *Purgatorio* with several layers of mediation and intercession. It is through witnessing a representation of Trajan's great act of humility in his forum that Pope Gregory intercedes on the virtuous Pagan's behalf, posthumously fast-tracking him to Paradise.[64] It is through God's artistic depiction of Trajan's act carved on the walls of Purgatory that Dante-pilgrim is witness to this same act, and Dante-poet is able to recount the story to his Trecento readers. But it is due to the widow's persistence, and her persuasive speech, that his actions move Gregory centuries later to intercede. The simple widow's prayers ultimately lead to the salvation not of her husband's soul but of a powerful emperor. Gregory may be the one who places Trajan in the eyebrow of the eagle, but it is the widow who began the process. Thus, when Trajan reappears in *Paradiso* XX, so does the widow: "Dei cinque che mi fan cerchio per ciglio, / colui che più al becco mi s'accosta, / la vedovella consolò del figlio" (Of the five who make a circle for my eyelids, / he who is closest to my beak / consoled the poor widow for her son; XX.43–45).[65] Now it is Trajan who is left unnamed, identified only by his relationship to the widow, "colui che . . . la vedovella consolò." The "vedovella" serves not only as an example to all Christians that prayer can work but as a specific example to widows of the remarkable potential of their persuasive speech.[66]

Dante paid careful, consistent attention to widowhood in both *Vita nuova* and the *Commedia*, highlighting the poetic potential both of the widowed poem and of widowed voices themselves. Building on the authority with which widows' words were endowed in earlier sources as well as the special role of women in contemporary mourning practice, he crafted a particular ethics around love inspired by the ideal of unending widowly devotion. Petrarch appropriates this in his own self-referential cycle of mourning poetry, as he constructs a glossary brimming over with "widowed words"—*sfogare, sospiri, sconsolata, cattivella, vedovella, vedova*—words that, as we will see, would become part of a widowed lexicon in writings by and about widows in the centuries to follow. As I demonstrate in the next chapter, Boccaccio was also attentive to the poetics and ethics of widowhood, often playing in his works with what might lie beneath the surface of a widow's disconsolate exterior.

CHAPTER TWO

Boccaccio's Many Merry Widows[1]

While Dante alludes to the dangerous sexual desire of widows through the figures of Semiramis and Dido in *Inferno*, and even to a certain degree through the figure of Beatrice d'Este and her remarriage in *Purgatorio*, he generally shies away from explicit depictions of the "merry widow." Boccaccio, on the other hand, routinely exploits societal anxieties around the sexual appetite of widows in his writing.[2] Here I analyze a selection of these Boccaccian countertypes, who offer us an additional layer of understanding into this early poetics of widowhood and the complicated relationship between widows and the civic order.

Widows are everywhere in the *Decameron*, and many of them are up to no good. Boccaccio might be considered master of the "merry widow" topos, from the many widows we see throughout the *Decameron* to the antagonist of the vexed *Il corbaccio*, in which readers are subjected to one of the most vulgar antiwoman diatribes of the Middle Ages.[3] While the "merry widow" of Boccaccio's tales is often read as a flat, misogynistic stereotype—a sexually insatiable woman without morals of any kind—the diversity of widowed characters imagined by the author across his entire oeuvre contradicts this unilateral characterization. I start with one of the first widows to appear in the *Decameron*, in the tale of the merchant Rinaldo d'Asti and the hospitable widow he encounters in Day II, Story 2. She is but one in a long, interrelated cast of characters. There is the quasi-widow of Day III, Story 8, who, believing her husband has been condemned to Purgatory, accepts consolation from the sly abbot, ends up pregnant, and then convinces her "reborn" husband the child is his. There is the notoriously deceitful Elena of Day VIII, Story 7, the fable of the scholar and the widow and the precursor to Boccaccio's most extensive, and controversial, treatment of the merry widow type in *Il corbaccio*.[4] There are also more sympathetic examples: Madama Beritola of Day II,

Story 6, who spends many years believing she is a widow and is rewarded for her patience and suffering by reunion with her beloved sons and husband; the noble Ghismonda of Day IV, Story 1, who eloquently defends her amorous appetite after her father refuses to find her a second husband. Then there are the noble widows in *De claris mulieribus*, from the ancient exempla of Dido and Artemisia to Camiola, the Sienese widow who decides it is better to remain a widow than to marry again to a scoundrel;[5] we might also remember the robust discussion of whether it is better to love a widow, a married woman, or a virgin in *Filocolo* IV.[6] A closer look, then, reveals that there is more to Boccaccio's liberal use of widows throughout his work than the apparent "good/bad" binary that animates his most extreme presentations on this theme.

Rinaldo d'Asti and the Welcoming Widow of the Castle

The fable of Rinaldo d'Asti and the welcoming widow who offers him "buono albergo" (good lodging) presents readers with a widow who inhabits a space between these two poles, in a tale concerning the nature of widowed sexuality, piety, hospitality, and life on the road.[7] The novella provides an entry point for looking at the ways in which Boccaccio approaches the ever-present theme of widowhood in medieval Italian life and literature, and the cultural hopes and anxieties traditionally bound up with it. Here, much of the story's humor is anchored in making explicit the implied sexual *connaissance* inherent to widows, a source of great anxiety in a society invested in controlling sexual access to its women. How does this tale speak to the widow's role in Christian hospitality, to public and private displays of mourning, and to broader questions of fortune and consolation in the *Decameron*?

In the second story of the Second Day of *Decameron*, we encounter the lucky merchant Rinaldo who, despite persistent naïveté, finds himself better off at the end of the tale than he was at the start. Like its neighbors across Day II, the second story offers us a narrative featuring travel, humor, and clothing, in addition to a "happy" ending.[8] The tale, narrated by Filostrato, opens with Rinaldo on his return home alone from doing business in Bologna, when he encounters a group of three thieves dressed as merchants on the road between Ferrara and Verona.[9] The geographical location alone should set the careful reader on edge, for he is passing through the lands of the Marchese d'Azzo, most likely the same Azzo VIII d'Este Dante condemns for killing his father (*Inferno* XII.110–112) as well as for having exchanged his political favor for sexual access to his neighbor's unwed sister (XVIII.55–57).[10] It is also in the Po Valley that Francesca da Rimini and her brother-in-law Paolo succumbed to their "dubbiosi disiri" (dubious desires; V.120) under the influence of the original *galeotto libro* (V.137). Filostrato's suggestion that the tale will be recognizable to those who have traveled through the "dubbiosi paesi d'amore" (dubious lands of love) refers both to allegorical lands as well as to the treacherous territory through which Rinaldo is traveling, which literature has already told us is notorious for sexually deviant activity.[11]

Unsuspecting of the thieves' real identities and motivations, Rinaldo rides happily alongside them through these dangerous lands. When they ask if he takes care to pray while traveling, Rinaldo replies that though he has not much knowledge in the way of prayers, he always says a Paternoster and an Ave Maria for the parents of Saint Julian, before praying to God and Saint Julian himself for his own safety (more on the saint below).[12] He adds that he has often encountered danger on his travels but believes that Julian has long watched over him, for he always arrives safely at his night's lodging, no matter the troubles he faces during the day (*Decameron* II.2.8).[13] One of Rinaldo's thief-companions says that he too says prayers on the road, but somewhat different ones, which Branca suggests may allude "slyly" to their brigand lifestyle; it is a hint of what is to come of which Rinaldo takes no notice.[14]

When it is almost nightfall, the thieves make their move, robbing Rinaldo of his horse and everything else but the shirt on his back. They also tease him scornfully about his prayers to Saint Julian, which now seem to have been vain: "Va e sappi se il tuo san Giuliano questa notte ti darà buono albergo, ché il nostro il darà bene a noi" ("Now see whether the prayer you said to Saint Julian will give you as good a night's lodging as our own saint will provide for us"; II.2.13). Rinaldo's cowardly servant takes off as well. The forlorn merchant thus finds himself a sad victim on the road as night descends and, "dolente e isconsolato" (sorrowful and inconsolable; II.2.17), he bemoans his fate in piteous tones.[15] Saint Julian does, however, ultimately provide for the unlucky Rinaldo, through circumstances winkingly close to those of his own legend.

It is worth pausing here to rehearse the story of this Saint Julian, who plays a backstage but crucial role in the tale. There are echoes of his legend sprinkled throughout the novella, and Rinaldo serves as an unwitting double to Julian himself as well as to other characters in the saint's story. The saint, often known as Julian the Hospitaller, is the patron of hospitality and was a popular recipient of prayers in the Middle Ages and into the Renaissance, but he is perhaps most notorious for having unwittingly murdered his beloved parents. In the *Legenda Aurea* (*Golden Legend*), he is the fourth of five Saint Julians worthy of mention.[16] Hunting as a young man, Julian comes across a talking stag, who prophesies that he will kill his own mother and father someday. Julian tells no one about the encounter but, horrified by the stag's prediction, leaves his childhood home in secret and travels to a distant kingdom where he takes a position at court. He is soon rewarded with a knighthood as well as the hand of a rich and noble widow whose dowry includes a castle. Despite this good fortune, Julian cannot outrun his destiny; his parents, who have searched everywhere for their son, turn up at his castle and beg for shelter on their travels. He is away when they arrive, but his kind wife welcomes them in and recognizes them as Julian's parents. She offers them the marriage bed after their long journey and leaves them there sleeping when she goes to church the next morning. While she is out, Julian comes home and discovers the two asleep in his bed; assuming that his wife has betrayed him with another man, he kills them both in a rage. Only when his wife returns from church does he realize he has killed not his faithless wife and her lover but his own beloved parents, just as the stag had predicted. As penance for this grievous act, Julian and his wife abandon their comfortable life and take to the road; after making pilgrimage to Rome, they build a hospital for the needy. One night, Julian hears a poor leper along the road begging for help;

he takes the wretch in, offering him his own bed. The leper reveals himself to be an angel and tells Julian that his penance has been paid through his act of hospitality and kindness; soon after, both Julian and his wife die and go directly to Heaven.

The legend of Saint Julian provides both a roadmap and clear points of contrast for Boccaccio's tale. Julian, his parents, and the disguised angel are all embodied in the figure of Rinaldo, the dispossessed traveler who finds himself in need of consolation and hospitality and is rewarded for his consistent prayers—and who in turn rewards the widow for her welcome. Julian's widow-wife, who is presented as something of an afterthought in the *Golden Legend*, takes on new dimensions by implicit comparison with the figure of the hospitable widow who takes pity on Rinaldo's circumstances. After his servant runs off, Rinaldo makes his way to the town's fortress and finds shelter beneath an overhang, where he again prays, loudly and weepily, to his Saint Julian. His prayers are soon answered: the lady of the castle—who happens to be not only a beautiful young widow but the live-in mistress of the very Marquis d'Azzo who rules over the lands through which Rinaldo is traveling—hears his noisy lament and comes to his aid (*Decameron* II.2.19).

Like Rinaldo, the widow found herself in an unanticipated situation that evening, and she too is in need of consolation. She had been expecting to pass a romantic evening with the marquis, with a bath already drawn for the two of them and an elaborate, romantic dinner prepared, but he was abruptly called away, and she is left to her own devices. Described as "un poco sconsolata" (feeling rather disconsolate; II.2.21) by the news that her lover will not be joining her, the widow decides nevertheless to get into the bath, which is positioned close to the open window. It is from there that she hears Rinaldo's dolorous, "stork-like" wails (II.2.22) and sends her maid to fetch the wretched unknown traveler.[17] Rinaldo appears shivering before her, almost frozen to death, much like the disguised angel in the story of Saint Julian. In what we might classify as a kind of necromantic reanimation ritual, the widow and her maid get him into the warm bath where "e tutto dalla caldezza di quello riconfortato da morte a vita gli parve esser tornato" (he felt as if he were returning from death to life, II.2.27). She then loans him some of her recently deceased husband's clothes, which just so happen to fit him perfectly. Recovered and now dressed in finer garments than his own, Rinaldo does not forget to say a quick thank-you to God and Saint Julian. He is rewarded once again for his piety, this time with an act of sexual consolation that serves not only to restore him fully to good health but to resurrect, in a fashion, the widow's dead husband as well.

As Filostrato explains, the widow's insatiable sexual appetite—"concupiscibile appetito"—had already been whetted by her anticipated evening with the marquis (II.2.35), and when she sees Rinaldo in her husband's clothes, she finds herself overcome with desire. She consults with her maidservant, who eagerly encourages her to take advantage of what Fortune has delivered to her doorstep. The widow confesses to Rinaldo that he looks so much like her husband when dressed in his clothes that it is as though she is seeing her beloved again, and she has been holding back a strong desire to embrace him (II.2.37). Rinaldo replies with enthusiasm, welcoming her advances; before long, they are in bed together and pass the night fulfilling their every desire. The following morning, the widow takes back her husband's garments, gives Rinaldo money and more modest clothes to wear, asks him to keep their night of passion a secret, and sends him on his way. At the very moment he is happily reuniting with his servant and borrowing some of his clothes to wear, "quasi per divin miracolo" (as if by some divine miracle; II.2.41), the three robbers are brought to the castle and Rinaldo gets his horse and all his possessions back—other than, curiously, a pair of garters the thieves could not locate. Once more, Rinaldo thanks God and Saint Julian for protecting him and returns home restored of his property, having passed a very consolatory evening indeed. The thieves are hanged for their crimes (II.2.42).

Rinaldo's fortuitous appearance at the widow's door dramatizes a widespread societal concern about widowed sexuality and autonomy and, ultimately, the havoc it might wreak on masculine identity and patriarchal order. The hospitality Rinaldo receives from the widow is not simply an act of Christian charity extended to a wayward traveler—an example of which we will see in another Day II tale—but is instead emblematic of late medieval beliefs about widows' insatiable sexual appetites. Taken together, the absent marquis, drawn bath, and tasty delicacies offered to Rinaldo crudely caricature the circumstances of widowhood, in which a young woman might find herself living independently and "primed" for sex, wanting only for a partner, an example of which we see in the tragic tale of the young widow-returned-home Ghismonda in IV.1. Rinaldo is too naïve to be put off by the widow's attempts to upturn the natural order of things by treating him as a kind of mannequin, no more than an embodied stand-in for her late husband. Neither Rinaldo nor the widow expresses any hint of guilt or penitence, even though their night of passion arguably cuckolds two men, the marquis and her late husband, though one might alternatively argue that by sleeping with Rinaldo while he wears her husband's clothes, she cuckolds the marquis with two different men, one living and one dead. The story is presented as a comedy and not a tragedy precisely because Rinaldo is wholly restored to his previous identity—save for the pair of garters, the story's last indication that not everything, Rinaldo included, is as it should be.

Anxieties around widowed sexuality thus bleed into the theme of hospitality as key to salvation, which is so central to the message of Saint Julian's legend. Julian's widow-wife embodies the ideal of Christian hospitality that was expected of good widows: in 1 Timothy, we are told that a *vere vidua*, or "widow indeed," must not only pray all day and reject earthly pleasures but also readily take in strangers in need of shelter.[18] Though Julian's widow-wife fulfills that requirement by offering her bed to Julian's parents, she is still not above his suspicion, most likely due to the fact that she remarried after her first husband's death—even if it was to him.[19] Julian's unwitting act of double parricide is not simply a capricious if violent reaction to finding strangers in his marital bed but rather is grounded in a profound mistrust of his own wife, a beautiful widow who warmly welcomes his parents to her castle. It is fitting that Julian ultimately pays penance for his sins through offering his own bed to a stranger: Wayne Rebhorn observes that the "hospitality" of Saint Julian in the Middles Ages and Renaissance "often included the furnishing of one's guest with a bed companion."[20] This specific type of intimate hospitality collides in *Decameron* II.2 with unbridled widowed sexuality: Rinaldo's hostess offers him a perversion of both the traditional Christian hospitality Saint Julian offers the angelic messenger on the road and that expected of widows themselves in the Christian tradition.

That the widow, who is "un poco sconsolata" after learning that the marquis cannot make their rendezvous, is so quickly consoled in Rinaldo's arms reflects further societal anxieties around the authenticity and lasting power of widowed grief and whether "inconsolable" women could ever be trusted. "The merry widow," Sandra Cavallo and Lyndan Warner write, "was usually portrayed as rich, worldly, ready to enjoy her independence and satisfy her sensual appetite."[21] This literary type reflected broader trends in society. Christiane Klapisch-Zuber argues that in Florence the typical Renaissance widow was considered a grave risk due to her sexuality, an unsupervised time bomb like the lascivious, sinful widow of *Il corbaccio*.[22] Widows represented a "liminal state between the carnal world of marriage and the perfection of intact virginity," which had been underlined in the writings of Paul, Augustine, and Jerome.[23] Neither virgins nor married women, they were generally viewed as suspect, their sexual knowledge and experience placing them on a slippery slope of desire they could slide down at any moment, whether through a remarriage or an extramarital dalliance.[24]

Widows in the *Decameron*—a text whose proclaimed purpose is the consolation of women—are frequently described as "sconsolate," though not always due to grief over their husbands. To the contrary, from the first time we see the adjective used in the *Decameron*, in this very tale, widows across the *novelle* are generally disconsolate over the loss of their *lovers* instead. Teodolinda Barolini argues that for Boccaccio consolation itself is "an interactive process in which, through the offices of others, one who has experienced suffering . . . is able to reattain a baseline of sufficient existential comfort to carry on."[25] For the widows of the novelle, this existential comfort is generally amorous and indulgent; they are thus set up in opposition to the cultural ideal of the pious widow who spends her days mourning her husband's loss alone. In the lead-up to Day IV, we see Lauretta lead the ladies in a dolorous ballad, which begins "niuna sconsolata / da dolersi ha quant'io" (no disconsolate lady / has suffered more than I have; III.Conclusione.12).[26] The ballad is, significantly, told from the perspective of a widow; she mourns not the loss of her husband, however, but the happy time she spent as a widow.[27]

The widow Elena in VIII.7 is described as "sconsolata" only once Rinieri tricks her, trapping her atop her own tower in the blazing sun (VIII.7.109). As Barolini observes, Elena is Boccaccio's "most disconsolate heroine," "a woman whose own actions rather than bad fortune" have made her a *sconsolata*.[28] D'Asti's widowed hostess, too, is described ironically as "un poco sconsolata" when faced with the prospect of an evening without sex, but unlike Elena she receives her sexual consolation without being punished for it. For this we can thank fortune as well: Barolini reminds us that "while the wheel is on the ascendant and the ladies are heading toward the *Valle delle donne*, the *novelle* make erotic *consolazione* available to women as well as men," the inverse of what women experience in the *Decameron*'s second half.[29]

With no harsh *contrapasso* imposed upon her, Rinaldo's widowed hostess fits neatly into the category of what Heather M. Arden describes as the "grieving but easily consoled" widow, an "archetypal embodiment of deeply rooted male attitudes toward women and female sexuality."[30] It is a category frequently illustrated by medieval retellings of Petronius's story of the Widow of Ephesus, a woman once renowned for chastity who resolved to stay at her husband's grave and starve herself so she could join him in death. In only a few days' time, she is swayed from her plan by two fiddling characters: her faithful maidservant and a soldier stationed nearby to guard the crucified corpses of some thieves. Despite her initial grief, she is seduced first by the soldier's offer of food and then quickly also by his offer of sex, egged on by her maidservant. It doesn't take much for her to go from protecting her husband's body to willingly desecrating it, offering it to the soldier to replace that of a crucified thief stolen under his distracted watch. This cautionary tale underscores the cultural worry not only that widows possess insatiable sexual appetites but that these appetites can do serious damage, both to individual bodies and to the body politic. The echoes of the Widow of Ephesus in the story of Rinaldo d'Asti—the enabling maidservant, the executed thieves, the replacement of one man's body for another, all in the service of a widow's rampant sexual desire—interweave with the elements lifted from the story of Saint Julian to reinforce the idea that a widow's hospitality can be more layered than Pauline doctrine prescribed. Rinaldo's hostess is a far cry from Julian's chaste widow-wife, who offered hospitality to her husband's parents, but she is nevertheless following the lesson of Saint Julian, even if it is with an Ephesian twist.

Equally complex is the widowed hostess's peculiar devotion throughout the tale to the memory of her dead husband. While it would be far-fetched to suggest she is an exemplary loyal widow, she still treats her dead husband as irreplaceable and unforgettable in a way that neither the marquis nor Rinaldo is. Dressing Rinaldo up in her husband's clothes, she performs a perverted version of widowed grief, honoring his memory through sexual intercourse with an avatar, a stranger to whom she has offered refuge. Rinaldo is more than anything a body onto which she can impose her own latent desires, purposefully transforming him from the cold, shivering traveler on the road into a simulacrum of her dead husband. She does not seem interested in the possibility that the stranger might be a divine figure, Christ on the Road to Emmaus or Julian's disguised angel. Her focus is instead personal, fixed on her memorialization of her husband through a privately performed ritual in which, for one night, she brings him back to life by bathing Rinaldo (a makeshift baptism), feeding him, dressing him in her husband's clothes, and, finally, sleeping with him.

That she does all this in private, away from public view, may well speak to the highly litigated role in public mourning practice of widows as performative *sconsolate* whose uncontrollable wails and weeping were viewed as a possible catalyst for civic unrest.[31] As we have seen, in precisely the period Boccaccio was writing, the question of how society should mourn—in particular, how and where *women* should mourn—was being continually debated and legislated, including in his own city.[32] In this story, the widow, cooped up inside her lover's castle, unable to mourn publicly for her husband, can expiate her grief only in strange, unusual, and sexual ways, perverting the widow's obligations as a hostess. Outside the watchful eye of the community, Filostrato's story seems to suggest, Christian hospitality can morph into necromantic sex ritual in the blink of an eye. Whereas in Day III, Story 8, the abbot tricks the woman into thinking that her husband is dead so that she will sleep with him, here the story is flipped: the "sconsolata" has found a doppelgänger on earth who can help her bring her husband back to her, if only for a moment. Indeed, Filostrato is sure to tell us that when Rinaldo puts on her husband's garments, they fit him perfectly, as though they were tailored to him specifically (*Decameron* II.2.27). For Sergio Zatti, the Second Day is "un trionfo del corpo *deguisé*, del corpo camuffato" (a triumph of the disguised body, of the camouflaged body);[33] for Elissa Weaver, "clothes are the objective correlative of one's fortune [on the Second Day], and are, along with one's fortune, lost and regained."[34] Over the course of the novella, Rinaldo loses and ultimately regains his good fortune, with one small exception. The garters or *cintolini*—rather, their absence—signify a change. It is a small loss, but a loss nonetheless; without them, the clothes that make the man can literally fall away from the body. As garters are visible only in men's outfits, their noticeable lack means that Rinaldo loses a signifier of status as well as a very practical bit of wear that would otherwise keep his legs covered and protected on the rest of his journey home.[35]

Weaver points out that the story of Rinaldo is the only one of Day II in which "dressing and undressing" "account[s] for each progression of the plot."[36] There is a stark, and most likely intentional, contrast between the tenor of the widow's care for Rinaldo and that of the good woman who restores Landolfo to health two stories later. In Day II, Story 4, the "povera feminetta" or "poor little woman" (II.4, 22) who discovers Landolfo after he washes up on the shore takes care of him as though he is a little child ("come un picciol fanciullo"; II.4, 24); she too bathes the unfortunate stranger and feeds him, giving him back life and strength after his arduous journey. He is given new clothes, however, not by the woman but by kind merchants, and Landolfo rewards both the woman and the merchants financially for their kindness. There is no suggestion in Landolfo's story that the woman might offer him sexual consolation, despite all his bad luck, nor that he will repay her with his body; while we do not read of a husband, that she is described consistently as a "feminetta" and a "femina" is itself revealing, and not only of her class status.[37] Widows are nearly always labeled as such: they are a specific category of person, and when a character in the *Decameron* is a widowed woman, the reader is made to know about it.[38] Despite coming to a man's rescue, the widowed hostess of Story 2 shares little else in common with the "feminetta" of Story 4. Instead, she is tied through multiple linguistic indicators to other widows in Boccaccio's works, from Elena and the widow of the *Corbaccio* to the tragic Ghismonda, her "concupiscibile appetito" chiming with the widowed Ghismonda's self-proclaimed "concupiscibile disidero" (IV.1.34).[39]

Whereas Ghismonda's tale ends tragically, readers are given no hint that the widow of Day II, Story 2, will (or should!) suffer any consequences for her sins. While we learn first that the young women and men of the *brigata* praise Rinaldo's devotion and prayers to God and Saint Julian, more revealing is their reaction to the widow's choices. "Né fu per ciò (quantunque cotal mezzo di nascoso si dicesse) la donna reputata sciocca, che saputo aveva pigliare il bene che Iddio a casa l'aveva mandato" (Nor, moreover, was the lady considered to have acted foolishly [even though nobody openly said so] for the way she had accepted the blessing that God had left on her doorstep; II.3.2). The brigata is tickled by the sexual fortunes of the widow, the "buona notte" (good night) she is afforded as payment for providing Rinaldo with "buono albergo" or "good lodging." While she is not the first widow to be introduced in the *Decameron*, she is the first described as "sconsolata." Rinaldo is also "isconsolato" when rescued by the widow; their night of passion serves as mutual consolation, an example of the "interactive process" Barolini identifies, which can return Boccaccio's many characters to a state of "existential comfort," even if they come away with less clothing than they had at the start.

The Merry Widow Turned Tragic

The multifaceted problem of a widow's place in society is further evident in the complex tale of Ghismonda referenced above, the first of Day IV. The day is devoted to tragic love and ruled over by the unhappy lover Filostrato, and the tales are expected to move the audience to affective response—namely, tears.[40] The first story, told by Fiammetta, does not disappoint: Ghismonda is the beautiful, eloquent, and beloved daughter of Tancredi, Prince of Salerno, whom he is reluctant and slow to marry off, but marry her off he does. She is soon widowed and returns home. While few words are devoted to her brief marriage, her husband's death, and her subsequent return to her father's house—all these events are relayed in one sentence (*Decameron* IV.I.321)—it is her status as a widow that serves as the catalyst for her tragedy. She hopes to marry again, but she soon realizes that Tancredi has no intention of finding her a second husband, and so she takes the manservant Guiscardo as her lover. The two conduct their affair discreetly, but her jealous father, who happens to have fallen asleep in her room while waiting for her to return, overhears their lovemaking. Enraged and hurt, he orders his guards to seize Guiscardo and then confronts his daughter about her betrayal.[41]

It is his confrontation with his widowed daughter that bears analysis in the context of our discussion here. Tancredi confronts his daughter, as wounded as a jealous lover, and weeps continuously as he voices his accusation "come farebbe un fanciul ben battuto" (as though he were a child who had been soundly beaten; IV.I.29). In stark contrast to her father's gratuitous emotional display, Ghismonda remains in control of her emotions and does not give in to her feminine proclivities, despite feeling the desire to make apparent the "dolore inestimabile" she feels inside. Rather than break down, "con asciutto viso" (with a dry face) she launches into an eloquent and persuasive oration, in which she upbraids her father, defending herself as a woman entitled to her sexual satisfaction in her widowhood (IV.I.31). She reminds him that the "leggi della giovanezza" (laws of youth) are strong and hard to combat, which he should remember from his own youth. She is also "piena di concupiscibile disidero" (full of concupiscible desire; IV.1.34) as a result of her marriage, much like Rinaldo's widowed lover, who possessed a similar "concupiscibile" appetite. At the end of her speech, she turns the tables on the traditional alignment of gendered emotion, mocking her father for his distinctly feminine lack of control over his tears: she tells him to go "va con le femine a spander le lagrime" (go and shed your tears among the women; IV.1.45).

Despite her passion, Tancredi is not persuaded, and his men brutally murder Guiscardo. They cut out his heart, which Tancredi then bestows upon his daughter in a beautiful golden goblet. Ghismonda, heartbroken, resolves to die and sends for poisonous herbs, but we see her grief again contained—described here, specifically, as unfeminine in its silence. "Senza fare alcun feminil romore" (suppressing all sound of womanly grief; IV.1.55), she makes another impassioned speech, this time to her maidservants, weeping throughout; her tears are contagious, and her women cry along with her, creating a virtual fountain of tears (IV.1.56). Boccaccio here gives readers a group of women weeping together collectively in response to the grief of one person, after Ghismonda's earlier scornful suggestion that her father go weep with the women. The young widow then mixes and drinks a poisonous concoction in the goblet and lies down to die, her lover's heart placed atop her own. Her father, overcome with grief at her death, buries the two lovers together, as is her wish, so that they may remain together in death.

The story of the doomed Ghismonda plays with widowhood, sexuality, and emotion in a very different way than that of Rinaldo and his widowed hostess. Though she too is a rich, noble widow who falls into bed with a man of a lower class, the care and eloquence with which Ghismonda negotiates her fate move the brigata to compassion and tears: "aveva la novella dalla Fiammetta raccontata le lagrime più volte tirate insino in su gli occhi alle sue compagne" (more than once had Fiammetta's story brought tears to the eyes of her fair companions; IV.2.2). Yet Ghismonda herself insists on remaining dry-eyed throughout her initial speech to her father and silent even when she does break down in tears. Rather than succumb to the "feminil romore" with which widows were commonly associated, she speaks in front of her father only when she is able to be in control of her emotions and breaks down only when she is in a protected, all-female place—a privileged space much like that in which Dante imagines his poems finding good company.[42]

It is worth noting that Christine de Pizan took up the Ghismonda tale in her *Livre de la cité des dames*, one of only three stories she borrowed from the *Decameron* (as compared to the seventy-four she took from his *De claris mulieribus*). Carla Bozzolo has argued that Christine's choices from the *Decameron* represent "the incarnation of praiseworthy virtues," examples for her female audience; Ghismonda's rhetorical acumen, honesty—even her sexual frankness—are presented as qualities to emulate in Christine's text.[43] Hers was the version of Ghismonda that many vernacular readers in France first encountered; *Livre de la cité des dames* was read early on as a literal translation of Boccaccio's *De claris*, which allowed for a more pro-woman version of the stories to circulate for several years, in a text designed more as a true handbook of examples for women than one aimed at a male humanist readership. Only when Boccaccio's Latin text was fully translated into French in the mid-fifteenth century did Christine's text stop being copied and read as regularly. The tale of Ghismonda became increasingly popular in the Renaissance, in both Italy and France; Leonardo Bruni (1370–1444) translated it into Italian in 1438, making it more widely available to a vernacular audience, and it was versified in France by 1493.[44]

Nasty Widows: Elena and the Widow of *Il corbaccio*

The unusual affective discipline and spirit with which Ghismonda conducts herself before her suicide, which made her such an appealing example for Christine, is especially noteworthy when compared to the ostentatious, loud, and empty performances of grief by two of Boccaccio's thorniest characters, the related widows of *Decameron* VIII.7 and the *Corbaccio*. Unlike those who reside at the Marchese's castle and Tancredi's court, these two widows are creatures of the city—specifically, Boccaccio's own Florence, with all its laws and worries about gendered grief. In *Decameron* VIII.7, commonly known as the tale of the scholar and the widow, the widow Elena is first described, pointedly, by her provenance, as "una nostra cittadina" (a gentlewoman of our city; 3). Elena has resolved of her own accord never to remarry: she is economically independent and sexually satisfied by a lover she has chosen herself ("a sua scelta inamorata"). The scholar Rinieri, recently returned from his studies in Paris, catches sight of Elena at a party in her widow's habit ("vestita di nero sì come le nostre vedove vanno" [dressed in black as our widows are]; VIII.7, 6) and falls in love with her immediately.[45]

Pampinea describes Elena as a woman who "non teneva gli occhi fitti in inferno" (was not in the habit of keeping her eyes fixed to the ground; VIII.7, 8), suggesting she does not spend much time praying for her dead husband or considering the afterlife as a vere vidua should; instead, her eyes are fixed firmly on the fleshly world of Florentine society. She is therefore quick to notice Rinieri's amorous glances and, vainly delighted to have ensnared him, she decides to have some fun to entertain both herself and her lover. Using her faithful maid as a go-between, she leads Rinieri to believe that she is in love with him but that she cannot risk her good reputation as a widow and that they must therefore meet in secret. Pampinea, narrating the story, exclaims, "Ahi, cattivella, cattivella, ella non sapeva ben, donne mie, che cosa è il mettere in aia con gli scolari!" (Ah, what a poor misguided wretch she must have been, dear ladies, to suppose that she could get the better of a scholar!; VIII.7, 13).[46] The maid and the widow convince Rinieri to wait for Elena in the courtyard the day after Christmas. It begins to snow, and Elena and her lover spy on Rinieri from a window, an image that calls to mind the earlier tale of Rinaldo and his widowed hostess, who heard his cries through the window and took pity on him by having her maid bring him to her. Rather than welcome him, Elena lies again, saying that her brother is inside and she cannot risk her reputation as a chaste widow by letting him in. After a miserable frigid night in the courtyard—he is compared to a stork due to his chattering teeth, like Rinaldo outside in the woods—Rinieri finally realizes that he has been tricked by the widow. He is furious but does not reveal his anger, instead plotting future revenge.

Six months later, his body finally recovered from the ordeal, Rinieri is visited by the widow's maid for help. Elena's lover has left her for another woman, the maid says, and she hopes Rinieri has picked up some necromantic skill during his studies in Paris that might help her win him back. Seeing his chance for revenge, Rinieri invents an absurd ritual for her to perform, whereby she must dip herself and an image of her lover in water seven times and then climb onto a high point, naked, and face north. The widow listens to his every word; conveniently, she happens to have a nearby estate that abuts the Arno. Once she has bathed in the river, she climbs naked to the top of her estate's tower; Rinieri, mirroring her earlier secret surveillance of his humiliation in the courtyard, hides in the bushes and watches her perform the meaningless ritual. He then quietly enters the tower and removes the ladder, leaving the widow trapped and naked. After she has recited the bogus prayer, she waits, but nothing happens, and she soon realizes that, like the scholar six months earlier, she has been tricked. The following morning, when Rinieri awakes, the two engage in a long conversation in which the scholar holds forth on the evils of women in a misogynist tirade outdone only by the *Corbaccio*. After much back and forth, Rinieri abandons her and she is left alone, humiliated, weeping, and tortured—her skin scorched by the hot July sun, her dangerous beauty destroyed.

For all her beauty, wealth, and sexual satisfaction, the widow's violent (and excessive) punishment is not just for her deceit but for living in a way not befitting a widow—her body set on fire a simulacrum of the hellfire she deserves because of the way she has conducted herself as an unattached woman in society. As Barolini observes in her analysis of the tale, "Perhaps a widow's need of instruction is in proportion to her greater social liberty."[47] Rinieri's brutal treatment of the widow has a clear, Dantean logic, underlined by the widow's burning atop the tower: it is the logic of the contrapasso, in which one's eternal torment reflects one's sin on earth. The widow left the scholar outside to freeze, nearly deforming his body through cold, and so he leaves her outside to burn, destroying her beauty through a literal scorching.[48] Not just any humiliation will satisfy Rinieri—he must punish the widow physically for her cruelty, destroying the beauty that made him fall in love and that makes her such a dangerous widow. That he manipulates the situation so that she is also nude is more than just a brutal humiliation on his part. He fell in love with Elena when she was dressed in the clothes of a Florentine widow: "vestita di nero sì come le *nostre* vedove vanno" (dressed in black as *our* widows are; emphasis mine).[49] Punishing her at her country home outside the city walls, he strips her of her identity as *both* "cittadina" (citizen) and honest "vedova" (widow).

The brigata's verdict on the two wretched characters in VIII.7 is that neither is blameless, though they allow Elena some sympathy, while judging the scholar quite harshly. Indeed, Regina Psaki suggests that they may find much in common with the disgraced widow, who is treated so harshly for her actions.[50] Barolini goes further, and I agree with her analysis: Boccaccio himself, she suggests, "is more critical of the scholar than of the widow," and builds Rinieri into an "anti-Boccaccio": an intellectual totally out of touch with the human compassion at the ethical core of the *Decameron*.[51]

When Boccaccio expands the tale into *Il corbaccio* in 1355, he deprives the widow of the cushion of compassion offered her by the frame commentary of the brigata, and of the larger context of a community of women who are also "pushing back" and making their voices heard, leaving her as naked and alone as Elena on top of her tower.[52] The story of a lusty Florentine widow, her bitter dead husband, and the narrator, her angry spurned lover, *Il corbaccio* replicates both the youthful anguish and devotion of the *Vita nuova* and the fantastic voyage and pious condemnation of sinners found in the *Commedia*. The story has been the subject of much critical debate and indecision. Millicent Marcus, forgiving Boccaccio's characters in the *Decameron* their misogyny "as a literary tradition and as a premise for storytelling," cannot look past the baldness of the *Corbaccio*'s narrator's loathing for the widow: "For whatever reasons, be they autobiographical, as most critics argue; spiritual . . . or cultural . . . the writer of the *Corbaccio* becomes the Rinieri of *Decameron* VIII, 7 whose revenge changes from roasting the widow on a tower to embalming her in abusive prose."[53] Marilyn Migiel has observed that "[it] tends now to be read as an ironic fiction, an immense joke at the expense of those who would advance extreme misogynist views."[54] Robert Hollander also argues that the story is a "prolonged joke."[55] Sara Díaz has recently observed that whatever the author's motivations, "within his antifeminist narrative lies a damning critique of the philosopher-type," another "anti-Boccaccio," to borrow Barolini's description of Rinieri.[56] Here, I am most interested in the way the book's widow is proffered by her dead husband as an avatar for all the worst female qualities the misogynist narrator can imagine and verbalize and how we might understand Boccaccio's depiction of the widow as both subtly sympathetic and socially engaged.

As the *Corbaccio* opens, we are presented with a narrator overwhelmed by amorous grief, much like the Dante of the *Vita nuova*. This time, however, the (not so young) man, a scholar like Rinieri, is the victim of a manipulative, lecherous widow who has made a fool of him and broken his heart. Again like the young Dante of the *Vita nuova*, he cannot stop his lamenting and spends his days in his room weeping over his rejection; like the pilgrim of the *Commedia*, he is at an existential impasse.[57] On the verge of suicide, he finds himself on a road in a dark and forbidding forest; the narrator is approached by a solitary figure, who becomes his guide through the "laberinto d'amore," an otherworldly, purgatorial space for those who suffer the torments of love.[58] His mysterious guide is, it turns out, the dead husband of the woman with whom the narrator has been so in love; he is now a shade stuck in Purgatory because, like Buonconte and others before him, his widow is not spending her time praying him into Heaven but instead cavorting with other men.

Where Virgil is Dante's literary forefather, the Spirit-Guide is the narrator's amorous one, an earlier victim of the widow's cruelty. Rather than take the lovelorn pilgrim on a tour of this strange underworld and introduce him to other men destroyed by love, however, the narrator's guide launches into a long, grotesque tirade not only against the widow, but against all women, whom he lambasts as an inferior, deceptive, and physically revolting sex, a crude expansion of Rinieri's tirade in *Decameron* VIII.7, and it does not make him look any better than the scholar. The shade tells the narrator that his wife deceived him constantly when they were married: through financial manipulation, cosmetics to falsify her appearance, and adultery.[59] When he died, she put on a histrionic and convincing performance as a grieving widow: she took to the role with dedication, he continues bitterly, openly shedding "false tears" or "le 'nfinte lagrime" (as opposed to "infinite lagrime," which a true widow might shed), and ostentatiously wearing widow's weeds. What is more, she began to describe herself with the familiar vocabulary of widowhood—"misera, abbandonata e sconsolata e dolente" (wretched, abandoned, and disconsolate and mournful)—despite only truly caring about holding on to his money and enjoying herself.[60]

This deceptive self-presentation by the widow as "misera, abbandonata e sconsolata e dolente" underlines the societal anxieties over the authenticity of a widow's outward performance of grief. (As Strocchia has noted, there were even concerns that widowed Florentine women were hiding revealing and immodest garments underneath their mourning attire, a sartorial representation of the deeper fear that widows who *appeared* to be in mourning were secretly enjoying themselves.)[61] The widow's husband himself seems to be most angry not over her sex life but over the fact that she uses her feigned despair over his death to get what she wants—in this case, an independent life, in which she lives with neither her husband's family nor her natal one, but instead in a modest house ("alcuna picciola casetta") where she might devote herself ("vedova e sola" [widowed and alone]) to solitary prayer.[62]

While the Spirit-Guide explains that her entire argument is composed of lies ("suo finto parlare")—including that her expressed desire to be close to a church is only so that she might amuse herself with the friars—it bears stepping back from the way she is presented by her angry husband to consider the widow's underlying strategy here, as it is written by Boccaccio within the sociohistorical context of fourteenth-century Florence. Left alone after her husband dies, without children of her own, and aware she will not be able to survive on the dowry that is hers alone, she negotiates a way to remain a widow and keep herself financially secure and independent, by separating herself from both her husband's family and her own.

Although a widow's dowry and patrimony were legally released to her after her husband's death in Florence, in practice the widow often became caught in a game of tug-of-war, in which her husband's male relatives and her own fought over who got to keep the widow—and, consequently, the money.[63] In response, widows adopted numerous strategies to maintain some semblance of self-determination for themselves and their children, which nearly always included avoiding remarriage.[64] The *Corbaccio*'s widow seems to be rather shrewdly negotiating her situation through the public performance of her grief, insisting that she be allowed to grieve as a "vedova, e sola," so she might maintain control over both her and her husband's wealth.[65] Intriguingly, Katherine

Clark Walter suggests that the widow of the *Corbaccio* is a spoof of the celebrated Florentine widow Umiliana de' Cerchi (1219–1246), who fled from the second marriage her merchant father had arranged for her and lived as a Franciscan tertiary until her death. Boccaccio's widow, Clark Walter argues, is an "anti-saint"—"a model of vice rather than holiness, and a parody of a Florentine tertiary who exploited her position as an ostensibly chaste widow to pursue vanity, greed, and lust."[66] For the Spirit-Guide, her great sin is not that she sleeps with other men but that she spends the social capital of her widow's grief on herself—not on his children from a previous marriage, whom she dumps on his family, nor to secure his eternal salvation.

We might think back, here, to the widow in the story of Rinaldo d'Asti, who is not criticized by either the narrator or other characters for jumping into bed with a stranger—she keeps her husband's memory alive, albeit in an unusual way, and is portrayed as a humorous and welcoming widow. But neither Elena nor her successor in the *Corbaccio* has much concern for their husband's reputations, nor for their eternal destinies. We see this underlined in the Spirit-Guide's final appeal to the narrator, in which the shade begs him to pray on his behalf: "La malvagia femina, che mia moglie fu, è tutta ad altre sollecitudini data, come puoi avere udito, che a ricordarsi di me . . . parente altro non ho, che di me mette cura . . . e perciò alla tua libera profferta imporrò che ti piaccia, quando di questo viluppo sarai dislacciato . . . che tu, a consolazione di me e ad alleggiamento della mia pena, alcuna elimosina facci, e facci dire alcuna messa nella quale per me si prieghi; e questo mi basterà" (That horrible woman, who was my wife, is devoted entirely to other concerns, as you may have heard, and does not keep my memory alive . . . I have no other relatives to take care of me, and therefore I will take you up on your kind offer, if it so pleases you, when you are freed from this knot of yours . . . that you might console me and lessen my pain, by giving some alms, and having some masses said for me; and this will be enough for me).[67]

His words to the narrator here chime with those of Buonconte da Montefeltro in *Purgatorio* V, who tells Dante the pilgrim that he has been abandoned by his wife Giovanna, and with those of Nino Visconti, who asks the pilgrim to tell his daughter Giovanna to pray for him because his wife has remarried. Most importantly, perhaps, the words contrast sharply with the service performed by the devoted widow Nella Donati, who deploys her "pianger dirotto," "prieghi devote," and "sospiri" to move her husband Forese quickly up the Mountain of Purgatory. The widow of the *Corbaccio* is her direct opposite, deploying her grief to secure her own destiny, not that of her husband. The Spirit-Guide is thus forced to be his own ambassador, put in the humiliating position of begging his widow's scorned lover to pray on his behalf. This gives us a deeper understanding of the dangers of the "wailing woman," who could create such disorder in society—not only just after her husband's death, in the instigation of violence and "vendetta" in the streets, but sexually and financially, throughout the long years she remained a widow. The *Corbaccio* ends in a far less dramatic way than *Decameron* VIII.7, with the Spirit-Guide returning to Purgatory and the narrator finding a new lover, unnamed, and warning the "picciola operetta," in a reversal of his opening to the *Decameron*, not to end up in perfidious female hands.

Through the representations of widows in Dante, Petrarch, and Boccaccio considered in this chapter and the previous one, a framework emerges for how we can think about both the ideals and the perceived dangers of widowhood as they related to the broader community on earth, and to the afterlife, in the Italian literary canon. In the next part of this book, I consider historical widows who, like Umiliana de' Cerchi, were celebrated by their communities for their conduct and who contributed to the development of a new authorial voice—the widow's voice—which would come to fruition in sixteenth-century Renaissance literature.

PART II

Context

Model Widows, Holy and Historical

CHAPTER THREE

Sacred Role Models from Judith and Anna to Birgitta of Sweden

In 1614, at the age of sixty-one, the poet Francesca Turina moved to Rome. She was a widow and something of a refugee—at least in her own view—having been forced from her home in Città di Castello in Umbria by her two grown sons, despite stipulations in her husband's will that she would remain in control of his estate until her own death. Luckily, she had friends in high places, and when she arrived in Rome she fell upon the mercy of the noble Colonna family. She became a lady-in-waiting to Lucrezia Tomacelli and tutor to the noblewoman's young daughters with Filippo Colonna, Anna and Vittoria; she remained in Rome until Lucrezia's death in 1622, then returned home.[1] Her *Rime*, published in Città di Castello in 1628, are dedicated to her former charge Anna Colonna, who had been recently married to Taddeo Barberini, the nephew of Pope Urban VIII. In the volume's dedication, Turina praises the Colonna family as her saviors, saying that with them she found "a safe port" from the raging tempest of trouble she had encountered in her widowhood.[2]

The volume, published when she was seventy-five, contains poems in praise of members not only of the Colonna but of the Borghese, Farnese, Orsini, and Aldobrandini families, as well as then-pope Urban VIII and the former popes Paul V and Gregory XV. She ends the collection with two poems dedicated to the king of France, Louis XIII; praising his military victory over the Huguenots at La Rochelle on October 28, 1628, she presents herself as a politically engaged and internationally attuned writer.

Turina's 1628 *Rime* punctuated a long career of survival diplomacy, in which she fashioned herself as a widow in need of help, a sometimes-aggrieved mother, and a secular but pious poet. In chapter 5, I look closely at Turina's poems centered on her widowed grief. Here, I draw attention to a poem in which she addresses a different aspect of widowhood: the sacred role model. The poem transcribed and translated below is one of two in the *Rime* labeled as having been written "sopra le scale del convento di S. Francesca Romana"—on the steps of the convent of the beloved Roman saint Francesca Romana (1384–1440).

> Vedovanza mi tien, sì come lei,
> già di molt'anni carca e 'l crin di neve.
> Francesca anch'io mi chiamo;
> prole ho per cui vivo egra i giorni miei
> e di servir a Dio sol cerco e bramo.
> Con queste qualità, che pari sono,
> qual' désti a lei, Signor, non ti sia greve
> dar anch'a me de la tua grazia il dono:
> ché, quando d'ottenerla io sia mai degna,
> seguiterò sua gloriosa insegna.

> (I have been burdened with widowhood, just like her, for many years, and have a brow of snow. I too am called Francesca; I have children, for whom, sick, I live out my days, and I seek and desire only to serve God. Possessing these qualities, which are the same as hers, Lord, would it not be too much trouble for you to grant me your grace as well? For, if I am ever deemed worthy of it, I will follow her glorious example.)[3]

Francesca Romana was a widow for the last four years of her life, though she is generally described as having lived *like a widow* for many years before, in a "matrimonio bianco" or "chaste marriage" with a husband who suffered from terrible wounds sustained on the battlefield.[4] In the poem, Turina draws an explicit comparison between herself and the fifteenth-century saint, who was canonized while Turina was living in Rome in 1608. Like the saint, she too is a widow, and an old one—she is also a mother and a devoted servant to God, and by happy coincidence she is also named Francesca! Speaking directly to God, Turina points to the established model of the famous Roman widow (one of many designated patron saints of widows) in order to be granted His grace—and to be afforded legitimacy of all different kinds by her readers, who included some of the most influential men and women of seventeenth-century Roman society.

Turina's husband's family boasted a chapel at Santa Maria in Aracoeli just down the road from Santa Francesca Romana's convent Tor de' Specchi; she would have passed the convent every time she visited the church, just beside the Campidoglio. This proximity surely helped inspire her belief in the strong connection with her saintly, widowed Roman predecessor. Through her self-comparison to Francesca Romana, moreover, the secular, widowed poet from Umbria is also aligning herself with a longer lineage of celebrated saintly widows closely tied to the city's identity, which would have been immediately legible to contemporary readers of her poetry. Turina thus authorizes her own civic engagement in Rome.

Holy Models of Widowhood in Late Medieval and Early Modern Italy

In the first part of this study, I discussed the various ways in which Dante, Petrarch, and Boccaccio engaged with widowhood in an ongoing literary laboratory for thinking through *how* and *why* widows were central to civic life—from the metaphorical widow originating in Lamentations to the lyric poems of elegy by Dante and Petrarch and the widowed characters in Dante's *Commedia* and Boccaccio's *Decameron* and *Il corbaccio*. In the two chapters that make up part II, I turn to a discussion of the many figures from the Bible and classical history who were proffered as role models for widows—and thus widowed writers—in Renaissance Italy. These chapters straddle literary history and adjacent fields, including but not limited to religious and political history and the history of emotions. The interdisciplinary nature of these particular chapters is a matter of necessity: it is not possible, nor is it productive, to separate entirely the historical context in which widowed writers lived and worked from the literature of the period or from the writing produced by widows themselves—especially when many of the widows doing the writing were also players in some of the most significant historical events of the day. Before turning to how widows presented themselves, which I consider in part III, it bears considering the textual evidence of widowed women who engaged directly with the saintly and secular role models who surrounded them. As a result, the current chapters also include the analysis of works both by and about widowed women, including Birgitta of Sweden (1303–1373), Christine de Pizan (1364–1431), Lucrezia Tornabuoni (1427–1482), and Vittoria Colonna (1490–1547), in addition to the aforementioned Francesca Turina (1553–1641; sometimes referred to as Francesca Turini Bufalini).

This chapter, specifically, examines the role of holy widows in the development of the engaged, public mode of widowhood we see emerge by the sixteenth century in Italy. I first offer a broad consideration of two biblical prototypes: the Hebrew widow Judith, who rescues her people from Nebuchadnezzar's army through the cunning assassination of the general Holofernes, and the prophetess Anna of Phanuel, a silent witness to the presentation of Jesus at the temple. I then turn to consider how these two models of the civic-minded holy widow are elaborated and celebrated in late medieval and early modern Italy, especially in the case of Birgitta of Sweden and her Italian descendants. By the mid-fourteenth century, we see a new kind of saintly widow emerge in the Italian civic space, whose gaze is directed not inward like the Pauline *vere vidua* but instead outward to the welfare of her fellow citizens. Many of these women played a central role in the articulation of their own identities and legacies through visions, letters, and the establishment of religious orders.[5] I pay special attention to the unique authority of the widowed holy woman with political visions, her authority grounded in her life experience and her role in the community. Holy widows act, I argue, as a hinge between the earlier, binary perceptions of widows we have seen—the devoted mournful steward of a husband's memory and the sexually rapacious or "merry" widow—and the secular widowed writers who forged a new kind of widowed identity in sixteenth-century Italian literature, to which the remainder of this study attends.

Reading the Role Models: Judith and Anna in the Bible and in Italy

A holy widow's identity in the late Middle Ages and Renaissance was informed by a panoply of exempla from the Old and New Testament and late antiquity, all of whom could be mined for select qualities. Like the widow Paula so praised by Jerome, the most popular holy-widow exempla—found in the Bible, the *Golden Legend*, popular and conduct literature, and visual art—were celebrated for channeling their grief into a new identity characterized by an outward-facing focus, to society and God. The two figures to whom they were compared most frequently—the Old Testament's Hebrew widow Judith and the Book of Luke's Anna of Phanuel—embody to a degree the widowed authority inherited from the mournful city in Lamentations itself. They also align with the Pauline model of the ideal Christian widow, the *vere vidua*, who prays all day and isolates herself from others, all while managing to contribute to the greater glory of their people through their actions.

Elena Ciletti observes that Judith has been the recipient of an astonishing variety of "opposing identities and symbolic usages imposed on her across the centuries, from patriot to Virgin Mary prototype to femme fatale."[6] It is perhaps this multitude of identities and symbolisms that has made her such an appealing figure upon which to project a specific ideal. The version of Judith familiar to medieval and Renaissance Italian readers was a flattened one—a role model for Christian women repackaged by the same Jerome who so praised his widowed friend Paula.[7] The Book of Judith, an apocryphal section of the Hebrew Bible, appears in an abridged form in Jerome's Vulgate. Here, Jerome purposefully recenters and recasts the eponymous widow Judith in the role of what Ciletti and Henrike Lähnemann describe as "[a] 'mulier sancta' (holy woman; Jdt 8:29), one who is defined by a single virtue, chastity, of which she is made a moral example, for men and women alike."[8]

Jerome introduces the Hebrew widow Judith in chapter 8 of her own book; the well-known story is as follows. She is a beautiful and rich widow; after the death of her husband, Manasseh, Judith retreats to a "private chamber in the upper part of her house" with her maidservants (Judith 8:5–6) but is compelled to leave her life of widowed isolation when she observes that her community's male leaders are not effectively defending against the Assyrian general Holofernes and his army.[9] She upbraids the men in a long, impassioned speech and then prepares herself for battle, trading her simple widow's weeds for "the garments of her gladness" (Judith 10:3)—removing all external indicators of her widowed identity and returning to the way she dressed when she was a married, sexually active woman. She makes her way to the enemy camp, accompanied by her maidservant, and convinces the guards that she is there to help Holofernes; struck by her beauty and eloquence, they allow her in, and she soon wins the general's trust and admiration as well, as she promises that she will help him round up the Hebrews "as sheep that have no shepherd" (Judith 11:15). On her fourth day in the camp, she accompanies Holofernes to a banquet, dressed to seduce him. Bewitched by her beauty, the foolish general drinks himself into a stupor and passes out once they get back to his tent; Judith then takes his scimitar and decapitates him with two blows, an astonishingly bold political assassination that would become a much-used and highly effective subject of Renaissance art. She then wraps his head in the bed's canopy and passes it to her faithful maidservant waiting outside the tent, and the two of them escape. She delivers his head to the Hebrews, who hang it from the ramparts of Bethulia and then, inspired by her violent act, raid the enemy camp and overcome their oppressors. The Book of Judith concludes with her return to a chaste widowed life apart from society: "And chastity was joined to her virtue, so that she knew no man all the days of her life, after the death of Manasses her husband" (Judith 16:26). She lived to be 105 and was buried next to her husband.[10]

Judith was tremendously popular in the Italy of the Middle Ages and Renaissance, and her identity as a widow was presented as inseparable from her virtuous character and her heroic act of politically justified violence.[11] Hers was a dual resonance: a chaste model for widows as well as inspiration for collective political action against tyranny.[12] We see echoes of Judith, some explicit and some implicit, throughout texts praising Christian widows as well as in texts that served to advance specific political messages.[13] The Judith story was a predominant one in Florence, and artists and writers under Medici patronage made liberal use of the tale after the family's victory over the Pazzi in 1466.[14] Of particular note, Donatello's 1460 bronze statue of Judith in the act of beheading her victim stood in the Medicis' private garden for over thirty years before it was placed on public display, directly in front of the Palazzo Vecchio, in 1495. Allison Levy points playfully to the complexity of what Judith represents in this context, a chaste widow who used her sexuality for a broader civic goal: "Cutting across behavioral boundaries, [Judith] both mourns and plays tricks, tempting Holofernes with her will she / won't she performance just long enough to dismember him."[15] As Sarah Blake McHam has noted, along with his *David*, Donatello's statue of Judith conveyed the message that the ruling Medici family was as heroic as Judith and other "venerable Old Testament tyrant slayers and saviors of their people," which worked to counteract growing resistance in Florence to Medici tyranny.[16] The artist's version of Judith stands with Holofernes's sword raised high above her head, clutching her victim by his hair as she delivers a second, fatal blow to his neck (see Figure 3.1). The base of the statue bears an inscription commissioned by the ruling family's patriarch Piero de' Medici, identifying Judith as a woman who stood up to tyranny, a crucial symbol of liberty and fortitude—a theme his wife Lucrezia Tornabuoni would soon take up in her sacred narrative *The Story of Judith, Hebrew Widow*, as I discuss below.[17]

Although Donatello's sculpture exemplifies efforts to promote Judith as a symbol of Florentine civic identity, contemporary debates about the statue's proximity to the physical seat of Florentine civic power, the Palazzo Vecchio, reflect entrenched cultural fears about widows. In 1504, during the debate over where in Florence to place Michelangelo's statue of David, the architect Francesco Filarete "argued that the image of a woman

Figure 3.1. Reproduction after Donatello (Donato di Niccolò di Betto Bardi), *Judith and Holofernes*, ca. 1455–50, bronze. Piazza della Signoria, positioned in front of Palazzo Vecchio, Florence, Italy. Photo: Stefano Ravera / Alamy Stock Photo.

killing a man was a deadly symbol . . . an omen of evil that had brought only bad luck to the city."[18] Judith, once given pride of place in front of the town hall, was removed to the adjacent Loggia dei Lanzi, where she was repeatedly shuffled around among other public works; Levy has, importantly, observed that she is not visible in Baldessare Lanci's 1569 *View of Florence*, in which we can see both the Loggia and the Palazzo Vecchio.[19] Mary Garrard and others have argued that Donatello's Judith was especially sidelined in art under the rule of Cosimo I (r. 1537–1574) when two pieces depicting violence against women made their way into the civic space of the Loggia: Cellini's *Perseus Slaying Medusa* (1545–1554) and Giambologna's *Rape of the Sabine Women* (1581–1583).[20]

Despite, or perhaps *because of*, the fickle relationship between Judith and the ever-changing face of Renaissance Florence, it is worth considering her appropriation in a literary work by one of the most powerful widows of the Medici family, Lucrezia Tornabuoni. When Piero died in 1469, he left his wife, mother to Lorenzo il Magnifico, a widow at the age of forty-two. Jane Tylus has suggested that the Medici matriarch began writing her sacred narrative of Judith after her husband's death, when she herself was already a widow: in Tornabuoni's version, Judith is "timorosa" and a "vedovetta," a meek "little widow" who strikes out for a greater cause.[21] And yet we see here that "widowed" women can be, as it were, rather divorced from their husbands' legacies, the stars of their own stories. Tornabuoni makes no mention of Judith's husband in the narrative; her actions are centered, while the importance of the husband himself has dissolved. Tornabuoni also omits any mention of the public glory Judith experienced after her heroic act in the Book of Judith, simply reporting that she returned to her quiet isolated existence.[22]

It is, of course, remarkably suggestive that the widow Tornabuoni, who possessed notable political capital in the period of her writing, chose to write about a little "vedovetta" who left her quiet widowed existence to rescue her people in a dramatic, violent, and cunning way before returning to her isolated life. It is worth considering Tornabuoni's portrayal of the heroic Judith in conversation with her letters to both political leaders and Florentine citizens, in which, as Gerry Milligan has pointed out, she is "a promoter of peace as well as of reconciliation."[23] Her correspondence demonstrates a clear belief in her role as a political advocate for the Florentine people; she often writes to her son Lorenzo, then ruler of Florence, to intercede on behalf of poor widows and others in need of help from the ruling family. In a letter dated November 18, 1476, for example, Lucrezia writes to Lorenzo on behalf of the widow Mattea di Francesco, whom she twice characterizes as "poor" in as many lines: she is first "una povera vedovella" (a poor little widow), then a "poverissima donna" (a terribly poor woman), with just one son, Puccio di Francesco. Puccio has been arrested—she does not say why—and put in prison. She beseeches Lorenzo to have the man released because it is charitable and because the man is Florentine, "non altro" (not from elsewhere).[24] On June 9, 1477, Tornabuoni writes to Lorenzo that she has just received a letter from him, in which he has told her he is well, which has given her great comfort.

She then tells him that she plans to leave Bagno a Morbo soon for Florence and will stop at the house of another widow, Madonna di Tita, for the evening on her way back.[25] A year later, in March 1478, Madonna di Tita writes to Lucrezia on behalf of one Leonardo de Broscio da Colle, indicating that the two widows were close enough that she had reason to believe Tornabuoni would trust her recommendation. Tita's letter is appropriately humble given their discrepancies in station but indicates an intimacy with Lucrezia: "sapendo che la Vostra Magnificenza . . . mi vuole bene, [de Broscio da Colle] me à preghata che io ve lo raccomando" (knowing of Your Magnificence's affection for me, he begged me speak to you on his behalf).[26]

Other widows write to Tornabuoni with greater urgency. The widow Antonia di Niccolò writes from Poggibonsi on October 12, 1474, asking that Tornabuoni help her in her struggles to maintain ownership of her only field. On June 16, 1477, Caterina di Niccolaio writes to her beseechingly, admitting that she is in great need or "gran bisogno": "mi trovo hora con 4 figliuoli e senza el marito mio" (I now find myself with four children and without my husband), hoping that Lucrezia can help her "di qualche cosa" (in some way).[27] While her own widowhood is not addressed directly in this correspondence, the number of letters to Lucrezia from marginal women, especially widows, suggests she had a reputation for empathy toward widows and for effectiveness in helping them.[28]

Tornabuoni's self-conscious engagement with the figure of Judith alongside her own work on behalf of fellow Florentine widows highlights just how culturally ingrained the Hebrew widow was by the fifteenth century; in the city of Florence, she could operate as an allegorical symbol for the dynastic self-fashioning of Medici Florence writ large as well as for its matriarch personally. As we will see in the next chapter, Judith was also a figure who bridged the secular and religious, making appearances in multiple texts as the only biblical figure alongside women, especially widows, from antiquity.[29]

For now, however, we will remain in the world of saintly widows and turn to a complementary biblical model, Anna of Phanuel, with whom Judith was often paired in the religious context in a programmatic way. Sarah Harris suggests that there is a clear intertextual link between the two widows and the pivotal roles they play, pointing out that Luke used the Septuagint and thus had access to the Book of Judith.[30] Like her Old Testament counterpart, Anna is an outward-facing model of widowhood, her husband's death opening up her life and allowing her to be of service to the broader community. Although the New Testament widow was used as the prime example of pious widowhood from the patristics onward, she makes only a brief appearance in the Book of Luke (2:36–38). In the few sentences devoted to her, we learn a number of important things about why Anna is granted such authority. Crucially, she is a prophetess who can experience visions. We also learn her heritage, her age, that she has long been a widow, and that she is pious and devoted to the temple. We know she was a virgin, was then married for seven years, and had been a widow for eighty-four years at the time of her prophecy. She has thus completed the three stages of a woman's life as articulated by Jerome and Augustine: she has been a virgin, a wife, and a widow. Fasting and praying at the temple night and day, Anna fulfills important social work; as we have seen, the devotional duty of a widow was often to supplement the spiritual efforts of those unable to devote themselves exclusively to prayer and worship.

In the last line Luke dedicates to her, we learn perhaps the most important thing about Anna: thanks to her prophetic gift, she is able to recognize Jesus as the savior of Israel when she sees him at the temple. Patristic writings and later conduct literature tend to focus especially on the first two of the three sentences Luke dedicates to her in the presentation of the temple, which cast her as an example of widowed piety. Her gift of prophecy, moreover, is often overlooked as an important component of her *widowed* identity. But it is from the last line that we learn the underlying source of her authority and relevance in the Christological narrative: "Now she, at the same hour, coming in, confessed to the Lord; and spoke of him to all that looked for the redemption of Israel" (Luke 2:38). Katherine Clark Walter argues that "the aspect of the 'true widow' in patristic thought was the notion of the widow's 'spirit of prophecy'"; this dual identity, both widow and prophetess, is surely at the root of Anna's important influence for later holy widows.[31]

Anna is introduced just after Simeon, who is told of Jesus's arrival by the Holy Ghost. When the newborn Christ child and his parents arrive at the temple, Simeon is there to receive them, take the infant in his arms, and speak aloud: "Now thou dost dismiss thy servant, O Lord, according to thy word in peace; because my eyes have seen thy salvation, which thou has prepared before the face of all peoples. A light to the revelation of the Gentiles, and the glory of thy people of Israel" (Luke 2:29–32).[32] We hear him pronounce his prophecy of Jesus as messiah in direct discourse; though Anna is described as announcing the same prophecy, we are not given direct access to her words. She thus remains apart from the reader, mediated through layers of reporting, in a way that Simeon is not.

Anna's status as a widow is what authorizes her to receive the prophecy and to deliver news about the future salvation of Israel.[33] It is her widowhood that allows her the time and space to pray at the temple continuously as well as to fast; while other women might be occupied with familial duties, she is able to serve as an ambassador—one of only two witnesses to Jesus's presentation at the temple who can report the news to others. Moreover, she occupies a meaningful symbolic space: as Andrés García Serrano argues, the widowed prophet at the temple embodies the widowed Jerusalem of Lamentations itself: "Luke's characterization of Anna as Jerusalem summarizes the entire history of Israel in all its stages: from Egypt before the marriage, until the exile, and during widowhood. Anna, embracing Jesus, shows that each of the stages of the history of Israel accepts Jesus."[34] Anna, Harris suggests, "stands as a pivot between the small line of recorded women prophetesses in Jewish history who speak on behalf of YHWH . . . and the time in history when the prophetic office is a gift of the Spirit."[35]

Anna was taken up as an important model of Christian widowhood early on; Paul is most likely referring to her when he famously insists that there is a specific kind of widow, the *vere vidua* or "widow indeed," who should be honored and cared for by the community: "Honour widows, that are widows indeed . . . she that is a widow indeed, and desolate, let her trust in God, and continue in supplications and prayers night and day" (1 Timothy 5:3, 5). Paul contrasts the widow who "trusts in God" and who, like Anna, prays "night and day" with other widows who "liveth in pleasures" and are thus "dead while . . . living" (1 Timothy 5:6)—the same group of widows he also suggests are better off getting married rather than being left to "burn" with desire outside the bonds of matrimony (1 Corinthians 7:9).

Paul's characterization of Anna as the ideal holy widow, praying day and night, is repeated by Augustine in his *De bono viduitatis* and by Jerome in his letter to Furia, pointing to Anna as the definitive answer to his question, "Do we wish to know what widows ought to be?"[36] These readings of Anna were reinforced by late medieval and early modern Italians, such as Bernardino da Siena (1380–1444), who wrote, "Hai di quella Anna . . . che non si partiva dal tempio, dì e notte, e stava in orazione et in digiuno. . . . E queste sono quelle vedove che, istando così, sono di Dio" (You have that Anna . . . who never left the temple, day and night, and was always engaged in prayer and fasting. . . . And these are those widows who, being like this, are of God).[37] Bernardino's description reflects the consistent ideal Anna embodied. She—this aged, pious, prophetic widow—is specifically "di dio" or "of God," rather than "of" her husband, much like the vere vidua described by Saint Paul.

We see consistent evidence of Anna as an important role model for Christian widows in Italian conduct and clergy writings throughout the Renaissance and well into the Counter-Reformation, from Girolamo Savonarola to Juan Luis Vives, the bishop Agostino Valier and the jurist Giulio Cesare Cabei. Taking Anna as his main example of the ideal devout and simple widow, Savonarola cautions widows throughout his treatise against speaking too often, too loudly, or, if possible, to men at all.[38] But Savonarola's insistence on widows' silence, which built upon centuries of patristic texts advocating that true widows such as Anna of Phanuel are seen and not heard, is contradicted in the real-world examples of holy widows who were praised, even canonized, for their outspoken devotion not just to God but to their communities. The remainder of this chapter focuses on one such widow during her decades-long tenure in Rome: the foreign-born Birgitta of Sweden (1303–1373) and her influence on women in Renaissance Italy.

"La vedova svecese": Birgitta of Sweden in Italy[39]

Birgitta of Sweden, or Birgitta Birgersdotter, arrived in Rome in the jubilee year of 1350 when the papacy was in the fourth decade of its "Babylonian captivity" in Avignon.[40] A devout pilgrim who received her calling vision from God shortly after her husband's death some years earlier, Birgitta became, in her own lifetime, an important political and religious figure in Italy, active in the debate over the Avignon Papacy, arguing for the pope's swift return to Rome even before Catherine of Siena.[41] As scholars have argued, she also came to represent for many the sacred widow par excellence, drawing her rhetorical authority from precisely that social identity understood as so intrinsically tied to civic and spiritual life. Her widowhood has been described by Renate Blumenfeld-Kosinski as a "second career" in which she crafted a new identity for herself as a visionary whose rhetorical authority stemmed from her position as a humble widow.[42] In visual works, she is depicted nearly universally in a widow's habit, with white wimple or *bianche bende* beneath a black veil, just as she appears in an early fifteenth-century depiction of Birgitta's ecstatic vision of the Nativity, which adorns the walls of Santa Maria Novella, Florence.[43] Her hands are generally folded in prayer, as she receives one of her visions, or she is seated in a writerly posture, pen in hand at a desk, while she accepts the Divine Word in beams of light from God and Mary.[44]

Who was Birgitta, and why did she become such a central role model as a widow in the Italian context? She was born in 1303 in the Swedish province of Uppland, the daughter of a noble family with ties to the Swedish-Norwegian royal family; although, according to her biographers, she wished to remain a virgin devoted to a spiritual life, she was married at the age of fourteen to Ulf Gudmarsson, and had eight children.[45] Despite her initial reluctance, it seems her marriage was a mutually beneficial and respectful partnership: at Birgitta's urging, they lived chastely and agreeably as fellow pilgrims for the last several years of their marriage. They went on pilgrimages locally in Sweden, as well as to Santiago de Compostela in Spain; Ulf eventually succumbed to an illness he picked up during their travels, in either 1344 or 1346.[46] God first appeared to Birgitta following her transition to widowhood, in her private chapel while she was engaged in solitary prayer, and told her she had been chosen as his "sponsa et canale" (bride and channel).[47] At God's instruction, she began to recount her visions to her confessor, Matthias; these visions would be compiled in the two decades following her death in the *Liber celestis revelacionum* or *Revelations*.[48] Her visions touched on politics, spiritual reform, and domestic affairs, and she made a name for herself in Sweden in the six years after her husband's death. She was directed by God to found the *Ordo sanctissimi salvatoris* or Order of the Most Holy Savior, which she envisioned as majority female but with an auxiliary male group; the order was to be presided over by a woman abbess.[49] She was also told by God to go to Rome, where she should wait for the pope and the emperor to meet there.[50]

Birgitta obeyed, arriving in Rome shortly before the jubilee year of 1350, to find the once-marvelous ancient city in disrepair and ruin, making the return of the papacy to seem all the more urgent. She stayed first in the convent of San Lorenzo in Panisperna and then moved to the house of the widowed noblewoman Francesca Papazzurri in Piazza del Duca (now Piazza Farnese, where the house shares a corner with the north end of the Palazzo Farnese). She lived in Rome for nearly twenty years and died there in 1373 shortly after her return from a pilgrimage to the Holy Land.[51] Papazzurri left the house to Birgitta's religious order in her will, and the Casa di Santa Brigida today remains home to a group of thirty-odd Birgittine nuns who oversee the rooms in which she lived and died.

Birgitta achieved sainthood less than twenty years after her death, in 1391, the first of the century to be canonized in Rome. While the pope had returned to Rome by 1377, the Western Schism began the next year, and it was in this troubled setting that the campaign for Birgitta's canonization took place. Birgitta's revelations, especially those arguing for the return of the papacy to Rome, were met with deep suspicion by ecclesiastical figures including the chancellor of the University of Paris, Jean Gerson.[52] Over the course of the two decades between her death and her canonization, her multivolume *Revelations* was transcribed across the Italian peninsula, especially in Naples, Rome, Florence, and Genoa, where convents of her order were opened with scriptoria, and by the fifteenth century she was an established figure and popular role model to Italian women.[53]

Over the two and a half decades she lived in Rome, Birgitta capitalized on her profile as a widow to model a particular rhetorical authority as she litigated for the return of the papacy to the "widowed" city of Rome. Unn Falkeid has shown that Birgitta purposefully connected her own widowhood to the broader "widowing" of Rome during the papacy's "Babylonian captivity."[54] In a letter to a prelate from just after her arrival in Rome in 1350, for example, Birgitta opens by describing herself as "ego vidua," or "I, a widow."[55] Echoing in the "ego vidua" of Birgitta's letter is also Judith's plea to God, "subveni quaeso te Domine Deus meus mihi viduae"—"Assist, I beseech thee, O Lord God, me a widow" (Judith 9:3)—in which the Hebrew widow speaks directly to God and asks him to help her act. In her letter, which expresses great alarm about the Church's precarious condition, Birgitta describes a vision she experienced in Rome's Santa Maria Maggiore, in which the Virgin appeared to warn her that "the church of God is tottering dangerously" with a foundation "so heavily deteriorated" that "she will suffer a downfall if she does not receive the help of repairs."[56] Falkeid suggests that the figure of widowed Rome may well have been of "great importance" to Birgitta on her arrival in Rome and argues that Birgitta's deployment of "ego vidua" in this letter is an instance of *personificatio*, in which she takes on the role of the widowed city itself.[57] Birgitta deploys the voice of the widow from Lamentations in order to underline the urgency of her message: she, a widow, is announcing the calamity about to befall the Church, and in her voice are echoes of the widowed cities and widowed women before her who have seen similar catastrophe.

Birgitta's letter to the Roman prelate fits into a broader pattern of how she uses her widowhood to bolster her rhetorical authority with male leaders of the Church. Allusions to the particular authority of widows in the Bible and patristic writings are woven into her letters and visions, from references to Judith and Anna to multiple mentions of the miraculous story of widow's oil. These references would be picked up by Birgitta's male champions, especially posthumously. In his sermon upon her canonization in 1391, Pope Boniface IX compared Birgitta to different kinds of biblical widows and mentions Judith and Anna by name.[58] Like Judith, Birgitta lived a life of solitary piety from her husband's death until her calling vision, at which point she left behind her isolated existence in the north and descended into the fray to help the godly city of Rome. Like Anna, she experienced prophetic visions revealing, so she claimed, the future of the Christian faith. Her canonization itself, Boniface adds, is partly an attempt to heal the Church in such a moment of great division.

There is a certain irony in her comparison by the pope to these two biblical figures and to his presentation of her as a unifier rather than a divider. Scholars have suggested that the pope focused so heavily on Birgitta's widowhood in his canonization sermon in order to downplay her controversial visions, which were often fiercely critical of the Church's rulership and would make her a target for misogynist philologians in the decades to come.[59] The pope may also have highlighted her place in a broader pantheon of widowed women because it was her widowhood itself that granted legitimacy and acceptability to her visions and that made her a central exemplum for later generations of Italian widowed women. In his defense of the legitimacy of Birgitta's visions that was published with her *Extravagantes* in the lead-up to her canonization, Birgitta's confessor, Alphonso of Jaen, also cites both Anna and Judith: "Were not Mary (the sister of Aaron), Judith and Esther gifted with the spirit of prophecy? . . . In the New Testament, too, Anna, daughter of Phanuel, prophesied, as did Elizabeth the wife of Zachary . . . and the Tiburtine Sibyl, the Erythraen Sibyl, and many others that you will find in great numbers in the books of Sacred Scripture and the Lives of the Saints."[60] Alphonso's defense of Birgitta is pragmatic and careful, linking her to the "good" female prophets sanctioned by the Church who spoke of Christ's arrival and anticipating the terms through which Jean Gerson would later attack Birgitta in his *De probatione spirituum* (1415) and *De examinatione doctrinarum* (1423).[61] Alphonso reminds his readers (who included, of course, the ecclesiastical authorities adjudicating Birgitta's canonization) that "the almighty God in the Old Testament as well as in the New chose the weak things of the world, of both the female and male sex, to show forth his might and put the wise to shame."[62] That Birgitta is doubly weak, as a woman and as a widow, makes her doubly effective as a channel for God's word. The Bible reminds us that widows are equal only to orphans in their vulnerability; Judith and Anna are both praised for their humility, and their impact is all the more glorious because they come out of their safe and isolated existence, devoted to prayer, in order to make societal contributions before returning to their solitary states.

Birgitta's awareness of the symbolic potential of widowhood is evident throughout her *Revelations*, as she works to craft herself as unique in her authority as a visionary. Shortly after her calling vision, God appears to her and explains that he has given her "spiritual eyes" and "spiritual ears" and allowed her to feel his spirit in "her living breast." In reply, Birgitta asks him, "O my Lord, Son of the Virgin, why have you condescended to come as a guest to so base a widow, who is poor in every good work and so weak in understanding and discernment and ridden with sin for so long?"[63] In response, God tells her that he is able to restore her heart, once focused on "worldly sensuality," to one "full of love on the inside that you want nothing and yearn for nothing but me." He compares her to the phoenix, who cyclically self-immolates and returns to life renewed; "burned . . . and purged from sin," she will "arise . . . having put off the skin of sensuality."[64]

While there is a familiar humility in Birgitta's question—women visionaries nearly always express amazement, wonder, and doubt when they are visited by holy figures and receive visions—God's answer works to reassure Birgitta and her readers of her authority and the true origin of her power.[65] His comparison of the widow to a phoenix is an early example of Birgitta's self-presentation as a unique, Christlike figure resurrected from the ashes of her husband's death.[66] She is thereby positioned as both the unique phoenix and a widow chosen by God in a very particular lineage of widows selected for special missions: Birgitta's task is to inform ecclesiastical authorities and temporal rulers of the true path forward for the Church in the Babylonian captivity, much as Judith the Hebrew widow's path was to slay Holofernes and deliver her people from the true Babylon and Anna of Phanuel's was to recognize the Christ child at the temple as the savior of the people of Israel.

Recent scholarship has expanded understanding of the Swedish saint's influence on late medieval and Renaissance Italy and the importance of studying her within the broader matrix of Italian holy women and mystics.[67] Here I would like to point especially to the fact that her appearance on the public stage in Italy as a widow—one who presented herself as being in conversation with God and the Virgin and with regular access to souls in Purgatory—significantly shifted how widowhood as a theoretical ideal intersected with the real widows walking around the streets of Italian cities. If, as we have seen, the metaphorical power of the widow's speech proved useful in the fractious political years of the fourteenth century, it was also powerful for a prominent real-life widow to argue on behalf of civic and spiritual issues on earth, offering herself as a living emblem of widowhood in the period.

Part of Birgitta's great appeal was that she offered herself as a hinge between the metaphorical widowhood exploited by writers and statesmen like Petrarch and Dante and the potential of "real widows" for the broader aims of the Church. In *Revelations* we see Birgitta's vision of her own husband appearing to her from Purgatory, an instance in productive contrast with the widows in Dante's purgatorial ecosystem. As we saw in the first chapter, Dante's ethics of widowhood demand the tireless attention by widows to their husbands' afterlives; those widows who do not attend to their husbands' salvation are condemned to literary infamy, from the historical figures Giovanna da Montefeltro and Beatrice d'Este castigated in Dante's *Purgatorio* to the unnamed widow of Boccaccio's *Il corbaccio*. Birgitta's encounter with her husband is a rare first-person account of a premodern woman engaging with her husband following his death and chimes with societal understandings of Purgatory that we see in Dante and other sources.

Birgitta's husband appeared to her from Purgatory shortly after she received her calling vision. Theirs is not an emotional reunion, nor one of wonder. It is instead an informative, transactional discussion. There is no "broken weeping" here—Ulf informs her matter-of-factly that he has "received the justice of the judge" and explains the reasons he must atone in Purgatory before ascending to Heaven.[68] Among his handful of transgressions is a notable one, concerning his own conduct with another widow: "I did not give that widow full payment for the property bought from her before my death," he confesses, "and this was due to my own negligence. So that you know I speak the truth, tomorrow she will come to you and ask for it. So give it to her, for she is only asking for the due amount."[69]

The mention of the unnamed widow is noteworthy for many reasons, of course: it is a particularly shameful act to shortchange a widow, in all her vulnerability, on a financial matter, and it is interesting that Ulf instructs Birgitta to make right on his behalf. He does not ask her to atone for his other minor sins, which include his making fun of an "idiot boy," whom Birgitta most likely had brought into the house in an act of charity, and other less-than-noble acts that certainly could have been smoothed over by a wife with Birgitta's political and financial capital. Instead, he beseeches her to work for his early release into Heaven through the more traditional tasks of the grieving widow: saying votive masses on his behalf for the next year and engaging in acts of charity, such as donating chalices for communion at their local church. Finally, he asks her to distribute their real estate among their children.[70]

Birgitta's vision of her husband is of a different character than her visions of God and the Virgin Mary, in which she is often overcome with emotion or terror. It is a comparatively mundane revelation, and she expresses no amazement at his appearance before her, speaking only to ask her husband what led to his salvation (he answers her with a banal calculus: his list of good deeds is longer than his list of sins). Once he has given her his instructions, he departs, and the vision ends. This single recorded instance of Ulf appearing to Birgitta is a neat example of what Clark Walter has described as "spiritual housekeeping," her helpful term for widows' Purgatory-related labors—he appears, tells her what business he left unfinished before his death, and commands her to take care of it.[71] He also gives her a clear schedule: she must have votive masses for a full year in the hopes that he is released. After that, however, it seems her work on his behalf will be over. This visitation from her husband thus reinforces her calling vision, in which she is made God's *sponsa et canale*: she faces no messy dual loyalties to husband and to God but can devote her attention fully to her new groom as soon as she has put her husband's final affairs in order.

Given the mundane and matter-of-fact nature of this vision, it is especially striking that Birgitta's other visions of Purgatory were often horrific, depicting a far less lyrical or orderly Purgatorial space than Dante's mountain. While Ulf does not tell Birgitta where in Purgatory he is, his list of sins is so mild that they would most likely place him near the top of the Mountain of Purgatory. Elsewhere, in a vision recounting the sufferings of her acquaintance Nicola Acciaiuoli (1310–1365), the high seneschal of Sicily and Naples, Birgitta describes Purgatory as layers of gradually decreasing torment; like Dante's realm, it is "an intermediary with an orientation," though one with a very different topography.[72] It is also a place where demons "can touch" souls, and "poisonous vermin and wild beasts" roam; "there is heat and cold, darkness and confusion, all coming from the punishment of hell."[73] There is, however, hope through intercession: "The more help a soul gets from her friends, the quicker she convalesces and is released from that place."[74]

Birgitta's relationship to Purgatory was not limited to litigating on behalf of her husband; as her biographers remind us, she was treated in her lifetime as a true intermediary, consistently asked for information from acquaintances concerning their relatives in Purgatory. During her time spent in Naples en route to her pilgrimage to Jerusalem, she affirms to the Archbishop of Naples that his relatives are in Purgatory and explains how to pray on their behalf.[75] Upon reaching Jerusalem, in a vision at the Church of the Holy Sepulcher, Christ tells her that many of her own family members have been sent on to Heaven because of her prayers: "And because of your labors and devotion, the souls of some of your kinsmen have today been set free and have entered into my glory in Heaven."[76]

While the seemingly successful widows of *Purgatorio* demonstrate their rhetorical authority through their affective performances, negotiating their husbands' salvation through tears and prayer, Birgitta takes a more expansive approach: she can negotiate her husband's ascent to Heaven, but that is the least of her many responsibilities. Instead, her visions offer her acquaintances in Sweden and in Italy particular insight into the bureaucratic divisions of the space and where their relatives reside within; she has an understanding of Purgatory's bureaucracy that looks beyond her own particular widowhood to her identity as a *canale* for her community on earth.

Birgitta incorporated multiple models of holy widowhood into her persona, crafting a hybrid identity in which the authority of her visions was grounded in her widowed identity. Modeling herself after the same lineage of Old and New Testament widows into which she is posthumously placed by Boniface and her biographers, she also expands the role of the widow in established theological and literary spaces, especially through her attention to Purgatory. Birgitta projects herself and her widowed authority beyond the personal (prayers for her husband) and into the political (continuous prayer on behalf of the collective). Much like her biblical predecessors, Judith and Anna, who possess a special connection to God possible only because of their status as widows, Birgitta outwardly extends her direct connection to God for the express benefit of her community.

Birgitta's Italian Descendants

As her cult grew in the century following her death, Birgitta became for many what Enrico Garavelli describes as "l'exemplum della perfetta vedova cristiana" (the exemplum of the perfect Christian widow): an embodied ideal of piety, prophecy, and widowed authority across hagiography, sermons, and literary and visual culture.[77] Scholars now recognize the widespread pattern of her impact on numerous holy women in late medieval and early modern Italy, from Catherine of Siena to the saint with whom we began this chapter, Francesca Romana. Romana was born Francesca Roffredeschi in 1384 into a noble Roman family who lived near Piazza Navona. She was baptized at the church of Sant'Agnese and married at the age of twelve to Lorenzo de' Ponziani, a relation of Pope Boniface IX. Her biographers note that like Birgitta, she was not eager to marry, but she obeyed her family, and as a married woman she moved to Trastevere, to a large house just down the street from the Basilica of Santa Cecilia, where she often prayed. She had three children; one of her sons married Mabilia Papazzurri, a relative of Birgitta's friend and host, Francesca Papazzurri. Francesca Romana experienced visions all her life—of numerous saints, the Virgin, and visions of Purgatory—and also performed numerous miracles, many of which benefited her local community in Rome. Like Birgitta, she founded an order, and there is a small group of nuns who continue her work today at Tor de' Specchi, close to the Capitoline Hill. Following her husband's death in 1436, she joined the order herself.

Francesca's narrative—and her self-fashioning by way of her reported visions—underscores the aspirational nature of widowhood for many devout women. Francesca modeled herself at least in part on Birgitta, whose presence was widespread and profound in Rome in the years following her 1391 canonization.[78] On July 23, 1432, Birgitta's saint day, the Swedish saint appeared to Francesca in a vision in which she explicitly compared the two of them, telling Francesca not to doubt her own visions and capabilities.[79] Birgitta reminded Francesca, who would have been well-versed in the Swedish saint's biography, that she also married but then was rewarded with widowhood, which Francesca would achieve four years before her death, when her ailing husband finally died; in this respect, Francesca's experience very much mirrored Birgitta's, as her husband was injured and ailing for at least eleven years. As Arnold Esch has pointed out, whereas Birgitta was a foreign noble widow and Catherine of Siena was from a different part of Italy when she came to Rome, Francesca Romana offered Romans a particularly *Roman* saint, a new and local Birgitta.[80] Though she was not widowed until close to the end of her life, Francesca became after her death a clear and beloved exemplum of widowhood for widows of Rome. In Francesca's vision of Birgitta, we see a similar framework to what Turina offers in her poem: two women in two different historical moments forge a connection through comparative affective and lived experiences that ensconce them in a broader emotional community of sacred widows, which, in turn, confers a specific kind of authority on them and their visions.

We see a continued forging of this expansive emotional community in the nun and mystic Domenica Narducci's remarkable 1533 sermon to the noblewoman Caterina Cybo, Duchess of Camerino (1501–1557), whose husband had died in 1527 of the plague.[81] Cybo was an influential noble widow with important connections and deep spiritual commitments, a friend and correspondent to other high-profile widows including Vittoria Colonna and Giulia Gonzaga. By the time Narducci (1473–1553; also known as Domenica del Paradiso) founded her convent La Crocetta in Florence in 1511, Birgitta was already something of a household name—particularly in Florence, home to the convent of Santa Brigida al Paradiso—and was viewed specifically as a role model for widowed women in search of a spiritual example to emulate. In letters as well as the 1533 sermon, Narducci implores Cybo with the specific directive to "learn" ("imparate") from Birgitta's unique example, on what Clara Stella identifies as "spiritual, civic, and intellectual terms."[82] Indeed, Narducci highlights Birgitta's example for her status not only as a holy widow but as a woman of the world: a "queen" who made the choice to abandon her material life following her husband's death and embrace a new life as a bride of God.

In the virtuosic, imagery-rich sermon, Narducci explains that she has called upon the Virgin to endow her with a vision to satisfy the duchess, who has come to visit the convent for spiritual counsel. The Virgin complies, and Birgitta is presented to Narducci following a parade of allegorical figures sent by God, strongly reminiscent of those in both Petrarch's *Triumphs* and de Pizan's *Book of the City of Ladies*. First come the three queens Faith, Hope, and Charity, clothed in spectacular and rich garments: "vestite molto resplendiente, incoronate di mirabil corone, piene di pietre pretiose" (dressed resplendently, adorned with wonderful crowns filled with precious stones).[83] They are followed by five allegorical senses including Light and Taste, and then by Birgitta, who sagely has incorporated all these virtues and senses into her own way of being. The saint is first introduced only as "una mirabile matrona" (an admirable woman) with "uno amanto nero, pieno di stelle e pietre pretiose" (a black cloak, full of stars and precious stones) and who leads a beautiful queen by the hand. Birgitta then introduces herself, as a saint and also a widow in the same breath: "Sappia ch'io son santa Brigida, la quale rimasi vedova, io ero maritata, che havevo tolto lo sposo celeste et havevolo sempre meco" (Know that I am Saint Birgitta, she who was left a widow, I was married and then took the celestial spouse, and He is with me always).[84] Birgitta then introduces the queen she leads by the hand as her own daughter, Saint Catherine of Sweden (1331–1381), who also became a bride of Christ after her own husband's death. As Narducci stressed in a separate letter to Cybo, the noblewoman can fully become "signora di voi" (owner of herself) only now that she is widowed, and thus she can discover her true self in the essence of God like Birgitta did ("come fece la gloriosa Santa Brigida").[85]

In her sermon, Narducci explicitly highlights Birgitta as a *widowed* ruler who was rewarded for her righteous conduct after her husband's death. Her descriptions of Birgitta cast the saintly widow as "resplendente e lucida" (resplendent and bright) in her widow's habit, her dark mantle decorated with stars and precious jewels.[86] In Narducci's vision, the saint's *panni vedovili*—so often viewed in other contexts either as drab or, conversely, as worthy of suspicion—are instead described as glorious, emblematic of the glamour Birgitta projected, and tightly linked to her identity as a holy widow reflecting God's light.[87]

Narducci's sermon to Cybo comes at a significant moment in the history of Italian widowhood, both literary and historic, and Cybo herself is an important hinge figure, a negotiator with significant political and spiritual capital. The year 1533 was, perhaps not coincidentally, when Cybo and Colonna fought together to save the Capuchin order from being expelled by the Church. The two widows were in a prime position to argue the case for the order: Pope Clement VII, the Medici pope who had been held prisoner during the Sack of Rome, was also Caterina's maternal uncle.[88] The women were regular interlocutors at the salon Colonna oversaw at the Convent of San Silvestro in Capite, alongside other important (and notorious) members of the *Spirituali* reformers, including Bernardino Ochino, the leader of the Capuchins; Juan Valdés; and the Cardinal Reginald Pole.[89] Through her own entanglements with Church leaders in the fourteenth century and the attention both she and followers of her cult paid to her identity as a widow, the Swedish saint offered well-connected Italian widows a model for a kind of widowhood that bridged spiritual devotion and secular—even civic—authority. Narducci sets forth a model, through Birgitta, for authorizing widows' *civic* engagement as well as engagement in the world of the sacred, through the eschewing of remarriage and devotion to God.[90]

Holy Widows and the Sack of Rome

As I conclude this chapter on holy widows, I pause on the figure of Ludovica Albertoni (1473–1533), a citizen of Rome and contemporary of Cybo and Colonna. In a posthumous 1672 *vita* of the Blessed Ludovica, Pier Mattei Paluzzi casts the city of Rome as a widow following the infamous Sack, the bloodiest single event of the Italian Wars: "restò vedova Roma per piangere incessantemente l'eminente occidio de' suoi cittadini" (the widow Rome was left to weep ceaselessly over the outrageous slaughter of her citizens).[91] The characterization of the devastated Rome as a "widow" would have been recognizable to Paluzzi's seventeenth-century readers, a direct nod to the long-standing Italian literary tradition that cast beleaguered cities as bereaved women on the model of the widowed Jerusalem in Lamentations. Paluzzi ties the widowed city of Rome directly to the noble widow Ludovica, who, like the grieving city herself, lamented the destruction and death that befell her fellow citizens.[92] He recounts that she mourned alone in her Trastevere house, dressed in haircloth, neglecting her earthly body as she prayed on Rome's behalf: "dimenticandosi affatto del sovvenimento del corpo, tutta dedicandosi alla oratione" (forgetting even to take care of her body, [she] dedicated herself entirely to prayer).[93] After the "furibonda tempesta" (fierce storm) of the Sack had passed, Paluzzi writes, Ludovica left her house and appeared to the people of Rome like a "nuova luce dopo lunga e spaventosa caligine" (new light after the long and terrible darkness), offering her fellow citizens emotional succor as well as material aid.[94] For her acts of charity following the Sack, Paluzzi reminds us, Ludovica was dubbed the "madre dei poveri," or "mother of the poor," in her own lifetime; in one famous painting by Baciccio from 1670, she is depicted handing out bread stuffed with gold and silver coins, wearing the white veil and black dress that marked her as a Franciscan tertiary (Figure 3.2).

Who was Ludovica Albertoni? She is best known as the subject of one of the last, most exquisite sculptures by Gian Lorenzo Bernini (1598–1680), in which she is posthumously depicted in the ecstatic throws of death (Figure 3.3). The statue, still in its original home in the Altieri family chapel of Sant'Anna in San Francesco a Ripa in Trastevere, was commissioned by her distant relative, the Cardinal Paluzzi Albertoni, shortly after her spectacular 1671 beatification in Saint Peter's presided over by Pope Clement X (himself an Altieri, 1590–1676, and thus also Ludovica's descendant).[95] In Bernini's sculpture, Ludovica is depicted lying down, an elaborately carved pillow propped up behind her head. Her right hand touches her breast, while the left clutches at her stomach; the shape of her bent knees can be made out through layers of carved skirts. Her head leans back, eyes and mouth both half open; her face is a mirror image of the artist's earlier, more famous sculpture of Saint Teresa of Avila (ca. 1647), found across the city in Santa Maria della Vittoria.[96] The similarities to Bernini's Teresa are a visual shorthand, connoting prophetic saintliness on a local level: Rome's own ecstatic holy woman with visions, to rival the Spanish Teresa, who was beatified in 1614 and canonized in 1622.

Bernini's statue of Albertoni represents a collision of public and private, universal and individual, central to the focus of this chapter and the next. While most scholarly work on Albertoni has been related to her role as the subject of Bernini's statue, she

Figure 3.2. Baciccio (Giovanni Battista Gaulli), *Blessed Ludovica Albertoni Distributing Alms*, ca. 1670, oil on canvas, 210.2×137.2 cm. Object number 70.PA.30, J. Paul Getty Museum, Los Angeles, CA. Photo: Carlo Bello / Alamy Stock Photo.

Figure 3.3. Gian Lorenzo Bernini, *Blessed Ludovica Albertoni*, 1674, marble. Altieri Chapel, San Francesco a Ripa, Trastevere, Rome. Photo: Stefano Ravera / Alamy Stock Photo.

was also an important figure in her own lifetime a century and a half earlier—an heir to influential saintly widows such as Birgitta and Francesca Romana and to biblical role models like Judith and Anna. Upon her 1494 marriage to Giacomo della Cetera, the twenty-year-old Ludovica moved from her childhood home near the Capitoline to Trastevere, where she raised three children; when her husband died in 1506, she became a Franciscan tertiary or *pinzochera* at San Francesco a Ripa, caring for the poor and sick of the neighborhood.[97] She was well-known in her lifetime for her ecstatic visions, many of which she experienced at her local church. Ludovica became, according to Paluzzi, a "mirror and model of saintliness" for other Roman matrons.[98] When she died in 1533, she was buried next to her husband in the family chapel that would later become home to Bernini's famous representation of her.

The cluster of literary and visual works I have described lauding Albertoni—by Bernini, Baciccio, Paluzzi—are all from the period around her beatification at the end of the seventeenth century. The vita by Paluzzi, Ludovica's distant relative as well as a Franciscan tertiary associated with San Francesco a Ripa, was part of a broader, coordinated campaign to raise her to the ranks of other widows celebrated as sources of hope and vision at moments of catastrophe in the city. Albertoni was represented by her biographer, by witnesses in support of her beatification, and by visual artists, using the specific vocabulary that connoted a hybrid model of solitary widowhood (hiding at home in mourning during the Sack) and active civic engagement (emerging to soothe the people of her city in the aftermath). Like Francesca Romana, who was also a member of the *popolo romano* class that ran Rome's city government, Ludovica embodied qualities that had already been celebrated, even codified, in the earlier widows analyzed throughout this chapter.[99] In Paluzzi's text, we also see how high-profile widows could be employed to suit political, as well as theological, narratives: Ludovica is presented both as metonym for the people of Rome following the Sack and as a source of comfort for that community.

We see models of saintly widowhood deployed with increasing frequency during the Counter-Reformation, when female saints became a particularly important pillar of Church strategy for reinforcing devotion and loyalty in reaction to Protestant menaces.[100] After a stalled canonization process following her death in 1440, Francesca Romana was sainted in 1608 under Paul V, in part thanks to the efforts of Francesco Peña (ca. 1540–1612), also responsible for the canonization of Counter-Reformation stalwart Carlo Borromeo (1538–1584). Following a period of obscurity that lasted a half century, Birgitta's texts burst back onto the publication scene beginning in 1606, and her *Revelations* and apocrypha were printed consistently throughout the century, including a popular hagiography, *La vedova svecese*, in 1648.[101] As Ludovica Albertoni's relatives litigated for her canonization in this environment, they were careful to underscore the qualities she had in common with these earlier sacred widows, who melded together the ideal traits of widowed life—piety, devotion, the eschewing of remarriage—with a remarkable *vita activa*, a life out in the open in Italian cities. As we will see in the next chapter, this new brand of civically engaged widowed life, forged by holy widows, took on a particular resonance during the Italian Wars.

CHAPTER FOUR

Dido, Death, and Exemplarity

Public Widowhood from Petrarch to Vittoria Colonna

As we saw in the last chapter, Rome was labeled a "widow" during and after the catastrophic Sack of Rome—a hearkening back to the "widowed" Rome of the Avignon Papacy and to the "widowed" Jerusalem of Lamentations. As an increasingly feminized—and victimized—character was imposed on the Italian peninsula itself during the Italian Wars (1494–1559), many widows in the public eye, especially those who had been personally affected by the violence and political turmoil, were looked to as examples of proper conduct not just for other widows but for society at large.[1] The sixteenth century thus saw a further expansion of the widow's traditional responsibilities, to include the facilitation of their communities' collective response to the death and trauma of the period. As this chapter elaborates, we see evidence of this expansion in multiple ways: through the exempla deployed in female biography and conduct literature, through individual widows celebrated for their actions, and through a broader phenomenon of what we might call "collective exemplarity," in which groups of widows were positioned as exemplary emotional bulwarks for their communities, sometimes replacing the classical and biblical widows who had been long proffered as exempla.

Providing further context on widows as role models in Italian Renaissance society, I offer here a framework for thinking through why Vittoria Colonna, Veronica Gambara, and other widowed poets, many of whose widowhood poetry I analyze in the next chapter, were taken seriously as cultural authorities for how to articulate and grieve loss. My discussion includes decidedly high-profile widows as well as less well-known figures who also contributed to the cultural ideal of what we might call "public widowhood" in the period by serving as affective emblems for their communities. As with chapter 3, this chapter thus straddles literary and cultural history, examining historical figures alongside many of the texts that solidified their reputations both in their own day and in posterity.

This chapter provides key historical and theoretical context for the final two chapters of the book, which analyze the power of widows' voices themselves. In the case of women like Caterina Sforza (1463–1509), Costanza d'Avalos (1460–1541), Vittoria Colonna (1490–1547), and Veronica Gambara (1485–1550), the expanded social role of the "public widow"—a woman who possessed both a public profile and political power during her widowhood—played out through triumphs organized in city streets, political and military action, the 1530 Congress of Bologna, and sonnets and letters to popes and princes with advice on governing. A necessary connecting thread in this chapter and the next is Colonna, recognized in her lifetime and in today's scholarship as the "ur-widow" of the Renaissance.[2] As I discuss in the following chapter, she was a primary literary role model for widowed women writers who came after her. What I am interested in here, however, is not the many ways in which Colonna stood out but rather how she also fit into a broader battalion or *schiera* of exemplary widows who were endowed with authority by their widowhoods and cast as both models of mourning and symbols of hope and strength for the community.

In the following pages, I first trace humanism's engagement with widowed exempla from antiquity and then with contemporary widows, who were transformed into exempla themselves by writers of female biography and conduct literature. I then present a case study of the little-studied *Triumphum novem viduarum* (*Triumph of Nine Widows*, ca. 1510), in which the poet Giosuè Capasso praises a group of nine noble Neapolitan widows who serve as a collective "honestate exempio" (virtuous exemplum) for their fellow citizens following the devastation wrought on Naples in the first decades of the Italian Wars. As I explore, it seems very likely Colonna not only read the poem when it circulated but may well have been thinking of it when she wrote her famous canzone "Mentre la nave mia," in which she presents herself as a unique exemplum. The chapter concludes with a second instance of "collective exemplarity" in Naples: a 1561 verse cycle by the best-selling poet Laura Terracina (1519–1577) dedicated to a new group of exemplary Neapolitan widows shortly after the Treaty of Cateau-Cambrésis, which put an official end to the Italian Wars in 1559 and confirmed Naples as property of the Spanish. As we will see, the protracted period of cultural and religious upheaval between 1494 and 1559 helped to codify a new and richly articulated model of Italian widowhood that women increasingly fashioned for themselves.

Exemplarity and Widows in Boccaccio and His Renaissance Imitators

In his *Tusculan Disputations*, Cicero describes the legendary queen Artemisia II of Caria (d. 351 B.C.E.) as having been destroyed by her grief over the loss of her husband, King Mausolus: "quam diu vixit, vixit in luctu eodemque etiam confecta contabuit" (while she lived, she lived in grief, and died of it, being worn out by it).[3] Before succumbing to her overwhelming grief, however, she seems to have been very productive. Artemisia honored her husband after his death through the daily ritual drinking of his ashes in order to make herself more like him in body and spirit; in addition to making her own body a living sepulcher for her husband, Artemisia erected an architectural marvel in his honor, a monument so spectacular that henceforth all burial buildings were called "mausoleums" and it was hailed as one of the Seven Wonders of the World.[4] She also became a fierce military commander in his stead: incorporating his virile spirit in her body through the consumption of his ashes, she grew powerful enough, *masculine* enough, to defend their kingdom at home and abroad.[5]

Artemisia was regularly cited as a paragon of widowhood for her fierce preservation of her husband's memory and the political power he had established. She was praised by Boccaccio in *De claris mulieribus* (1374) as "a lasting example of chaste widowhood and of the purest and rarest kind of love"; writing just a few decades after Boccaccio, de Pizan praised Artemisia in *Le livre de la cité des dames* (1405), drawing special attention to the widowed queen's military victories.[6] By the sixteenth century she was also a go-to point of comparison for the highest profile of Italian widows. Vittoria Colonna was famously praised by Ludovico Ariosto in the final version of *Orlando furioso* (1532) as "un'altra Artemisia" (another Artemisia) for her public devotion in writing to the memory of her husband, Fernando Francesco d'Avalos, who had died in 1525 following the Battle of Pavia.[7] Scholars have recently suggested that a Sebastiano del Piombo portrait now held at Harewood House in the United Kingdom depicting a historically vague woman holding up a solitary cup is of Colonna *as* Artemisia.[8] A generation later, Catherine de' Medici (1519–1589), the Italian queen regent of France, consciously modeled her own persona on Artemisia following the death of her husband, King Henri II, in 1559, solidifying her power through an ostentatious self-presentation as a "nouvelle Arthémise" (a new Artemisia) dressed in black widow's weeds.[9]

Renaissance widows were surrounded by exempla—both the holy widows explored in the last chapter and a host of classical widows lauded in conduct literature and female biography from Boccaccio onward.[10] Like Renaissance representations of saints, whose good works and devotion animated frescoed church walls and were meant to be emulated, examples from ancient texts served not just as models but as "describers" and "mirrors"—categories that encouraged a particular kind of reading, interpretation, and emulation.[11] "The evocation of an exemplary figure," Timothy Hampton argues, "constitutes that textual moment at which the authority of the past is brought to bear on the reader's response to the text. The exemplar can be seen as a kind of textual node or point of juncture, where a given author's interpretation of the past overlaps with the desire to form and fashion readers."[12] Sarah Kay points to the way exempla "accumulate": "Different stories may share the 'same' meaning as a crucial component of exemplarity. Both these forms of repetition—the same exemplum across time, and different stories in the same place—underline how the tellers and receivers of these stories are expected to be exemplary, as well as the stories themselves."[13] For Virginia Cox, exemplarity is "a language, a signifying system" unto itself, one "necessary to master in order to reach an adequate understanding of Renaissance humanistic culture."[14]

The humanist devotion to exemplarity evolved primarily with a male audience in mind—Florentine schoolboys learning about virtuous Roman men along with their

Latin grammar. It was also central to how widowhood was represented and promoted through literature and material culture. While the social position of a widow was often tenuous or fraught, to a great degree her role had already been fleshed out and was being performed all around her, through a continual and collective reading and rewriting of models both positive and negative.[15] Italian Renaissance widows had access to a broad catalogue of classical models, relayed in Latin and vernacular and appearing in epic and lyric poetry, dialogue, conduct literature, painting, emblems, and numismatics, illustrating how a virtuous widow might operate in public, outside the confines of her home or the convent.

A central component of this multimedia catalogue was female biography. Beginning with Boccaccio's *De claris mulieribus*, texts authored by male humanists brimmed over with examples from the Greco-Roman tradition offering Christian women the chance to outdo their pagan predecessors. As we have seen, Artemisia underscored the combined power of public devotion and military valor. The quasi-widow Penelope of Homer's *Odyssey* demonstrated the importance of marital fidelity and of evading pushy suitors.[16] Further examples of virtuous women—from Cornelia to Portia to the pre-Virgilian version of Dido rehabilitated by Petrarch and Boccaccio—offered reminders not only of the importance of serving (or even of leading) one's community but also of chastity and loyalty: the Pauline model of "true widowhood" applied to classical exempla. "Bad" widows from the classical tradition, on the other hand—those who, like the Widow of Ephesus, gave in to sexual appetites, remarried, or forgot their husbands—destroyed not just their own reputations but their husbands' as well.[17]

De claris mulieribus set the vogue for female biography; Boccaccio's compendium, dedicated to the Florentine noblewoman Andrea Acciaiuoli, was enormously popular, and in the two centuries following his death female biography developed into a rich and varied genre.[18] Following de Pizan's protofeminist French-language *Le livre de la cité des dames*, later fifteenth-century Italian male humanists produced a raft of works including *De laudibus mulierum* (Bartolomeo Goggio, 1487, dedicated to Eleonora d'Aragona); *Gynevera de la clare donne* (Giovanni Sabadino degli Arienti, 1489–1490, to Ginevra Sforza); and *De plurimis claris selectisque mulieribus* (Jacopo Filippo Foresti, 1497, to Beatrice d'Aragona). Whereas Boccaccio included only a handful of his contemporaries in *De claris*—including Queen Joanna II of Naples and the Sienese widow Camiola—Goggio, Foresti, and Arienti praised numerous contemporary women alongside the familiar ancient exempla, offering readers a new cohort of exemplary women.[19] As Cox has observed, the insertion of contemporary women into these compendia after Boccaccio "had the effect of far more clearly constructing the category of 'famous women' as permeable, in a way that encouraged a dynamic of emulation."[20] As the years progressed and the number of compendia grew, more and more contemporary public figures were codified as exempla; Giuseppe Betussi's 1545 *Libro delle donne illustri* celebrates contemporary women exclusively, with Colonna as the final example, surpassing all the classical exemplars to whom she is compared, including Artemisia, Cornelia, and Dido, queen of Carthage.[21]

The Two Didos

We will return to the idea of Colonna as the ultimate example of public widowhood later in this chapter. To understand how exemplary widows figured in the political and cultural consciousness of Renaissance Italy, however, we must consider the case of Dido, and her endlessly contested status as either "good" or "bad" exemplum—either ally or anathema to earnest Italian widows. The scholarship on the two versions of Dido, Virgilian and anti-Virgilian, is vast and comprehensive, and much has also been written on the way Italian canonical authors chose sides, with Dante following on the Virgilian version and Petrarch and Boccaccio pointedly refuting that model, instead arguing for the "truth" of earlier classical historians' version of the Carthaginian queen.[22] Her identity as a widow is a defining characteristic in both versions of her story and informs her successes—or failures—as a ruler, and thus as an exemplum for Renaissance widows.

In pre-Virgilian accounts, Dido's suicide is not a reaction to grief over a lover's rejection but rather an admirable act of self-sacrifice to avoid being forced into a second marriage with the neighboring African king Iarbas, partly to spare her subjects an unsavory political alliance.[23] The historians' Dido is a chaste woman who, through a combination of cunning and virtue, navigates treachery first in her home kingdom of Phoenicia and then abroad as she founds the city of Carthage. Having constructed a safe, new city for her displaced people, her final "act of defiance" protects her own bodily chastity, and also the legitimacy, even the "purity," of the Carthaginians, while also returning her to her rightful place beside her husband in death.[24]

It is this chaste widow to whom we see Colonna compared in the 1545 Betussi biography, the same version of Dido who killed herself in order to preserve her chastity and avoid remarriage, and was defended ardently by Petrarch and Boccaccio. This was certainly relevant for Colonna, a widow who did not remarry despite what seems to have been the best attempts of many of her male relatives. The Virgilian iteration of the tragic figure, however—the widow who did not manage to stay virtuous, acted out of lust then rage, and thus destroyed the future of her kingdom—tends to hover just beneath the surface whenever the virtuous version is invoked.[25] In her final speech atop the pyre before she takes her life in *Aeneid* Book IV, Dido looks back upon the great accomplishments, and the great shame, of her life:

> vixi et quem dederat cursum Fortuna peregi,
> et nunc magna mei sub terras ibit imago.
> urbem praeclaram statui, mea moenia vidi,
> ulta virum poenas inimico a fratre recepi,
> felix, heu nimium felix, si litora tantum
> numquam Dardaniae tetigissent nostra carinae.
>
> (I lived my life out to the very end
> And passed the stages Fortune had appointed.
> Now my tall shade goes to the underworld.

> I built a famous town, saw my great walls,
> Avenged my husband, made my hostile brother
> Pay for his crime. Happy, alas, too happy,
> If only the Dardanian keels had never
> Beached on our coast.) (IV.653–658)

We see in these lines both a tidy summation of her life's work and an index of accomplishments of which any exemplary widowed ruler in the Renaissance might have been proud: she has contributed to and improved the situation of her people, rescuing them from her tyrant brother Pygmalion and building a new and better city of her own; and she has stood in for her husband on earth, avenging his death and depriving Pygmalion of the fortune he coveted while fighting off other suitors. If it were not for her momentary lapse of loyalty to Sychaeus with Aeneas, her life as a widow—more precisely, a politically powerful one—would have been exemplary.

James Simpson suggests that Petrarch chose to fight so ferociously against the Virgilian version of Dido primarily in order to rehabilitate Aeneas, not only from the unsavory episode in Virgil but from the even more shocking *Heroides* 7 epistolary account by Ovid, in which we hear from Dido herself and learn more about her heartbreak, as well as about the child she may have carried from her liaison with Aeneas.[26] I would venture that Petrarch may also have been consciously working to recuperate Dido's own rhetorical and symbolic value as a virtuous political widow for his own time. In *Seniles* 4.5, Petrarch frames his perturbation as that of a historian frustrated by chronological and factual inaccuracies that he views as in bad faith: Virgil, he claims, "invented" the love affair between Dido and Aeneas even though he knew "[she] died out of zeal for chastity and the preservation of widowhood."[27] Boccaccio, too, performs outrage at Virgil's faulty chronology in *De claris*: "Even before the arrival of the Trojan Aeneas"—"(whom she never saw)," he pointedly insists—"Dido had already decided to die rather than violate her chastity."[28] She is his response to hypothetical Christian widows who might say they *had* to marry again for reasons beyond their control: "Dido's only brother was an enemy to his exiled sister—on whose help could *she* depend? Did Dido not have many suitors? Was Dido made of stone or wood any more than the women of our time? Certainly not! That is why she used her mental strength to escape in the only way she could—through death—the snares she lacked the physical strength to avoid."[29] The anti-Virgilian Dido is presented as not only earlier but "truer," both pedagogical tool and cudgel with which to chastise those less devoted widows Boccaccio imagines in his own fourteenth-century Italian audience.[30]

In verse, Petrarch is even more intent on the recuperation of Dido as a virtuous widow. His investment in a "poetics of widowhood," which we have already seen in the case of *RVF* 268, deepens in the *Triumphs*, as he enshrines Dido in an important collective of political widows including the "vedovella" Judith. Written in vernacular *terza rima*, Petrarch's six Triumphs—of Love, Chastity, Death, Fame, Time, and Eternity—took the Roman tradition of triumphant military spectacle and literary performance and twisted it into a humanist coil of classical and contemporary components. Petrarch chooses, pointedly, to locate Dido not among the lovers in the Triumph of Love (including her Carthaginian "heiress" Sophonisba) but in that of Chastity, where he rewrites her quick and cruel depiction from *Inferno* and locates her in a group of chaste lovers who help Laura to defeat Love.

As we might recall, Dido is referenced twice in *Inferno* V: first, as the nameless widow who broke her oath to her husband's ashes, then as the named leader of a pack of wanton lovers, the "schiera ov'è Dido." In contrast to Dante, Petrarch names her very early in the Triumph of Chastity, when he speaks of Love's victims, including, "Dido, / ch'amor pio del suo sposo a morte spinse, / non quel d'Enea com'è 'l publico grido" (Dido, whose pious love for her husband spurred her to death / not that for Aeneas, as the public cry).[31] The description of her love for her spouse as "amor pio" or "pious love" is pointed, of course, a play on "pius Aeneas" as we are told he was not the cause of her downfall. The "publico grido" or "public cry" is also pointed: Petrarch's knowledge of Dido's true fate is cast as more elevated, authoritative, than the popular version reproduced in Dante—one must be familiar with the historians' versions as well, it suggests, in order to know what really happened to Dido.[32]

The significance of Petrarch's move to enshrine Dido in his Triumph of Chastity, as a widow who killed herself rather than remarry, is made starker when we consider Petrarch's treatment of the Hebrew widow Judith. She herself is a "defining figure" in the *Trionfi*, mentioned a remarkable three times in the poem cycle, more than any woman other than Laura: first in the Triumph of Love, then Chastity, then Fame.[33] She is first introduced in the Triumph of Love as one whose power lies not only in her beauty but in her eloquence: "una vedovetta" who won over Holofernes "con bel parlar, con sue polite guance" (with beautiful speech, with her lovely cheeks; Triumph of Love, l. 54). As Eugenio Refini has shown, Petrarch's decision to describe Judith as eloquent was a late addition: in an earlier redaction of the Triumph of Love, Judith was cast not as eloquent but only as beautiful, the little widow "con sue polite et belle guancie" (with smooth beautiful cheeks) rather than "con bel parlar, con sue polite guance" (with beautiful speech, with smooth cheeks).[34] Petrarch's choice to include mention of both her physical beauty and her "bel parlar" in the final redaction reminds us that her story is not complete without an acknowledgment of how she used words to deceive the general, reminiscent of the "vedovella" in *Purgatorio* X who convinced Trajan to change course.[35]

In the Triumph of Chastity, she is made even more prominent: described as "Judith ebrea, casta e forte" (Hebrew Judith, chaste and strong; Triumph of Chastity, l. 142), she is included among the "sacre e benedette virgini" (sacred, blessed and pure women; Triumph of Chastity, ll. 127–128), the group of chaste women who join Laura to subdue Love. All the women who are included are famous for preserving their chastity, sometimes even sacrificing themselves in so doing, including Lucretia, Penelope, and Virginia. Moreover, Petrarch firmly absolves Dido here of the crimes Virgil and Dante attribute to her, by including her in the battalion that comes to Laura's aid:

Poi vidi, fra le donne pellegrine,
quella che per lo suo diletto e fido

sposo, non per Enea, volse ire al fine
(taccia 'l vulgo ignorante); io dico Dido
cui studio d'onestate a morte spinse,
non vano amor com'è 'l publico grido.

(Then I saw, amongst the foreign women
she who for her beloved and faithful
husband, and not for Aeneas, went to her end
[be quiet, ignorant crowd!]; I say Dido
who was driven to her death by loyalty and honor,
and not by vain love as the public cry.) (Triumph of Chastity, ll. 154–159)[36]

Judith and Dido are connected in the *Triumphs* as women who helped Laura preserve her chastity, chosen for the job because of a very specific pedigree. They are the only two widows mentioned, but every woman included safeguarded her body in the context of a broader *political* crisis. Other examples Petrarch includes make the point even clearer: Lucrezia, Hippo, the Teutonic women all killed themselves rather than submit to foreign, enemy men. The thesis of the Triumph of Chastity is thus that women, including widows, must not only preserve their chastity but go so far as to sacrifice themselves rather than to submit to sex with foreigners, even within the sacred boundaries of (re)marriage.

We see alternate revisions of the Dido story in Christine's *Mutacion* and her *Cité des dames*, in which Aeneas is allowed in the retelling, but there is less interest in their love affair and a stronger focus on Dido as the doomed founder of a doomed city.[37] Marilynn Desmond argues that in Christine's works the queen "is initially identified as a wise, powerful city builder—a woman who possesses masculine qualities and strengths—a figure much like the author Christine constructs in the *Mutacion*: a widow whose widowhood turns her into a man."[38] As Desmond observes, "As a political leader, [the Virgilian] Dido exhibits the qualities that are valued in a heroic, male figure. As a woman who succumbs to erotic desire," she represents the "elegiac stereotype of lovers."[39] We might understand the Petrarchan and Boccaccian version of Dido as the kind of bigendered widow figure that we have seen lauded in other cases, both the "heroic, male figure" and the stereotype of the ever-faithful, chaste widow.

In Dido's medieval and Renaissance incarnations, she "challenges any fixed categories of gender," oscillating between the flimsy and "libidinous" feminine paper doll of Augustine and Dante and the strong and virtuous masculine ruler in Petrarch and Boccaccio.[40] Her identity as a widow—not just a powerful foreign women, but an unattached one with sexual experience, appetite, and a known former consort—is always linked to her status as a ruler and city builder, a threat to the Roman imperial project and thus to the Italian literary one.[41] It is no wonder that she was a constant presence in the politically charged atmosphere of Renaissance Italy, when numerous elite widows had militias of various sizes at their disposal. While Judith would appear once more in Petrarch's *Triumphs*, in the Triumph of Fame, Dido is relegated to the Triumph of Chastity, shunted from one pole to another.

New "Good" Didos: Widowed Rulers from Caterina Cornaro to Veronica Gambara

These varied and contradictory versions of Dido bring to the fore the question of what, precisely, an exemplary widow is—the answer to which most certainly depended on the specific time and place in late medieval and Renaissance Italy. In 1519, the recently widowed poet and ruler Veronica Gambara had an inscription placed above her bedroom door with Dido's declaration from *Aeneid* IV, 28–29 that she would remain faithful to her husband's memory: "Ille meos primus, qui mi sibi junxit, amores abstulit, ille habeat secum, servetque sepulchro" (For he who first had joined me to himself has carried off my love, and may he keep it and be its guardian within the grave).[42] While the use of Virgil risked conjuring up the wrong version of Dido, who did in fact betray her husband's memory later in the very same book of the *Aeneid*, the lines themselves capture the spirit of the virtuous widowed ruler, so devoted to her husband and her people that she would rather kill herself than defile his memory and their city.[43] Gambara's claim to Dido as a role model was a natural one: she herself would become a high-profile example of a chaste political widow during her own lifetime, an image she cultivated and that was propagated in print. Born the daughter of Alda Pio, of the Pio family of Carpi, and Gianfranceso Gambara, lord of Pralboino, she was also cousin to the intellectual sisters Isotta and Ginevra Nogarola. She began exchanging poetry with Bembo as early as 1504, and he would become both a close interlocutor and a major supporter of her, along with Colonna, as crucial to the enterprise of Petrarchism. She married Giberto of Correggio as a very young woman, in 1509, and managed to remain Countess of Correggio from his death until her own over thirty years later, in 1550. In her widowhood, she hosted high-profile cultural and political leaders, including the emperor Charles V, to whom she dedicated a number of poems.[44]

The political and military conflicts of the Italian Wars continued throughout her entire life and regency. Attentive to the needs of the age and of her own court, Gambara fashioned her authorial identity not as a grieving widow but as a political poet and ruler, carving out "a unique space" with her poetry, as Martin suggests, "whereby she was able to foster not only her cultural reputation but her political prosperity as well."[45] As scholars have observed, and as I discuss at greater length in the next chapter, Gambara was also highly invested in cultivating Vittoria Colonna's reputation as a unique poetic talent.

Colonna herself was descended from a long line of politically savvy and publicly intellectual women, including her grandmother Battista Sforza, whose posthumous memorialization by her husband Federico da Montefeltro was certain to have influenced her perception of what it meant to be a public figure.[46] Vittoria was born into the hugely powerful noble Roman Colonna family in 1490 and was married to the famed Aragonese military leader Fernando Francesco d'Avalos from 1509 until his death in 1525 from wounds sustained during his triumph on behalf of Charles V in the Battle of Pavia. And yet while she certainly waded into high-stakes political and spiritual matters—her brother's Salt Wars with the pope, the *spirituali* reform movement—this was not the image she worked to project, nor was it what she was most celebrated for.[47]

Though Colonna was consistently heralded as unique by cultural giants from Bembo to Ariosto (as well as by herself), there is good reason why scholars often talk about Colonna and Gambara as something of a set. In their own lifetime, they were widowed cultural icons who had access to models pulled from several generations of Italian widows in the public eye, some in their own families. They became, as Cox has described it, "mutually reinforcing exempla," "consolatory icons" during the unrest of the Italian Wars.[48] As Jessica Goethals has argued, the two authors served a crucial purpose following the Sack of Rome, helping to "reinforce an image of *renovatio*" in Italy through their vernacular works at a moment the peninsula was suffering a crushing defeat politically.[49] Despite their superficial commonalities—elite noble widows of military men, poets, and close interlocutors of Bembo—they chose to cultivate strikingly different public profiles. The 1530 Congress of Bologna, a political event of the utmost importance as well as a virtual who's who of the cultural elite across the peninsula, serves as an excellent illustration of these differences. Scholars have identified Bologna, at which Pope Clement VII and Charles V agreed to reinstate the Medici as rulers of Florence, as the key moment when Gambara and Colonna shifted from well-respected poets to icons, especially through the reception of their work by Bembo.[50] It is also at this moment that they perhaps best solidified their public personae in relation to one another. While Gambara was in attendance, playing the role of widowed poet and ruler for all to see, Colonna, still too much in mourning to go among the "volgo," or common crowd, was absent, although her works circulated throughout the Congress in manuscript.[51] And yet it is important to note that Colonna was not known for the kind of hair-pulling, wretched grief that had been legislated right out of view in cities across the peninsula (although as we will see, some of her imitators did go that route); instead, Colonna was posited as exemplary because she expiated her grief, like Petrarch, through the proper medium—lyric poetry—and not in a deleterious public performance.[52] Her absence from the Congress itself served to reinforce an image of her in constant mourning, without her having to perform that mourning in public.

Colonna and Gambara were also prime fodder for contemporary female biography, in which they were routinely represented as the ultimate in womanly perfection, often due to excelling at more masculine arts than "lesser" women.[53] Giuseppe Betussi praises both for their intellect and rejection of womanly activities, such as sewing, in favor of writing.[54] In Lodovico Dolce's 1545 vernacular revision of Juan Luis Vives's *De institutione foeminae Christianae* (1523), *Dialogo della instituzione delle donne, secondo li tre stati che cadono nella vita umana*, Colonna is praised first by herself and then alongside Gambara: the speaker Flaminio asserts that the world has not seen a greater example ("esempio più nobile") than Colonna since Anna of Phanuel.[55] In the final words of the dialogue, he proffers Colonna and Gambara as ideal models, not just for widows but for "all women."[56]

While the two widow-poets became the most high-profile widows of the age, Italian widows had long held positions of political power in hereditary systems of government and became influential, even legendary, for their actions in dire circumstances. Many ruling widows, especially in northern Italy, gained political power and cultural capital through decisive leadership, even military action, after their husbands' deaths.[57] These women were generally aware of the power in their identities as widows, performed accordingly, and were often written into the new exemplarity literature, long before Colonna and Gambara. Sabadino degli Arienti (1445–1510), for one, dedicated his *Gynevera de la clare donne* to Ginevra Sforza (1440–1507), a widow remarried who had provided continuity from one de facto regime to the next in Bologna by virtue of her previous marriage to her second husband's political predecessor as well as the backing of her powerful father, Alessandro Sforza.[58]

The Venetian Caterina Cornaro (1454–1510) was married at the age of fourteen in a proxy ceremony to Giacomo II Lusignano, king of Cyprus, and was pregnant and widowed at nineteen. She reigned as queen of Cyprus, Jerusalem, and Armenia until 1489, when Venice took the island back, forcing her return to the mainland. Asolan historian Antonio Colbertaldo (1556–1602), praising Cornaro for refusing to remarry, compares her constancy to that of Scipione Africanus, the hero of Petrarch's *Africa*, and to Ulysses's faithful Penelope, who tirelessly refused the advances of men on Ithaca as she waited for her husband's return from the Trojan War.[59] This conspicuously bigendered comparison reflects the sometimes-fluid understanding of widows' gender, as we have seen continuously throughout this study, as well as entwined societal anxieties that informed the world in which Cornaro and other widows negotiated their power: first, that a sexually experienced widow would most likely engage in sex outside of marriage; and, second, that a widow would be tempted to remarry in order to experience sex again, forgoing honorable chastity for sexual pleasure within a marriage that might endanger her first husband's immortal fame as well as his earthly possessions. Cornaro, Colbertaldo explains, is exemplary because she "fled" from the possibility of remarriage, as from a grave threat, remaining widowed in order to fulfill her duties as a faithful servant to God; she deserves more praise than a virgin would, he stresses, because it is much more noble to resist a pleasure "incominciato a gustare" (begun to be tasted) than to spurn "il non gustato" (the never tasted).[60]

As compensation for the loss of Cyprus, Venice made their "figlia addottiva" (adopted daughter) the ruler of the small community of Asolo in the Veneto, and she reigned over a culturally vibrant court there until her death in 1510. Cornaro's natural exemplary model in Asolo was the anti-Virgilian Dido; in the 1507 *De situ et laudibus Asyli oppidi serenissimae reginae Corneliae*, a Latin poem of praise for Caterina, Giambattista Liliani writes that like Dido, Caterina has founded a new and important community in her widowhood and subsequent political displacement.[61]

Perhaps the most infamous example of a ruthless Renaissance widow is Caterina Sforza (1462–1509), a woman with an unusual historical record.[62] In the apocryphal account for which she is most known, Machiavelli describes Sforza's now-notorious response to threats to kill her children unless she complied with her captors' demands after the murder of her husband, the tyrant Girolamo Riario: "E per mostrare che de' suoi figluoli non si curava, mostrò loro le membra genitali, dicendo che aveva ancora il modo a rifarne" (And to show that she didn't care about the [fate] of her living children, she showed them her genitals, saying that she still had the means to make more).[63] The astonishing episode, highlighting fears around the unchecked sexual and reproductive power of widows in the most outrageous of fashions, marked but the beginning of her widowed career.[64] While Sforza's adventure in Forlì occurred before the beginning of the Italian Wars, she was one of many widowed women who participated in the complex maneuverings at the start of the conflicts in 1494, including the younger Gambara and Colonna.[65] In his recent analysis of her as a martial figure, Gerry Milligan observes that both Foresti and Arienti "allowed for a . . . flexible or blended gender performance of militant heroism" in their depictions of Caterina that stood in contrast to the later ones by Machiavelli.[66]

Sforza's embrace of masculine or feminine attributes as it suited her after her husband's death is illuminated by Foresti's account of her, which, as Milligan shrewdly observes, is a far more traditionally feminine portrait than that by Machiavelli; she is no mere "masculine avatar in a woman's body."[67] Foresti's description of Sforza's varied emotional performance is particularly intriguing when we think of her in terms of the sometimes curious gendering of widowhood. Though initially presented as "a tearful mother and widow" after her husband is killed and her children taken hostage, Foresti describes her as ultimately "reject[ing] feminine tears as would a man" when she enters the castle in order to negotiate with her husband's killers.[68] This kind of control over her tears when she is in a politically tenuous situation is reminiscent of Boccaccio's tragic Ghismonda, who, despite despair at her lover's fate, performs an impassioned speech "con asciutto viso" (with a dry face), defending the legitimacy of her sexual desire before mocking her father for his tears, telling him to go "va con le femine a spander le lagrime" (go shed your tears among the women; IV.1.45). In Foresti's depiction of her, Sforza, like Ghismonda, is attuned to when feminine tears are appropriate and when they must be suppressed in manly fashion.

From what we do know, Sforza was keenly aware of the political power widowhood offered her and worked to capitalize on it for the remainder of her time as regent of Forlì.[69] She became a kind of metonym for her husband, his earthly political representative, and consciously reinforced this through grand public displays. Of note, she staged her own triumphal entry into the city on the feast day of Forlì's patron saint, San Mercurialis; as Joyce De Vries observes, "This public forum allowed Caterina the opportunity to display her body—the body of a widow—as part of a larger spectacle of courtly power and rulership; her body replaced that of her husband's as the head of state."[70]

The strategic and symbolic role of the political widow became particularly potent in this period, as the peninsula saw unprecedented devastation that exposed not just the extent of Italy's vulnerability to the larger powers of France, Spain, and the Holy Roman Empire but also the perilously fickle bonds of the peninsula's many rulers. In *lamenti storici* of the period, cities were often ventriloquized and presented as *sconsolate* on the model of the widowed Jerusalem in Lamentations, crying out to the reader and describing the anguish they were experiencing, such as in the 1509 *Lamento de' venetiani*, which opens with a widowed Venice crying out "France and

Spain and the emperor have completely desolated me!"[71] In Marsilio Compagnoni's *Il lamento di Caterina Sforza* (ca. 1500), written about Sforza's capture by Cesare Borgia and the French in 1499, it is the widow herself who is ventriloquized, what Milligan calls "ostensibly recorded speech."[72] Throughout the *lamento*, "Caterina" urges the listener to "ascolta questa sconsolata" (listen to this disconsolate woman); Milligan observes that throughout the lament, Sforza's suffering is made to seem "common to all of Italy."[73]

Political widows, whether they were sconsolate or instead suppressed their grief "like a man," were often portrayed as symbols, or even repositories, for the grief or suffering experienced by a community. We see an interesting case of this in Castiglione's *Il libro del cortegiano* (1528), which includes a ruling quasi-widow in the figure of Elisabetta Gonzaga (1471–1526), the Duchess of Urbino, whose husband the duke, though still alive, was unable to perform his duties. Alongside the duchess are a slew of other examples provided to instruct not only widows or women more broadly but the peninsula at large at this critical and devastating juncture in Italy's history.[74] In Book III of the *Cortegiano*, which is devoted to the ideal court lady, a discussion of exemplary widows is embedded within the larger conversation on women's loyalty that comes shortly after it is affirmed that there is no greater good in the world than to "dar bon esempio" (be a good example; III.20). To illustrate how loyal women can be, the character of Giuliano de' Medici recounts the tale of Camma from Plutarch, another chaste-widow exemplum, whose husband was assassinated by a political rival and who killed herself and her husband's murderer rather than be forced to marry him.[75] Castiglione follows with the tale of another loyal widow, but with a humorous, Boccaccian twist that considerably softens the solemn impact of Camma's noble sacrifice. In response to Frigio's suggestion that women like Camma no longer exist, Giuliano tells the story of Tommaso of Pisa, a merchant captured by pirates. When his devoted wife Madonna Argentina learns that he is finally to be liberated, she is so overcome with emotion at the prospect of seeing her husband again that she dies immediately.

From this, the group returns to more serious examples of heroic women, and the womanly impulse to self-sacrifice on behalf of their communities, with Gasparo telling two modern-day Lucretia stories back-to-back in Book III.47 that hint at the dangers women faced in the occupied Italy of the Italian Wars. In the first, a young Capuan woman throws herself into the river to drown rather than be raped by her French captors. In the second, which Gasparo says happened only three days prior to their conversation, a young peasant girl from Mantua is raped when she asks for a drink of water at a young man's house; after she has escaped the brutal assault, she too throws herself into the river, refusing all offers of rescue from her sister on the shore. Unlike the Roman Lucretia, these two young Italian women are not married; it is the loss of their virginity that drives them to suicide. And yet there is a clear parallel between the sexual violence enacted against them as young and unattached women and the violence enacted upon the widow Camma, forced to kill herself rather than be married to her husband's killer. That the first girl is a captive of foreign soldiers and the second girl a native of the Duchess of Urbino's natal province highlights both the political underpinnings of sexual violence and the fact that it is always imminent, even near the protected space of the Urbino court.

These somber tales are quickly reinforced in III.48, when Messer Cesare recounts the story of a young woman who is tricked by a scoundrel working in collaboration with her maidservant and is cornered by him in one of the caves at the church of San Sebastiano in Rome. Despite her best attempts to fend him off, he murders her, and she is honored with a hero's burial. Clearly agitated by the injustice in his own tale, Cesare goes on to speak more broadly of the wrong perpetrated upon all women who find themselves without male protection. His indignation peaks as he says that their hostess the duchess has lived "come vidua" (like a widow) these last fifteen years, and risked "esilio, povertà ed ogn'altra sorte d'infelicità" (exile, poverty, and every other kind of unhappiness) rather than leave her husband, despite his compromised state.[76] Cesare is, conspicuously, interrupted in his tirade by the duchess herself, who redirects him, instructing him firmly to turn to another subject: "Parlate d'altro e non intrate piú in tal proposito, ché assai dell'altre cose avete che dire" (Speak of something else and do not return to this subject, as you have much to say about other things).[77] The earlier praise of exemplary women by Giuliano seems to lose its significance when, in answer to Cesare's protest, he is told by Frigio, "una non fa numero" (one example does not mean it is always the case) and the exempla are left behind. But an important point has been established: defining the duchess—whose husband Guidobaldo da Montefeltro (1472–1508) was, though feeble, still very much alive at the time the dialogue was supposed to have taken place—as "come vidua," Castiglione opens up the idea of widowhood to all women who find themselves in ambiguous or tenuous situations, suggesting that widow exemplars are useful models for a broader community of women.[78]

As Castiglione acknowledges with "qualche fastidio" (some annoyance) in the opening letter of the *Cortegiano*, he is moving to publish the dialogue in part because Vittoria Colonna, who was closely related to the ruling couple of the Urbino court, was already passing around his dialogue without his permission.[79] His high-profile gripe is a useful measure of the patrician widow's influence on literary culture, to which I will return shortly.

A Neapolitan "Schiera" of Exemplary Widows

Gambara and Colonna may have been those most routinely praised, but in practical terms the widows of any powerful men could serve as consolatory icons for communities, and geography mattered as the peninsula saw near-continuous violent political conflict between 1494 and 1559. Naples, the first front of the Italian Wars when it was invaded by Charles VIII of France, was the site of some of the fiercest battles between the French and Spanish until the Spanish wrested back dominance from the French in 1503. The city had no fewer than four hereditary kings in a span of two calendar years (1494–1496), and this chaotic situation made particularly clear the political value of queen consorts, queen regents, and dowager queens both as active rulers and as highly visible symbols of dynastic continuity.

In the first decades of the sixteenth century, the Bay of Naples also played host to an elite woman-led salon on the island of Ischia. Costanza d'Avalos, Colonna's aunt by marriage, was widowed in 1483 following the death of her husband Federico del Balzo (b. 1455), the brother of Queen Isabella of Naples. Costanza, renowned in her own lifetime and afterward for her martial and cultural prowess, ruled over Ischia after King Federigo (r. 1496–1501) left it to the d'Avalos family and defended it admirably from French hostilities twice.[80] In addition to her fame as a beautiful, intelligent, and powerful ruler on Ischia, Costanza played a crucial role in Colonna's life from the beginning of the younger woman's marriage: she signed the marriage contract between Colonna and her husband in 1507 and hosted Colonna in Ischia as he fought and again after his heroic death in 1525. The two women ran a salon on the island throughout the politically tumultuous period; as Rome was being sacked by the soldiers of their ally Charles V in 1527, they hosted writers like Paolo Giovio (1486–1552), whose works offered lengthy praise not only of Colonna herself but of numerous widows from Naples. These included women who had fled Naples after the fall to the French in 1494; the island community offered refuge to numerous elite women in need of political shelter, including Giovanna and Maria d'Aragona.[81]

While scholars have discussed these examples from the 1520s of high-profile widows influencing literature in Naples, less attention has been paid to the circa 1510 *Triumphum Novem Viduarum*, or *Triumph of Nine Widows*, by poet Giosuè Capasso (b. ca. 1466–1468). The poem is found in one extant manuscript in the Bavarian State Library in Munich, titled *Rime di Jacopo Sannazaro ed altri*, which was published for the first time only in 1990.[82] In addition to the triumph, the manuscript contains Capasso's other known writings, two allegorical *farse* and a *lamento*; works by Antonio Tebaldeo and Iacopo Campanile; and numerous poems by Jacopo Sannazaro, including his *Capitulo in la morte del Marchese di Pescara*, commemorating the death of Colonna's father-in-law, Alfonso D'Avalos D'Aquino.

Capasso's choice of triumph as the genre for his poem in celebration of nine worthy widows is significant. Triumphs, both visual and literary, saw momentous growth in popularity throughout Italy in the late fifteenth and early sixteenth centuries, as they circulated in high-end visual representations such as Piero della Francesca's Montefeltro diptych (1473–1475) as well as more quotidian productions such as wedding *cassoni*.[83] This was in large part thanks to Petrarch's poem cycle as well as to contemporary reenactments of Roman-style military triumphs, such as Battista Sforza and Federico da Montefeltro's real-life triumphal procession into newly conquered Fano in 1463; Pope Julius II's triumphal 1506 entrance into reclaimed Bologna; as well as Caterina Sforza's previously mentioned 1488 triumphal parade following her husband's assassination and her subsequent beating back of aggressors at Forlì.[84] Humanist Naples was integral to triumphs as a visual, public-facing genre in the fifteenth century, best evidenced in the spectacular triumphal arch at Castelnovo depicting Alfonso of Aragon's 1443 entrance into the city (Figure 4.1).[85]

It was in this local atmosphere that Capasso wrote his own version of the *Trionfi*, which featured a parade not of allegorical figures, ancient heroes, or military leaders

Figure 4.1. *Alfonso I's Triumphal Arch*, 1453–1462. Entrance to Castel Nuovo, Naples, Italy. Photo: Sérgio Nogueira / Alamy Stock Photo.

but of contemporary Neapolitan widows, a new, collective "honestate exempio" (honest or chaste example) for the city. The "gente gloriosa" (glorious people) he puts forth include some of the most famous and powerful widows in Naples, and Italy more broadly, including Giovanna d'Aragona (1454–1517), widow of King Ferdinando I of Naples (1423–1494), and Costanza d'Avalos herself. Every one of the women Capasso praises is the widow of a political figure and thus implicated in the suffering and the survival of Naples at one of its bleakest political moments.

The triumph's first of two *capitoli* opens with the narrator lovelorn in the springtime who, like Petrarch at the outset of the *Trionfi*, quickly lapses into a dream vision. Flying to the third sphere of Paradise, the heaven of lovers, he spies Venus, with Cupid fluttering his wings before her. As she often does, mother reproaches her son for his absence. In response, he invites her to descend with him to observe his latest masterpiece, a community of women without equal who, he claims, will render the gods' names eternal on earth ("darran memoria in terra al nostro nome"; l. 63). Venus accompanies her son to earth, and the second chapter treats the reader to a swooping aerial view of Italy before focusing in on Naples and its environs: Cupid identifies the islands of Prochida, Ischia, and Capri; Vesuvius; Cumae, where the Sibyl resides. He points out the Castel dell'Ovo, beneath which the siren Parthenope is said to be buried, and the Lago d'Averno in Lucrino, where Aeneas descended into the underworld and encountered Dido one last time.[86] The most glorious women in the world live here, Cupid tells his mother, in this city so rich in literary and mythological history. He instructs her to gaze upon them:

> Ecco la gente gloriosa,
> altera, più de ogn'altra famosa, excelsa e degna
> che adorna el mondo advolta in veste negra.
>
> (Behold this glorious and lofty people, honored and worthy, who adorn the world dressed in black.) (ll. 188–190)

In this initial description of what he will later term the "hornata schiera" (elegant squadron) of noble widows, Capasso casts the group of women as a discrete people unto themselves—*la gente gloriosa*—who "adorn" the world while dressed in black. This is a studied contrast to the conventional understanding of widow's weeds as dark and dreary, chiming instead with Domenica Narducci's description of Birgitta's bright and shining habit in her sermon to Caterina Cybo.[87]

Capasso offers a double reference to Petrarch in the specific description of the group of widows as dressed in black that is both innovative and especially worthy of consideration in the broader context of widowhood in poetry. As I discussed in the first chapter of this study, the words "in veste negra" bring to a close *RVF* 268, *Che debb'io far*, when the canzone itself is transformed into a "vedova, sconsolata" (disconsolate widow) after Laura's death; they are echoed in Petrarch's description of Death in the *Triumphs*. As Laura, dressed in white, leads her "brigata allegra" (happy band), which includes Judith and Dido, from the Triumph of Chastity into the Triumph of Death, she is greeted by Death herself, who is described as a woman wearing a black dress: "una donna involta in veste negra" (l. 31). After Laura and the lady in black exchange words, with Death announcing her intention to kill Laura, the poet describes the arrival of a mass audience of both the dead and living to witness Laura's death.[88] When Death takes Laura's life, it thus sets off a choral demonstration of mourning by the assembled crowd that would be familiar to readers of Dante; Laura herself remains the only one who is dry-eyed:

> Quanti lamenti lagrimosi sparsi
> fur ivi, essendo que' belli occhi asciutti
> per ch'io lunga stagion cantai et arsi
> e fra tanti sospiri e tanti lutti
> tacita e sola lieta si sedea,
> del suo ben viver già cogliendo i frutti.
>
> (How many scattered tearful laments there were, while those beautiful eyes remained dry, for a long season I sang and burned! And amongst many sighs and much mourning, silent and alone she sat happily, already reaping the fruits of her good life.) (Triumph of Death I, ll. 118–123)[89]

Laura's death is thus mourned, even on the allegorical plane in which it occurs, through the "lamenti lagrimosi" and "tanti sospiri e tanti lutti" of the "schiera" of living women who arrive to witness her death and who gather around her deathbed to lament the loss of "virtù, bellezza e leggiadria" (virtue, beauty, and gracefulness; Triumph of Death I, l. 146) that have died along with her. Petrarch transforms the figure "in veste negra" from a participant in the feminine mourning ritual so common to Trecento Florence, to the monstrous cause itself.[90]

By describing the nine widows of Naples as "adorning" the world "in veste negra," Capasso retains the power of the phrase but signals an intentional departure from the Petrarchan standard of the widow "in veste negra" as an ominous figure of mourning and death. Whereas Petrarch warned of the danger and aggravation sparked by women's public mourning, here the women dressed in black are celebrated as figures of public pride. Capasso's "gente gloriosa" are praised for making themselves and their mourning visible to society—they do not retreat from the world, as Petrarch urged in his poem, or cause chaos in the streets as he suggested in his letter to the Duke of Carrara, but instead lead the triumphal parade.[91] It is their very visibility that makes them so glorious, according to Cupid. Capasso's triumphant group of widows *in veste negra* not only are *of* the world but light it up, bringing glory and honor to their city as "consolatory icons," just as Colonna and Gambara would become two decades later.[92]

Capasso's Cupid explains to his mother that this has been a conscious project on his part. The nine widows make up the columns of a temple atop a new Parnassus; their valorous, exemplary behavior in widowhood has made them his ideal muses as well as role models for their fellow citizens:

> Sopra de queste nove, alte colonne
> ho fondato il mio regno e sacro tempio
> che advolte in manto obscuro e nere gonne
> fan di belleze e de honestate exempio.
>
> (I have founded my kingdom and my sacred temple atop these nine, lofty columns, who, dressed in dark veil and black skirts, are an example of beauty and virtue.) (ll. 420–424)

Capasso thus sets up the nine widows who populate Cupid's temple as a collective of exempla to learn from and emulate. The first is the former queen of Naples, Giovanna d'Aragona, married to King Ferrante (Ferdinando I) of Naples, who died at the start of the Italian Wars in 1494 after warning of the coming political catastrophe. We also see Giovanna, widow of Ferrandino (Ferdinando II) (d. 1496) and vice-regent of Naples; Isabella d'Aragona, widow to Gian Galeazzo Sforza of Milan (d. 1496) and later sovereign duchess of Bari; and Costanza d'Avalos, who, as we saw, ruled Ischia after the death of her husband Federico del Balzo. Rounding out the "schiera" are a set of close contemporaries and wartime widows, some of whom also ruled in their husbands' stead: Laura Sanseverino (widowed 1503), Ippolita d'Aragona (widowed 1498), Beatrice Sanseverino (widowed 1503), Barbara Gonzaga (widowed 1501), and Vittoria Terranova Cantelmo (widowed ca. 1506).[93] Belonging to the highest echelons of Neapolitan society, these were the widows of powerful men—some of whom were killed during the first years of the Italian Wars—and many of them were related to each other through marriage. The husbands themselves, significantly, are not identified by name, and their accomplishments (or defeats) are not the focus of the poem. The widows' collective duty as presented by Capasso is to bring glory not to their husbands but to Naples itself, serving as an embodied representation and reminder of Naples's history and an indication of its future.

In Capasso's praise for the members of his schiera, he continually emphasizes the unique hope and beauty they offer the world despite their personal encounters with tragedy. Their dark weeds of widowhood distinguish these women from all others, a visual marker of their difference and virtue. Isabella is "sì chiara e bella . . . in veste negra . . . gloria del mundo e del femineo sexo" (in black dress she appears so bright and beautiful, glory of the world and of the female sex; ll. 225–226). Costanza has remained a beautiful woman in her widowhood and is still widely, albeit "chastely," admired by men:

> Vedi sobto funeste e nere bende
> il lume de begli ochi che sintille
> d'amor pudico ogn'hom ch'el mira accende.
>
> (See below the mournful and black veils the light of the beautiful eyes that sparks chaste love in every man who looks at it.) (ll. 269–270)

Especially noteworthy, Capasso suggests, is how valiantly D'Avalos has served as the ruler of Ischia in times of trouble, exceeding both the exemplary Livia's fame (who continued to rule after her husband Augustus's death) and the warrior virgin Camilla's spirit.[94] Costanza's sister-in-law Laura Sanseverino is lauded for her "bel volto" (beautiful face), which "come lampegia il bel volto suave / quasi in serena notte biancha luna" (shines out much like a white moon on a still night; ll. 300–301) from beneath her black veil and dark dress. Capasso deploys the common trope of a ship in need of a pilot or "nocchier": whereas widowed Rome was so often described as *senza nocchier* or without a helmsman, Sanseverino is here cast as the trusty "nocchier" herself, who "con lieta voce e prompta l'assicura / il mar quieto e poi tranquil il porto" (with her happy and decisive voice ensures a calm sea and a tranquil harbor; ll. 306–307). Capasso seems to hint at a significant gender transformation here, reminiscent of Christine de Pizan's mutation into a man following the "shipwreck" of her husband's death. Cast in the masculine-coded role of ship's captain, Sanseverino is no longer in need of her husband to guide her and her people to shore.

Though Capasso first attends to his subjects individually, describing them each as virtuous in their own way, they are, ultimately, presented as a group that possesses a *collective* power: a "gente gloriosa, altera" (a glorious, lofty people; l. 188), nine new muses for the city of Naples. The final fourteen *terzine* of the poem are devoted to this group, a "gente valerosa et magna" (a great and valorous people; l. 383), who possess a singular "volto angelico et iocondo" (angelic and laughing face; l. 386) that can transform, Medusa-like, when necessary.[95] His nine widowed muses together form a sturdy, reliable foundation for Cupid's temple, a description that chimes with numerous poems in the decades to follow; indeed, it may well have influenced later works coming out of Naples. While the poem is characterized as a triumph, the temple imagery also ties it to the genre of the literary *tempio* or temple, which was regularly used as an encomiastic genre directed to women in the sixteenth century. Given the placement of Capasso's triumph in a manuscript that contains poems by influential Neapolitan poets connected to the d'Aragona family and Costanza and Colonna's Ischian salon as well as the similarities in theme and tone, it is certainly likely that the triumph influenced later *tempi* to which Diana Robin has drawn attention, especially Campanile's 1522 *Tempio d'amore*, dedicated to Costanza d'Avalos, in which the poet describes a temple constructed from thirty female "columns," with Vittoria Colonna in the place of honor, a central, load-bearing column.[96]

In comparison to Campanile's later temple, however, Capasso offers up a more specific type of colonnade, constructed of women whose widowhood has granted them a particular kind of cultural liberty. Their public identity as devoted, mourning widows of prominent social stature is directly linked in the triumph to the character of the city of Naples itself. In the concluding line of the poem, Capasso declares that the nine women "fan di belleze e de honestate exempio" (are an example of beauty and virtue; l. 425), underscoring the utility of the triumph: Capasso proffers these women as a group who have survived loss and emerged as shining lights, who can be emulated as exempla at a moment of great loss and hardship for the community. The adjective "honestate" echoes Petrarch in the Triumph of Chastity when he insists that Dido killed herself not due to "vano amor" but instead "onestate"—not vain love, but honor, or even uxorial fidelity. Capasso's Triumph praises not just the widows per se but their *visibility* in the community as they keep their widowly virtue intact. They do not retreat from the world to mourn in solitude but are instead on full display, shining brightly in their widow's weeds.

The collective identity of the nine widows is affirmed through their emblem: a golden phoenix on a black background. The motto below the phoenix reads, "D'ambrosia e nectar sol mi cibo e pasco / perché le stelle, el ciel m'han facto tale / che sola vivo e poi morta rinasco" (I graze and feed on ambrosia and nectar alone, for the stars and the heavens have created me to live alone and then, dead, am born again; ll. 197–199). If Artemisia kept her husband's memory alive through the ritual ingestion of his ashes after his death, becoming a living monument to his memory, the phoenix-widow goes even further, rising from the ashes of her husband, reborn as a new—perhaps better—version of him. As we saw in the last chapter, Birgitta of Sweden reports in her *Revelations* that God compares her to the phoenix. Vittoria Colonna would also take up the symbol in her own widowhood—both in coins in which she is depicted on one side in widow's habit, with a phoenix on the flip side, and in the canzone "Mentre la nave mia," in which she compares herself to a host of exemplary classical women.

There is an important difference, however, between the phoenix as a unique emblem for individual widows and Capasso's use of the mythical bird to represent his coterie of widowed rulers. His phoenix represents "questa triumphale schiera," a group linked through their widowhood. This is a paradoxical setup: a phoenix is, by definition, a species of one. And yet Capasso intentionally crafts his triumph for this phoenix-like species as praise of nine women who act as one body and who serve, together, as a singular "honestate exempio."

Vittoria Colonna, Veronica Gambara, and Widowhood beyond the "Schiera"

It is revealing to read Capasso's triumph against Colonna's ambitious *canzone*, "Mentre la nave mia," authored in her widowhood, in which she surveys and then rejects the many exemplary wives and widows of antiquity as models to emulate. In the final line of the poem, she claims that in her grief she has become a phoenix herself and has found her own ambrosia and nectar: "m'è nettar il foco, ambrosia il pianto" (the fire is nectar to me and my weeping ambrosia to my lips; l. 76).[97] "It is difficult to escape the conclusion," Cox remarks, "that by the last decade or so of her life, Vittoria Colonna no longer needed *exempla* to figure herself, classical or religious. Phoenix-like, she had become an *exemplum* in herself."[98]

What, then, might we make of the similarities between her words and those of the phoenix in Capasso's triumph? It seems very possible that Colonna read Capasso's words, which celebrate so many women she knew, some to whom she was even related. Perhaps she read it shortly after it was written, when she was still a young bride living on Ischia under Costanza's watch (she married d'Avalos in 1509). Perhaps her repurposing of the widowed group's emblem in Capasso for herself is a conspicuous rejection of the model of collective public widowhood he presented to the Naples elite in her young married life. In her highly self-conscious musing in "Mentre la nave mia," she mentions numerous classical exemplary figures she might model herself after, looking first to wives before turning to widows: Laodamia, Penelope, Ariadne, Medea, and Portia.

> Esempi poi di veri e falsi amori
> ir ne veggio mill'altri in varia schiera,
> ch'al miglior tempo lor fuggì la spene
> . . .
> Onde a che volger più l'antiche carte
> de' mali altrui, né far de l'infelice
> schiera moderna paragon ancora,
> se 'nferior ne l'altre chiare parte,
> e 'n questa del dolor quasi fenice
> mi peggio rinovar nel foco ognora?

> (I see a thousand more examples of true and false love troop past in a diverse horde, all of whom saw their hopes dashed in the midst of their joy . . . why continue to turn the ancient pages that tell of others' ills, or to look for peers in

the unhappy ranks of modern lovers? I may be less than these heroines in their other fine qualities, but in my pain I am like the phoenix, eternally renewing myself in the fire.) (ll. 49–51; 61–66)[99]

Colonna makes two scornful allusions to the "schiera" in the section cited above: first, the "varia schiera" of historical examples of faithful lovers and, second, the "infelice schiera" of her contemporaries. Neither group appeals to her. Colonna here abandons the need for a role model altogether—she, like the phoenix, is an immortal creature, and a singular one, who has been reborn from the ashes of her husband.

A comparison between the subjects of Capasso's triumph, written when Colonna was a young and newly married woman, and the outsized figure Colonna crafted for herself in her later years, helps to articulate two strands of widowhood as it was performed and understood in the sixteenth century. While Colonna became the zenith of this cultural type, famed in her widowhood and after her own death for her devotion to her dead husband's memory and her poetic excellence, we see a specific rejection in "Mentre la nave mia," not just of examples from antiquity but of her contemporaries. It is also worth remembering that despite this rejection in verse of the collective, Colonna lived happily in collectives of women more than once: in Ischia under Costanza's protection and in the Clarissan convent of San Silvestro in Capite in Rome multiple times during her widowhood.[100]

Another of our exempla was also focused on promoting Colonna's unique nature. Veronica Gambara praises Colonna in a much-published sonnet exchange as "la nostra etade unica gloria" (the sole glory of our age), reinforcing an image of Colonna as a singular entity, an example for other widows of *personal* conduct, not political. In a familiar turn, Gambara declares that the female sex should build a temple to Colonna's memory:

O de la nostra etade unica gloria,
donna saggia, leggiadra, anzi divina,
a la qual reverente oggi s'inchina
chiunque è degno di famosa istoria:
ben fia eterna di voi qua giù memoria,
né potrà il tempo con la sua ruina
far del bel nome vostro empia rapina,
ma di lui porterete alma vittoria.
Il sesso nostro un sacro e nobil tempio
dovria, come già a Palla e a Febo, farvi,
di ricchi marmi e di finissim'oro,
e, poiché di virtù sete l'esempio,
vorrei, Donna, poter tanto lodarvi
quanto vi riverisco, amo, ed adoro.

(Oh unique glory of our age! Wise and graceful lady—nay, divine—before whom all those living who are worthy of fame's annals bow in reverence, your immortal-

> ity on earth is now quite assured. Time with all his ruination will not now be able to snatch away your lovely name; instead, you will carry off a fine victory over him. Our sex should erect a sacred and noble temple to you, as once they raised to Pallas and Phoebus, adorned with rich marble and the most refined gold. And since you are the epitome of virtue, I would wish, lady, to be so capable of speaking your praise as I am of revering, loving, and worshiping you.)[101]

Gambara's poem shares with those by Capasso, and later Campanile, the evocative metaphor of a collective of women who together construct a temple that serves both to worship women and to bolster women's role in poetic production. Gambara points to this project as one the female sex should undertake collectively, suggesting an all-female literary construction project, perhaps even an exclusively female community with Colonna as both its ideal exemplar and its figurehead.[102] Her proposal for collective worship of Colonna is, however, markedly different from what Colonna articulates in her own poetry: a desire to memorialize her husband and to stand alone. She is less interested in the collective and more in the individual, solitary world widowhood can offer. It was for this attitude and project that she was most imitated after her death, as I discuss in the next chapter.

Laura Terracina's *Settime rime sovra tutte le donne vedove di questa nostra città di Napoli titolate e non titolate* (1561)

Colonna's midcentury rejection of any schiera is neatly bookended by Capasso's triumph on the one side and by a second poetic cycle in praise of Neapolitan widows on the other. More than a decade after Colonna's death, Laura Terracina, born in nearby Chiaia, published a collection of poems with striking similarities to the triumph Capasso had penned half a century earlier. The *Settime rime sovra tutte le donne vedove di questa nostra città di Napoli titolate e non titolate* (1561) were also published two years after the Treaty of Cateau-Cambrésis was signed, marking the official end of the Italian Wars and leaving Naples, along with much of Italy, firmly in the hands of the Spanish. In the poem cycle, Terracina names over fifty Neapolitan widows and praises them for their virtue, their devotion to their husbands' memories, and their dedication to the city of Naples.[103] At the height of her career, Terracina had already received considerable acclaim when the *Settime rime* were published: she was a member of the distinguished Accademia degli Incogniti, and was the day's best-selling female author in Italy.[104]

Terracina begins the *Settime rime* with a prefatory letter to the dedicatee of the work, the recently widowed Marianna de la Cueva y Cabrera, princess of Ascoli. The poet assures the princess that her husband, the late Don Luigi de Leyva, second Count of Monza and the prince of Ascoli, is no doubt enjoying his eternity in Heaven. Marianna should therefore rejoice and celebrate his death rather than mourn, for he has passed on to a better life.[105] The poet allows, however, that the widowed princess might still be inclined to spend her time mourning her husband and therefore offers

Marianna some verses dedicated to her specifically as well as verses she says she has composed over the years and addressed to various worthy Neapolitan widows. In the preface, she apologizes to her dedicatee and to her readers, admitting it has taken her some time to complete the endeavor; as a result, she explains, some of the widows she mentions in the collection are now dead and some have remarried. Terracina's *Settime rime* addresses a schiera for the new generation, a remarkable fifty-seven Neapolitan widows, including the influential cultural figures Maria d'Aragona (1503–1568; widowed 1546), Giulia Gonzaga (1513–1566; widowed 1528), and the younger Costanza d'Avalos, Duchess of Amalfi (the daughter of Laura Sanseverino, d. 1575; widowed 1565); Isabella, Portia, and Vergilia Colonna; and numerous women from the prominent Neapolitan families of Carafa and Sanseverino. Vittoria Colonna goes unmentioned, despite Terracina admitting that while she meant to include only living widows, the project took her so long that some of the women have died. The poems addressed to the widows themselves, all in *ottava rima*, are notably repetitive, echoing Capasso's praise of his own nine widows: beneath each widow's black veil can be found an honest and beautiful face, a clear brow, a devoted heart. The tone shifts at the end of the poem cycle, however, morphing from banal encomium to an ambitious polemic about the crucial role of widows in poetic production, as she addresses the widows as a group worthy of praise by the greatest poets of Naples, past, present, and future.

Both Capasso and Terracina work to immortalize a group of women whose fame is derived from, and to a certain degree dependent upon, their widowhood. Each presents these groups as a collective, or even a type of emotional community, around which literature should be organized and produced. Terracina's poem pushes this concept of a community of widows even further than Capasso. Her *Settime rime* present each individual widowed subject as part of a broader project—a building block, or column, in a *tempio* dedicated to the concept of widowhood itself.[106] Tropes of lost love and wifely devotion return again and again, each widow's virtue building on the last, resulting in a firm foundation for her final argument. Whereas Capasso concludes his poem with Cupid proudly praising his newfound widowed muses, Terracina ends hers by turning to address her widowed subjects directly as a group. In a coy protest against her own poetic talents, she reassures her dedicatees that if her "roz[z]o stil" (rough style) and "inchiostro indegno" (unworthy ink) have not been enough to do them justice, they should not fear: greater poets than she will now know how to speak of them.[107] Her collection's project, she explains, has been but to highlight her subjects briefly to offer inspiration to other (male) poets, who, she says, will write far better poems in praise of these women now that she has introduced them. She pointedly identifies several potential poets still living at the time the *Settime rime* were published, including two who had been part of the d'Avalos/Colonna salon on Ischia: Luigi Tansillo (1510–1568) and Berardino Rota (1508–1575).[108]

Terracina, is, in effect, suggesting a temple-like project for honoring these widows, though one that cuts across social rank and class. By identifying lesser-known women alongside women of elite social, political, and intellectual status, she also systematically legitimates *nontitolate* (untitled women), elevating them as worthy of praise by male poets alongside more famous contemporary *titolate*. They too, it is implied, contribute to the broader civic good through their successful public mourning.

While there is an element of feigned humility at play throughout Terracina's performance, the *Settime rime* also argue for a broader poetic project celebrating the widows of Naples, that would take the voices of multiple authors, of both sexes, to be considered a true success. In the poem's final octave, she circles back to the dead: this time, to Naples's most famous poets now gone, whose words, she suggests, might have been most powerful of all in constructing the tempio she imagines. If Sannazaro and his peers were alive, she laments, their verses would make the seas tremble far beyond the local shores of Naples ("farebbeno tremar, non sol queste onde / ma quanti liti, e scogli il mar circonde").[109] Terracina thus memorializes her poetic influences while also inserting herself into a pantheon of famous Neapolitan writers, allying herself most especially with Sannazaro, whose connection to Vittoria Colonna during her days in Ischia was well-known.

Colonna remains a conspicuous absence throughout Terracina's poem cycle. Her ties to Naples through the d'Avalos family, her major influence on Neapolitan writing through the Ischia salon, and above all her legendary status as a widowed poet make it especially curious that Terracina did not include Colonna alongside other famous widows. Perhaps she took seriously Colonna's rejection of a public profile as a widow as well as her self-fashioning as an entirely unique figure and thus left her to the world of her own private grief.

As I have argued over the past two chapters, the work of widowhood—on individual and societal levels—was highly dependent on reading and replicating established role models, both sacred and secular. In the sixteenth century, widows with a public profile were increasingly cast—and cast *themselves*—as models of mourning as well as symbols of reconstruction after personal and political crisis, building cities allegorical and temporal on the model of Dido's Carthage. Capasso's triumph is, similarly, architectural in its approach to historical continuity and cultural instruction, consciously pointing up the still-extant landmarks of the ancient world and fashioning his exempla of widowly virtues seemingly endemic to the war-torn region into a classical "tempio" formation. Terracina's endless *Settime rime*, meanwhile, reflect the sheer number (and popularity) of "worthy" widows in Naples at the end of the Italian Wars. In the next chapter, we turn from the widowed schiera to a genealogy of women who, like Colonna, constructed their authorial and widowed identities through the genre of *rime vedovili*, or widowed lyric verse.

PART III

The Widow's Voice

CHAPTER FIVE

Widowed Verse

Christine de Pizan, Vittoria Colonna, and Francesca Turina

The third and final part of this study, made up of this chapter and the one to follow, focuses on the widow's voice as it is mediated through literary texts. This chapter also continues my analysis of sixteenth-century widows and widowhood, through a focus on the microgenre of widowhood poetry. I would suggest that widowhood poetry can be considered a category distinct from the broader one of *in morte* Petrarchan lyric, which has generally included poems of loss and mourning by widows to their husbands alongside all other mourning verse in the style of Petrarch.[1] Poetry by widows either to or about their spouses has a long and unique enough history, with enough examples, to be understood as a separate category worthy of consideration on its own. Indeed, Tatiana Crivelli and Maria Serena Sapegno have argued that Colonna's *rime amorose* (amorous verse) to her husband after his death should be categorized more specifically as *rime vedovili*, or widowed verse.[2] I would advocate that the term be used for all poetry written by widowed women to their husbands in the lyric tradition. Here, I explore a broad galaxy of such rime vedovili, arguing that widowed poets exploited long-standing tropes of widowhood in poetry to forge their own identities as authors and public figures—while also making grief expressed by women's voices through poetry acceptable, even admirable.[3] Through the lyric form, these writers consciously embodied the poetics of widowhood developed through poems of mourning by Dante and Petrarch, appropriating the vocabulary and conceptual framework of lyric mourning, with a twist: unlike Dante and Petrarch, they had no need to "widow" their poems. The widow was always already present.

Christine de Pizan's *Rime Vedovili Avant La Lettre*

While the bulk of poems analyzed here fall under the umbrella of sixteenth- and early seventeenth-century Petrarchism, I start by returning to the late Middle Ages and the widowed writer Christine de Pizan, who wove her personal experience of the loss of her husband throughout her oeuvre. Her most striking reference to the metamorphosis she experienced in widowhood may be in *La Mutacion*, with which I began the introduction to this study, where she describes her transformation after her husband's death as an explicitly embodied shift from woman to man. But she also forefronts her experience as a widow in her *Cent ballades*, a set of one hundred poems believed to have been composed between 1395 and 1401 following the death of her husband Etienne de Chastel in 1389, this time casting herself as a distinctly female widowed figure.[4]

The autobiographical character of Christine's poems on her husband's death is strikingly similar to that of poems written by sixteenth-century Italian widowed writers such as Colonna and others including Laura Battiferri, Chiara Matraini, and Francesca Turina. Kevin Brownlee has argued that Christine organizes a "provocative combination of gendered subject positions—virtuous widow, caring mother and female author" to "establish her authority within the discursive public space of the fifteenth-century Parisian literary establishment."[5] As we have now seen, the three subject positions Brownlee identifies were often interlinked for widows: any virtuous or "true" widow who had children had to be not only a caring mother but also, as so many argued, a mother *and* a father to their orphaned children. This required both avoiding remarriage and embracing any masculine qualities that might help get children closer to a full set of parents, one male and one female.

From the very beginning of her career, Christine established an authorial identity linked to her self-presentation as precisely this kind of virtuous widow. Brownlee argues that this was part of her broader project to establish her authority as an author by divorcing her identity, and her work, from the theme of sexual desire so present in court poetry in the time she was writing.[6] While I agree that this is an important part of her strategy, we should not conclude that she presents herself as a grieving widow *only* as a means to desexualize herself. Rather, as an attentive reader of Dante, Petrarch, and Boccaccio, Christine clearly understands the rhetorical potential of the widowed voice and engages directly with the poetics of widowhood established by the *tre corone*.

We see this throughout her poems in the *Cent ballades*, in which she presents herself as a widow who will never stop grieving for her one true beloved. In Ballad 14, she laments her husband Etienne's death across three stanzas, each concluding with the refrain "Qu'a tousjours mais je pleureray sa mort" (For I will weep for his death forever). In the body of the poem, she articulates the feelings of fear and abandonment she suffers as a widow, comparing herself to a ewe left behind by the shepherd who becomes the prey of the hungry wolf ("com brebis que lop tache a occire, / Qui s'esbaïst quant son pastour la laisse"; ll. 17–18) and asking, "what else can I do but weep and sigh?" ("qu'en puis je mais, se je pleure et souspire?" l. 8).

The physical expression of her lament through verbs of mourning such as "pleurer" (to weep) and "souspirer" (to sigh) is repeated throughout the poems, notably in Ballad 15, line 8, "plaindre et plourer je doy bien mon affaire" (to lament and weep is what I must do). The verbs "to weep," "to sigh," and "to mourn" recall poetic traditions of lament and resonate in particular with the way Dante and Petrarch fashion grief in the *Vita nuova* and the *Rerum vulgarium fragmenta*, respectively, as we saw in the first chapter of this study. In *Vita nuova*'s "Venite a intender li sospiri miei," which follows on the explicitly widowed canzone "*Li occhi dolenti*," Dante invites his readers to "venite a intender li sospiri miei" (come and listen to his sighs), which "li quai disconsolati vanno via" (issue forth disconsolate; ll. 1, 3). This mournful sighing is repeated in *Purgatorio*, when Forese Donati praises his wife's effective performance of grief that pushes him up the mountain, which includes "pianger dirotto" (broken weeping) and "prieghi devoti e . . . sospiri" (devoted prayers and . . . sighs; *Purgatorio* XXIII, ll. 87–88). From the proemial sonnet of Petrarch's *Canzoniere*, we see an invitation to readers to listen to his "sospiri ond'io nudriva il core" (sighs with which I nourished my heart; *RVF* 1, l. 2), the audible breath of his unrequited love for Laura. These "soavi sospiri" or "gentle sighs" are transformed following Laura's death into "gravi sospiri" or "heavy sighs" in *RVF* 332. The "dolce stile" of his earlier works—with the clear and intentional reference to Dante and the *stilnovisti*—is lost to the grief that follows Death's conquest of Laura, replaced by a "doloroso stile" or mournful style. Unlike Orpheus, who sang to rescue his love Eurydice from the underworld in an effectively "pietoso stile" (pitiful style; l. 49) Petrarch can no longer sing at all: instead, his singing is converted to weeping ("cantar converso in pianto," l.34). In Christine's poem, she is similarly robbed of the breath that might allow her to sing throughout the *Cent ballades* and is left only with weeping to express her deep sadness.

Christine uses her widowed grief to control the narrative around her character and her words: writing as a chaste and grieving widow, she presents herself as concurrently unthreatening and possessing a deeply rooted authority. In Ballad 17, Christine observes, "If all my writings are about sadness, it's no surprise, for a heart in mourning cannot have joyous thoughts."[7] She explains that while she might like to, she is unable to write "sweet things," for grief consumes her heart:

> Si ne pourroye doulcement
> faire dis; car, vueille ou ne vueille,
> m'estuet complaindre trop griefment
> le mal, dont fault que je me dueille . . .
>
> (I cannot write sweet things. Whether I want to or not, I must complain bitterly about the evil which I must bemoan . . .) (ll. 17–22)[8]

These lines are part of a broader project of self-justification evident across her widowhood poems, such as in Ballad 8, the refrain of which is "C'est bien raison que me doye doloir" (There is good reason for me to grieve). Poems 11 to 15, as Walters argues, are an extended metaphor of shipwreck in *La Mutacion*, where she describes the loss of her husband and her subsequent transition from woman to man.[9] The nautical metaphor—whether through the loss of the helmsman or the trauma of the shipwreck itself—is seen in poetry from Homer onward, and we might think especially in these circumstances of Ulysses in Dante's *Inferno,* punished for his "folle volo" or "mad flight."[10] We have also seen the allegory used before to describe the state of widowhood, beginning with Dante, as well as in fourteenth-century murals depicting Rome at the time of so-called Babylonian captivity of the papacy as a widow in a small craft on a raging sea. As I discussed in the last chapter, in his "Triumphem Novem Viduarem," Capasso describes the widow Laura Sanseverino as a *franco nocchier* guiding her people, no longer in need of her husband to steer the ship, and Colonna's canzone, "Mentre la nave mia," opens by describing her ship, "longe dal porto, / priva del suo nochier che vive in Cielo" (far from port and deprived of her helmsman, who is now in Heaven).[11] Shipwreck—and what comes after—offers numerous interpretive possibilities for the widowed writer, emphasizing above all the isolation of the widowed state, which can be interpreted as either devastating or, perhaps, liberatory. In this next section of this chapter, I look beyond "Mentre la nave mia" to consider Colonna's foundational contribution to the genre of rime vedovili.

Colonna, Gambara, and a New Poetics of Widowhood

Christine's use of the phrase "bien raison" or "good reason" in Ballad 8 as she justifies her widowly grief should be familiar to readers of Colonna's rime vedovili, written a century and a half later. The proemial sonnet "Scrivo sol per sfogar l'interna doglia," perhaps the most well-known and analyzed of Italian widowhood poems, announces and explains her poetic project of mourning for her husband:

> Scrivo sol per sfogar l'interna doglia
> ch'al cor mandar le luci al mondo sole,
> e non per giunger lume al mio bel Sole
> al chiaro spirto, a l'onorata spoglia.
> Giusta cagion a lamentar m'invoglia;
> ch'io scemi la sua gloria assai mi dole;
> per altra voce e più sagge parole
> convien ch'a Morte il gran nome si toglia.
> La pura fe', l'ardor, l'intensa pena
> mi scusi appo ciascun, che 'l grave pianto
> è tal che tempo né ragion l'affrena.
> Amaro lagrimar, non dolce canto,
> foschi sospiri e non voce serena,
> di stil no, ma di duol mi danno il vanto.

(I write solely to salve the suffering that those bright eyes, peerless in this world, caused my heart, and not to add luster to my lovely Sun, to his radiant spirit

> and honored remains. A just cause leads me to lament, and it sorely pains me that I may detract from his glory; his great name deserves to be rescued from death by a loftier voice and wiser words. May my pure faith, my ardor, my intense grief excuse me, for my mourning is such that neither reason nor time can restrain it. Bitter weeping, not sweet song; dark sighs, not a serene voice, my verse boasts not of style but of woe.)[12]

At the start of the second quatrain, Colonna defends the decidedly mournful tone of her amorous verse: "Giusta cagion a lamentar m'invoglia" (a just cause leads me to lament). Her use of the phrase "giusta cagion" or "just cause"—similar to Christine's "bien raison"—establishes what Maria Serena Sapegno has identified as a "legitimate ethics" for her poetry.[13] As we saw in the last chapter, Colonna was highly attuned to models as she fashioned her unique phoenix-like poetic identity. While she cast her particularly zealous focus on widowed grief as singular, it is useful to recognize that we already see, in de Pizan's poems, a woman writer who is using a paradigm honed by Dante and Petrarch in order to express her distinctly feminine, widowed brand of grief. Whereas Christine established her authorial identity as a widowed writer through the mournful ballads dedicated to her late husband before expanding her writing to other literary genres, including political writing, Colonna's renown became explicitly tied to the way she grieved the loss of her husband in verse.

In Colonna's proemial sonnet, now considered something of a classic of the genre, she lays out the motivations behind her ambitious literary project to document her widowed grief after the loss of her husband Fernando Francesco d'Avalos in 1525 following the Battle of Pavia. Like de Pizan, Colonna declares that there is no expiration date on her grief and that she may well mourn forever: "La pura fe', l'ardor, l'intensa pena / mi scusi appo ciascun, che 'l grave pianto / è tal che tempo né ragion l'affrena" (May my pure faith, my ardor, my intense grief excuse me, for my mourning is such that neither reason nor time can restrain it). From the outset, Colonna privileges the authenticity of her grief over poetic style and glory, declaring that she writes not to amplify the fame of the man she describes throughout her work as her "Sole" or "Sun" but "only" to expiate the terrible pain she feels. Proper glorification of her husband, Colonna declares, should be left to "a loftier voice and wiser words": she can offer but her "pure faith," "ardency," and "intense pain" as the motivation for her "grave lament." The final tercet underlines that she is not the right writer for the grand memorialization project her beloved husband deserves: her words are not the "sweet song" necessary to bring him eternal fame but rather base, "bitter weeping"; her voice is not "serene" but filled with "dark sighs."

The reader, of course, has been in on the joke from the very first line. As Abigail Brundin has observed, Colonna is asking her audience to collude with her in this poem by proclaiming her lack of style in masterful Dantean and Petrarchan language, interlacing her protestations of being no more than a pitiable widow who writes only to relieve her grief with a poetic mastery and elegance few others could hope to achieve.[14] She competes ably with her male models both in the depths of her grief over the loss of the beloved and in the poetic manifestation of that grief.[15]

After her husband's death, Colonna devoted thirteen years to the composition of doleful Petrarchan *in morte* poems, which circulated across the peninsula. It is for this body of work that she was heralded by her peers as at the same time a new ideal of a poet and a new ideal of a widow. These years culminated in the pirated publication of her *Rime* in 1538; Rinaldo Corso's 1543 commentary on the collection, commissioned by Gambara, was the first commentary ever published on the work of a living writer—male or female. Her renown was articulated by others and, critically, self-fashioned around her *private* widowed experience.

Her most enduring praise comes from Ariosto, who, as I noted in the last chapter, singles out Colonna in Canto 37 of the definitive version of *Orlando furioso* in 1532, identifying her as the ultimate woman poet because of her marvelous devotion to her husband's memory.[16] He defines her poetic grief-project, which she suggests is simple catharsis, as one of poetic immortalization, characterized above all else as a perfect blend of commemoration and "dolce stil" (tying her not only to Petrarch but to Dante). When he compares Colonna to the classical exemplar Artemisia, he locates Colonna's eclipse of the loyal widow par excellence precisely in this specifically *literary* project. I include the relevant passage again here from *Orlando furioso*, which we saw in the last chapter, specifically in order to draw attention to the connection Ariosto makes between her grief and her writing:

> Questa è un'altra Artemisia, che lodata
> fu di pietà verso il suo Mausolo; anzi
> tanto maggior, quanto è più assai bell'opra,
> che por sotterra un uom, trarlo di sopra.
>
> (She is another Artemisia, who was praised for devotion to her Mausolus: indeed, she is so much the greater in that to rescue a man from the grave is a feat so much more splendid than to bury him.) (37.18, ll. 6–8)[17]

Ariosto is specific in his praise, and this specificity is crucial for our understanding of why Colonna was so admired as a widowed poet during her lifetime and after. More than simply mourning her husband, she turns her grief into poetry and thus makes her husband immortal—in the process transforming herself from an everyday widow into an exemplary one. Her feminine mourning is also made acceptable, even admirable, through its transformation into verse.

Colonna offered widowed writers a robust model for imitation that brimmed over with hybrid vigor: Petrarchan lover mixed with heroic woman. Several critics have observed that the public nature of Colonna's widowhood provided her with a remarkably free space in which she could write, correspond, and contemplate spiritual ideas without having to fulfill the usual duties of an aristocratic woman, unlike Costanza d'Avalos or Veronica Gambara.[18] It also provided, perhaps, a strategic way to avoid remarriage when her relatives wanted to marry her off. Who, after all, wants to marry a woman famous for being the most spectacularly grief-stricken widow the world has ever known?

With her rime vedovili, Colonna adopted a central role in the long-established lineage of widows advocating publicly for their husbands postmortem in the Italian literary tradition. Her widowed voice, and the important role of the proemial sonnet in the shaping of that voice, was reinforced by the print editions that shaped her works into a digestible, clearly ordered *opera*.[19] From the first pirated edition of the *Rime* by Filippo Pirogallo in 1538, the proemial sonnet remained in pride of place despite numerous reorderings in later editions, and, as we will see, it is her artful self-positioning in this sonnet that seems to have resonated more than any other with other women poets under consideration later in this chapter. Sapegno has also noted that it is with the new print editions that Colonna's image "began to evolve relatively independently from her poetic activity."[20]

We return here to the role in print and outside of it of Veronica Gambara, also a widowed aristocrat and talented Petrarchist. Of special note, it was Gambara who commissioned the Corso commentary on Colonna's work, effectively promoting Colonna as the ideal widow poet despite having herself written poems on the same subject.[21] In the last chapter, we saw how Colonna and Gambara served as "consolatory icons," deployed to inspire cultural pride after the devastation of the 1527 Sack of Rome. They were also central to Bembo's Petrarchist project in the same years; Virginia Cox has observed that "the pairing of Colonna and Gambara, and their twin 'canonization,' was critical to the literary dynamics of Petrarchism in its formative period. It worked particularly well because the two women, though very different as poets, had sufficient in common as social and ethical models to work as mutually reinforcing exempla."[22] As Molly Martin points out, in contrast with Colonna, Gambara wrote comparatively few rime vedovili, devoting herself to political poems instead: "Gambara's political position proved a shaping influence on her poetics," Martin argues, "not only by facilitating her rise to recognition in the literary landscape, but also in determining her creative choices as a lyricist; the production of poetry served as a key site in the construction of her image as a legitimate widow ruler and as an icon of feminine virtue."[23]

Their divergence in authorial identity is crucial here. The two widowed poets themselves highlight the key differences between their poetic identities in a sonnet exchange from circa 1532, published by Bembo in his 1535 *Rime*, and also included after their deaths in the 1559 Domenichi anthology. In the *proposta*, we see Gambara announce conspicuously that she has given up writing amorous poetry—the "vaghi e giovenil penseri" that once "nourished" her—recalling the opening sonnet of Petrarch's *Canzoniere*:

> Mentre da vaghi e giovenil penseri
> fui nutrita, or temendo ora sperando,
> piangendo or trista ed or lieta cantando,
> da desir combattuta or falsi or veri,
> con accenti sfogai pietosi e fieri
> i concetti del cor, che, spesso amando
> il suo mal assai più che 'l ben cercando,
> consumava doglioso i giorni intieri.

Or, che d'altri pensieri e d'altre voglie
pasco la mente, a le già care rime
ho posto ed a lo stil silenzio eterno,
e se, allor vaneggiando, a quelle prime
sciocchezze intesi, ora il pentirmi toglie,
la colpa palesando, il duol interno.

(While I was nourished by wandering and youthful thoughts, now fearing, now hoping, now crying in pain, now singing in delight, grappling with both false and true desires, with fierce and pitiful tones I vented the affairs of my heart, which, seeking its own pain over well-being, spent entire days in agony. Now that my mind feeds on different thoughts and different desires, I have placed my once dear rhymes and style in eternal silence; and if then in my nonsense I devoted myself to those youthful follies, now my repentance, by revealing my guilt, relieves the inner pain.)[24]

Gambara here describes her own rime vedovili using multiple words that chime with the poetic vocabulary of widowhood we are by now familiar with: "sfogai," "piangendo," "doglioso," "duol interno." Strikingly, she expresses impatience with her earlier self, bemoaning the fact that her love and grief for her husband often consumed "giorni intieri" (entire days)—when she might have been dedicated to something more productive, like political negotiation.[25]

"Mentre da vaghi e giovenil penseri" is a conscious performance of renunciation, one further mitigated by Gambara's choice to address the poem to Colonna, with whom she shared so much in terms of class, marriage status, and poetic reputation. Colonna's *risposta,* in contrast, is an articulated refusal to join Gambara in renouncing her "vaghi e giovenil penseri" and, thus, is also a tacit assent to carry on the work of modeling widowed grief in poetry. She is simply not finished with her own mourning and has not yet purged her heart of grief. Indeed, while Gambara utilizes the classic verb from Dante and Petrarch for grieving—*sfogare*—in the past tense ("sfogai"), Colonna uses "sfogando" in her *risposta,* a grammatical indicator of her ongoing, endless, grief project:

Lasciar non posso i miei saldi pensieri,
ch'un tempo mi nutrir felice amando;
hor mi consuman misera cercando,
pur quel mio sol per altri alti sentieri.
Ma tra falsi pensieri e pianti veri,
la cagion immortal vuol che, obliando
ogn'altra cura, io viva al fin sperando
un giorno chiaro, dopo tanti neri.
Onde l'alto dolor le basse rime
muove, e quella ragion la colpa toglie,
che fa viva la fede e 'l duolo eterno.

In fin a l'ultim'hora a quella voglie
saran sole nel cuor, che furon prime
sfogando il fuoco honesto e 'l duolo interno.

(I cannot leave behind my fixed thoughts
That once nourished me while I happily loved;
Now they consume me, miserably searching
For that sun of mine on other high paths.
But, between false thoughts and true weeping,
The immortal cause wants me, forgetting
All other cares, to live till the end hoping
For one bright day after so many black.
Thus my lofty pain moves my lowly verse,
And reason removes the blame that keeps
My faith alive and my sadness eternal.
At the end of the final hour, those desires
Will be alone in my heart as always,
Venting my honest flame and inner pain.)[26]

Her grief is not just internal, as is Gambara's ("duol interno"), but also *eternal*—"duol eterno." The fervent poetic demonstrations of grief employed by Colonna in verse—the sighs and bitter weeping—bear, like Christine's before her, a close resemblance to the tools used by Nella Donati to negotiate her husband's swift ascent up the Mountain of Purgatory. Tasked with both her husband's legacy in death and her reputation on earth, Colonna weeps and sighs her husband to eternal fame.

From one angle, Gambara's sonnet to Colonna can be seen as an invitation to her fellow widowed poet to join her in the larger world. It also might be read as a kind of entreaty, a plea that Colonna will continue her widowed poetic project so that Gambara can focus less on her own internal and eternal pain and more on the world around her. She has already purged the grief from her heart ("con accenti sfogai pietosi e fieri / i concetti del cor"; ll. 5–6).[27] Gambara shifts the focus away from herself, working to impose the ideal model of poetic widowhood on Colonna, positioning herself, by contrast, in a different light: as a political poet, not one defined by her widowhood.

An examination of one of Gambara's three widowhood poems suggests that she views the aims of marriage itself in a different light than does Colonna. The sonnet "Quel nodo, in cui la mia beata sorte" is similar to Colonna's rime vedovili in many respects: in it, she claims that her only cause for happiness, her husband, has left her, and admits that there have been moments when she has longed for death.[28] Her focus is less on the man himself, however, than on the "nodo" or marriage knot, which has been untied. She explains that the only reason she decided not to kill herself was because she feared ending up "in parte troppo lontana" (in a place far away) from her husband, and she hopes that she can remain a good enough Christian to end up alongside him in Heaven.[29] That it is "fear alone" ("tema sol") that kept her from suicide, and not "ingegno od arte" (intelligence or art), recalls the dyad Colonna points to in "Scrivo sol per sfogar l'interna doglia," that of style on the one hand and grief on the other.[30] However, Gambara would choose a different path: when she declared herself done with the amorous poetry of her youth, she turned not inward to spiritual poetry, as Colonna would in the last ten years of her life, but outward to the broader political world.[31] Indeed, Gambara's renunciation of her earlier widowed verse seems contingent upon Colonna's continued performance of widowhood; her support of Rinaldo Corso's commentary, too, suggests an exceptional commitment to building up Colonna's particular brand of widow-poet, which would become the example par excellence for widowed poets later in the century.

New Colonnas

The next section of this chapter considers how Colonna's legacy as the ideal widowed poet influenced the self-presentation in poetry of three later widowed poets who not only imitated her but placed themselves in stylistic and affective competition with her, especially through allusions to her proemial sonnet. As the study of Colonna as a poetic and cultural influencer has blossomed over the past two decades, much has been written about her contemporary fame and her own careful self-fashioning as a figure to be imitated.[32] We now have a remarkably clear picture of just how high profile Colonna's reputation as an ideal widow was during her lifetime as well as the particular ways in which her verse was printed and organized for the reading public following the first pirated edition of 1538.[33] Here I explore how Laura Battiferri (1523–1589), Chiara Matraini (1515–1604), and Francesca Turina (1553–1641) engaged with and borrowed from Colonna's poetics of widowhood in order to elevate their own widowed verse and their status as women poets. A look to these three poets also significantly elongates the timeline of Colonna's influence, proving just how late Colonna's rime vedovili were being imitated and explored: deep into the Counter-Reformation, Matraini and Turina were still engaging directly with her work as a way to legitimate their own authorial voices, with Turina praising the honor she brought to women as late as her own *Rime* of 1628.[34]

Battiferri, Matraini, and Turina all engage with Colonna's reputation and poetry in their work, each establishing a dialogue in verse based on emulation of the poet despite no hope of a return sonnet or letter.[35] All three pick up, especially, on the richness of the proemial sonnet, providing the reader with variations on a theme and reminding us not only of Colonna's influence but of the breadth and potential of the innovation she offered as a model for later Petrarchists. It is most enlightening to look at the three sonnets in chronological order, which demonstrates how Colonna's influence evolved from mid- to late sixteenth century.

In addition to being the earliest of the three poets under consideration here, Laura Battiferri (b. 1523) is also the most celebrated and studied. Like Colonna, Battiferri is known for her highly cultivated image as an illustrious poet, as the famous 1560 Bronzino portrait of her makes clear.[36] Battiferri was attentive to her connections to the influential: a native of Urbino, she aligned herself with the powerful Grand Duchess of Florence, Eleonora de Toledo, through an important verse collection, *Il primo libro dell'opere toscane* (1560).[37] Despite her aristocratic pretensions, Battiferri was born out of wedlock and was married twice to commoners, a far cry from Colonna's noble lineage and illustrious marriage to the Spanish military leader d'Avalos. Battiferri wrote just nine widowhood poems, none of which were published, after the death of her first husband, the organist Vittorio Sereni, in 1549.[38] She was remarried the following year to Bartolomeo Ammannati. The early place of these widowhood sonnets in her poetic chronology is worth noting: they came at the beginning of her career, and it seems likely that they were an attempt at experimentation, crafting herself as a new Colonna, a young noble widowed poet with important friends. Her husband was even fortuitously named "Vittorio," allowing her to pun on his name and Colonna's at once.[39]

It is the first of Battiferri's nine poems that begs the closest attention in the context of Colonna's influence, due to its clear allusions to the proemial sonnet and its play with dissimulative language, as she vaunts her grief over her poetic merit:

> Non scrivo, alma mia stella, perch'io voglia
> o pensi alla gran luce tua infinita
> giunger punto di lume, ma m'invita
> amore, mi sprona mia sfrenata voglia.
> Ragion ognora a ragionar m'invoglia,
> di te, ch'or godi in ciel beata vita,
> dal vero oggetto tuo mai disunita,
> u' morte o tempo non fia che ti rispoglia.
> Così ponga omai fine al dolor mio
> l'alta felicità, la tua memoria,
> ch'ognor fa andar altier mio basso stile.
> Non è d'acquistar lode il mio disio,
> ma s'io parlo di te, alma gentile,
> avrò di morte e dello oblio vittoria.
>
> (I do not write, my bountiful star, because I
> want to add a touch of shine to your infinite light,
> or think I can, but love invites me,
> my unbridled will spurs me.
> Reason ever makes me want to speak with reason of
> you, who now enjoy in heaven blessed life, never
> disjoined from your true object, where death or time
> will not be there to despoil you again.
> Thus may lofty felicity, your memory,
> whichever makes my lowly style go proud, now
> put an end to my sorrow.
> It is not my desire to acquire praise, but if I

speak of you, noble soul, I shall have victory over death
and oblivion.)[40]

The poem is a frank nod to Colonna's "Scrivo sol per sfogar l'interna doglia," though it begins not with the affirmative "I write in order to" but instead with the negative "I do *not* write," introducing something of a defensive posture from the opening line. Addressed directly to her husband ("alma mia stella"), Battiferri echoes her role model while twisting Colonna's language to craft a protestation rather than an explanation—she does *not* write to "add a touch of shine" ("giunger punto di lume," echoing Colonna's "non per giunger lume").[41] Battiferri insists, like her poetic model, that she does not write mourning poems in order to advance her dead husband's reputation but because of unstoppable love and her own "unbridled will." The reasoning remains the same as Colonna's; it is the wording that is inverted.

Evident in this sonnet, however, are some small signs of ambition that Colonna would not have admitted to. Indeed, Battiferri's becomes a bolder poetic performance than that of her model overall, as she both imitates the rhymes of Colonna's quatrains (the original doglia/spoglia/invoglia/toglia transformed to voglia/voglia/invoglia/rispoglia) and builds on them, demonstrating stylistic flair through her use of *rima equivoca* (voglia/voglia) and inclusive rhyme (voglia/invoglia). Battiferri asserts that her grief and the memory of her love elevate her lowly style; if she speaks of him, she says, she will have "vittoria" or victory over death and oblivion, with the obvious allusion to Colonna's name.[42] While this victory is largely psychic, it is a far more martial choice of word than Colonna's choice of "sfogar." She is looking not to expiate her feelings but to conquer them.

Even balder ambition is on display in the next two poets under consideration here. Chiara Matraini was born in 1515 to a family of commoners in Lucca and died in 1604; her poems were published in two different versions, both under her direction, forty-two years apart, in 1555 and 1597.[43] Matraini published a remarkably diverse array of texts over her long life, including an oration in praise of the art of war, printed in her 1555 *Rime e prose*, and her *Dialoghi spirituali* of 1602.[44] Because of her social status, she operated in a less well-connected world than Colonna and Battiferri.[45] She was married to Vincenzo Cantarini by 1530, widowed by 1542; it is rumored that she engaged in a scandalous affair following her husband's death with the married Bartolomeo Graziani, who was murdered somewhat mysteriously.[46] In 1555, Matraini published her *Rime e prose* with the Lucchese publisher Busdraghi; much of it is a *canzoniere* of widowed mourning poems, although the identity of the object of said mourning remains up for some debate. Critics have often believed the poems to be directed not to Cantarini but rather to Graziani; Cox has recently argued that wordplay on "Vincenzo" in the opening sonnet points to her husband instead as the dedicatee of the poems.[47] While this makes for a less salacious biography of the poet, it does make more sense when we consider how she allies herself with the chaste and ever-devoted widow Colonna.

In her revised 1597 edition, Matraini includes a *cento*, a poem composed of lines from poems written by other poets, which lifts the first four full lines from Colonna's

"Occhi miei, oscurato è il vostro Sole." Another poem worthy of study for its Colonnesque attention to fame is Matraini's "Alto mio sol, se l'anima beata," in which she avows that if she could allow her mind to be enamored of her sun's rays, a new light would be born to the world, suggesting that she might receive reflected glory if only she could see her beloved Sun—indeed, following Colonna's model, she uses *Sole* throughout.[48] The most important sonnet for our purposes here, however, does not appear in either the 1555 or the 1597 edition but instead is available only in a manuscript in the Vatican library.[49] In it we see, for the first time, a direct comparison to Colonna by a poet in her widowed verse.

> Quanto l'alta Colonna il suo gran sole
> avanzò in Ciel mentre che i santi carmi
> cantava in terra, e ne' più saldi marmi
> l'opre di lui intagliava eterne e sole,
> tanto l'alto suo stile avanzar suole
> mio ingegno, onde non posso a tanto alzarmi.
> Però conviensi e la vettoria e l'arme
> rendere a lei, che 'l mondo onora e cole.
> Ella qui morta e in Ciel bella e viva
> merita sol la gloriosa palma
> E corona di lauro, edera, oliva;
> ma voi di ricca e preziosa salma
> meritate, e di fiamma ardente e viva
> ornate aver di me sempre mai l'alma.

> (Just as the lofty Colonna advanced her great Sun in heaven as she sang her holy songs here on earth and sculpted his eternal, peerless deeds in the most lasting marble, so too does her lofty style advance my intellect: I cannot rise so high, and must give the victory and surrender my weapons to her whom the world honours and worships. She alone, dead on earth and beautiful and living in heaven, merits the glorious palm and the laurel, ivy and olive wreath, but you deserve me to adorn your soul with a rich and precious body, and with live and ardent fire.)[50]

Here Matraini specifically name-checks Colonna as the ideal widow poet, weaving together both Colonna's own language ("il suo gran sole") and the Artemisian comparison from Ariosto: her role model "sculpted" her husband's deeds in marble on earth while singing in order to advance his glory in Heaven. She also borrows Colonna's canny rhetorical strategy and insists that she cannot achieve such lofty stylistic heights herself; conspicuously, she says little about the depths of her own grief. She lays poetic "victory" at her role model's feet, punning on Colonna's first name as few can resist doing; unlike Battiferri, however, she aggrandizes her verse by declaring that her own style is made better by Colonna's influence. The poem ends somewhat defiantly, with a direct address to her beloved, declaring that despite her inability to reach Colonna's heights, her lover still deserves her own poetic efforts, inferior though they may be. Yet eleven of the poem's fourteen lines are devoted to Colonna; the poem's dedicatee—be he Graziani or Cantarini—is effectively an afterthought, even as Battiferri reassures him of his worth. The true aim of the sonnet is not to memorialize her lover but to compare herself to Colonna. In this particular poem, widowed verse changes, becoming less about the commemoration of the beloved and more about direct stylistic and affective competition with Colonna herself.

This focus on Colonna rather than the poet's own dead beloved is repeated in a madrigal by the final poet to whom I draw our attention and on whom I will then linger: the Umbrian poet Francesca Turina, whose poems to Santa Francesca Romana are discussed in chapter 3. Turina was born in 1553, six years after Colonna's death; like Matraini, she lived to an old age, dying in 1641.[51] She was married in 1573, at the age of twenty, to Count Giulio Bufalini, who was seventy years old at the time; the count died nine years later, leaving Turina with young children. She spent the remaining fifty-seven years of her life a widow.[52] In 1595, Turina published the first of her two books of verse, the *Rime spirituali sopra i misteri del santissimo rosario*, dedicating them to Pope Clement VIII (1536–1605, pontiff from 1592). In the introductory letter to the collection, Turina presents herself to the pope as a poor "vedovetta," casting herself as an abject figure in dire need of patronage and material assistance for the care of her children. She states that she offers Clement the poem cycle, a collection of spiritual poems divided into three parts—the *Primo misterio del santissimo Rosario detto Gaudioso, Secondo misterio del santissimo Rosario detto Doloroso*, and *Terzo ed ultimo misterio del santissimo Rosario detto Glorioso*—in the hope that he will take pity on her. She reminds him that, as a woman, she cannot protect her land like a man would, "with his labor and blood," but only "with the sincerity of my feelings, and with devotion in ink."[53]

Following the last poem of the *spirituali*, which heaps glorifying praise on Clement VIII, Turina elaborates on her declared feminine vulnerability, showcasing her widowed grief through twenty-four supplementary poems lamenting the loss of her husband. The poems, *Della medesima in morte de l'illustrissimo Signor Giulio Bufalini suo consorte* (Poems by the same author on the death of her consort, the most illustrious Sir Giulio Bufalini), constitute a remarkable cycle of rime vedovili, clearly informed by Colonna's widowed verse. The final poem of the collection is a madrigal addressed to Colonna, which closely mimics "Scrivo sol per sfogar l'interna doglia" and places her in direct affective competition with her predecessor:

> Porti, Vittoria, il vanto
> di stil, non di dolore,
> ché de la vena onde si strugge il core
> l'arte ho minor, ma non minore il pianto.
> Tu chiamasti Parnaso; e ti rispose,
> al suon di dotte, angeliche parole,
> con rime alte e famose,
> adornandone il ciel del tuo bel Sole.

Misera, io piango, e male
Pindo ascolta il mio dire semplice e frale;
ch'io crederei, s'egual
fosse 'l mio stile a la pietade e al zelo,
ornar anch'io d'un novo Sole il cielo.

(Vittoria, you carry the palm of style, not of sorrow, for in the vein that melts the heart, my art may be lesser, but my affliction is not less. You called Parnassus, and Parnassus responded to the sound of learned, angelic words, with sublime famous verses, adorning heaven with your fair Sun. Poor wretch that I am, I weep, and Pindus barely listens to my simple, frail voice. But, if my style were equal to my devotion and passion, I too would think to adorn the heavens with a new sun.)[54]

This madrigal—a poetic form rarely used by Colonna and which came most fully into vogue after her death—directly challenges Colonna's claim in her proemial sonnet that she writes only to relieve her grief and not with any great style. Turina flips the script on her role model, asserting that Colonna may well be the mistress of poetic *style* but not of grief; Turina's feelings of widowed woe are far greater, though the muses of Pindus pay her words no heed. Just below the surface of the poem is Turina's winking enticement to her own readers to collude with her, as Colonna urged her own readers to do. Her own style, she seems to imply, may someday overtake Colonna's as well as her grief.

Further to the message of the madrigal alone, the poem's positioning and the overall intention of this published work are important in order to fully understand its sophistication and innovation. Whereas Battiferri's "Non scrivo, alma mia stella, perch'io voglia" and Matraini's "Quanto l'alta Colonna il suo gran sole" circulated only in manuscript, Turina's madrigal concludes a public-facing text with multiple, interlocking aims: to secure patronage from the pope, demonstrate her acumen as spiritual poet, and showcase the authentic nature of her personal grief in verse. The publication as a whole is a bold presentation of herself as a new Colonna for her age. She inverts the traditional print order of Colonna's *rime amorose* followed by *rime spirituali* as they were so often published, beginning instead with rime spirituali and then moving to her widowed verse; rather than initiate Colonna's rime vedovili with a poem declaring that her woe is greater than her style, she ends with one; rather than address Vittoria in sonnet form, she chooses a madrigal. She offers herself as an even *more* devoted widow poet than the legendary Vittoria whom the pope can claim as his own, with a style as fresh as her grief.

The Widowed Poet Endures

Unlike Battiferri and Matraini, Turina chose Colonna not as a way to explore her grief in a handful of widowhood poems but instead as a jumping-off point for a lifelong self-fashioning as a grieving widow, which she continued for forty more years. While Colonna shifted her poetic project away from widowhood in at least the last decade of her life, Turina dug in on the psychic, physical, and economic hardships widowhood brought to her. Despite her declaration in verse that Colonna is the role model par excellence for how to mourn in a public, literary way, Turina's style is markedly different, defined by an attachment not to celestial concerns but to the body and the earth. Her poetry touches on breastfeeding, child-rearing, the relief of leaving behind her grim childhood for her marriage, and the assorted agonies of a decades-long widowhood.

Her substantial corpus of widowhood poems reveals the accumulated rhetorical potential of the identity of the "widowed poet" by the time she was writing. Consider poem 152 of the 1595 volume, in which Turina meditates on yet another emblem of widowhood, alongside the phoenix we saw multiple times in the last two chapters: the "atro abito" or "dark habit" of widow's weeds themselves, which she describes twice over as emblematic, a "dolorosa insegna," or "external expression" of that which she hides within her heart ("ch'albergo entro nel core").

> Ne l'atro abito mio si rappresenta
> la mestizia ch'albergo entro nel core
> che, vie più dentro che non mostra fuore,
> lassa, m'ancide insidïosa e lenta;
> né scema il grave duol che mi tormenta
> per volger d'anni, anzi si fa maggiore:
> Ond'amo sol quel funeral colore
> ch'il mio vedovo stato mi rammenta.
> Oh dura impresa, oh dolorosa insegna
> de l'empia Morte e sol de la mia vita
> e del grado presagio afflitto e mesto!
> Ahi, chi mi fa d'ogni letizia indegna
> ne l'età mia più verde e più fiorita?
> Come il ben tardi viene e fugge presto!

> (My black garb pictures the sadness I harbor in my heart, which is killing me, alas! insidiously and slowly, far more than my outward guise shows. Nor does the grave sorrow that torments me wane with the years; rather it grows, so that I love alone that funerary color, which reminds me of my widowed state. Oh harsh device and dolorous ensign of cruel Death, sole presage of my life and my miserable, afflicted state. Alas, who is it that makes me unworthy of all happiness, in the greenest and most flowering age of my life? How good comes to us late, and flees soon!)[55]

In this melancholy sonnet, Turina stresses that her external appearance reflects the grief she feels within, emphasizing the power of her widow's habit as *both* "dura impresa" (harsh device) and "dolorosa insegna" (dolorous ensign). As Cox has pointed out, there is precedent for a mention of a widow's black clothes in poetry written by widows: Colonna herself alludes to having loved her husband in both "chiari" and "oscuri panni" (light and dark garments), and Matraini describes "dolci rime" (sweet rhymes) transformed into tears "sopra il negro e triste manto" (upon [her] black, dreary robe).[56] Despite superficial similarities to these earlier examples, however, Turina's poem, Cox notes, is "unusual in thematizing her mourning dress as symbol of her grief."[57] Playing with the Renaissance trend of the device or emblem that represents a person's essence visually as well as with the idea of the military insignia, Turina elevates her dreary black clothes, giving them an almost supernatural power—they allow outsiders a window into what she feels inside her heart, while also turning her into a kind of emblem herself, a living embodiment of grief.[58]

Turina's nod to the widowly ensign recalls the many ensigns we saw in the last chapter. As readers will now be familiar, in Petrarch's Triumph of Death, the figure of Death is described as "una donna involta in veste negra," the same words the poet uses to describe his widowed canzone, *RVF* 268, the "vedova, sconsolata, in veste negra."[59] When we encounter Death in the *Triumphs*, we first see her insignia, which is contrasted with the "brigata allegra" of heroines led by Laura:

> così venia quella brigata allegra
> quando vidi un'insegna oscura e trista:
> et una donna involta in veste negra
>
> (and as that happy group was moving forward I saw a dark and sad ensign: and a woman draped in black garments) (ll. 29–31)

The nine illustrious widows of Giosuè Capasso's "Triumphem Novem Viduarem" also share an insignia: a golden phoenix on a black background, beneath which read the words "D'ambrosia e nectar sol mi cibo e pasco / perché le stelle, el ciel m'han facto tale / che sola vivo e poi morta rinasco" (I graze and feed on ambrosia and nectar alone, for the stars and the heavens have created me to live alone and then, dead, am born again; ll. 197–199). This collective symbol offers them as an antidote to the figure of Death in Petrarch's Triumph of Death—they represent rebirth for the city of Naples and perhaps for all of Italy, a triumph *over* death, a triumphant reimagining of the female figure "in veste negra."

Turina does not present her own "dolorosa insegna" as a victory over death; instead, the poet's "atro abito" is imbued with a kind of reliquary power, an outward manifestation of her endless grief and connection to her husband. Her obsessive devotion, still evident in poems written as late as fifty years after Bufalini's death, at times recalls the more macabre side of the exemplary Artemisia, who enshrined her husband's literal remains within her own body. In Sonnet 167 in the 1628 *Rime*, "Diletto mio, che 'l sol mi rassomigli," Turina speaks directly to a portrait of her departed husband, expressing her fear that she may go mad with grief.[60]

This is not the only time when she speaks to her husband's form. In poems 180 and 181 of the same volume, Turina returns to the motif of her husband's physical appearance. Both poems are titled in a way that informs the reader of the ghoulish scenario the poet presents: Sonnet 180 is "Nel vedere la sepoltura aperta" (On seeing the opened tomb); Sonnet 181 is "Nel medesimo suggetto" (On the same subject).[61] As in Sonnet 150, in Sonnet 181, Turina calls attention to her husband's physical features through a twisted Petrarchan index: "Quest'è la mano, amato mio signore" (Is this your hand, my beloved lord; l. 1); "Son questi gli occhi, ohimè, dal cui splendore / prendeva lume: or chiusi e atri e funesti?" (Are these the eyes, alas, from whose splendor he took light: are they now closed and black and woeful?; ll. 5–6); "Quest'è la cara bocca onde mi désti / così dolci ricordi a tutte l'ore?" (Is this the sweet mouth which once spoke sweet nothings to me at all hours of the day and night?; ll. 7–8); "Queste le braccia che con tal dolcezza / al tuo ritorno mi gettavi al collo, / cadenti, a me cagion d'aspra amarezza?" (Are these the arms with which you once embraced my neck with such sweetness and which, fallen, are now the cause of such dread bitterness?; ll. 9–11). As she asks, sequentially, if these are her beloved's hand, eyes, mouth, and arms that she sees, she stands not before a painting but before her husband's actual remains, years after his death, when the Bufalini family tomb was opened for an expansion. The poem ends with a plea that she might join him in the afterlife, echoing a common desire among widows in the classical tradition, including Artemisia herself, who was said to have wasted away from drinking her husband's ashes two years after his death.

There is not much to indicate Turina was interested in any kind of tidy end to her widowed grief. Indeed, from the conspicuous ordering of her 1595 publication, in which the rime spirituali are followed by the vedovili in an inversion of the Colonnesque model, to the continued focus on her grief throughout the 1628 *Rime*, Turina remained a melancholic poet—a decidedly indecorous choice and one quite different from that of the widowed poet she identified in print as her stylistic role model—who did, after all, eventually move on.[62] And yet she also fostered a personal connection to Colonna in the last decades of her life. After a period in Rome working as a tutor for the young daughters of Colonna's relatives, Filippo Colonna and Lucrezia Tomacelli Colonna, she returned to her Umbrian home in 1622, but she remained determined to keep ties to the Colonna family, valuable to her both as patrons and as a tangible connection to her literary role model.[63]

The 1628 *Rime* were dedicated to one of her former charges, Anna Colonna; in her dedicatory letter, she states that she has composed these verses "solamente per allegerimento delle passioni" (only in order to relieve her suffering), recalling yet again the opening sonnet to Colonna's rime amorose.[64] By declaring this rationale for the poems, she crafts from the very beginning a distinct kind of authorial voice that lends her a very particular kind of authority: that of the widow-author, an identity she had cultivated over the course of roughly fifty years. What emerges from the web of poems that make up the 1628 *Rime*—personal, political, spiritual—is a portrait of a woman mired in the details of everyday domestic worries while also tending faithfully to her own spiritual practice as well as a poet with strong political allegiances, who believes herself in clear need of patronage from the most powerful men and women of the day—and who can offer counsel and encouragement in return.

Turina dedicates numerous poems in the volume to members of the Colonna family, including Colonna's namesake, Vittoria, Anna's sister. She praises the girl for breathing life back into the name, declaring that she will be a new, magnificent Vittoria for her age.[65] She lauds the original Vittoria as "that lofty Colonna, who with her wise and resounding verses made herself immortal and gave honor to all women."[66] Here there is no mention at all of d'Avalos, of Bufalini, or of a shared grief over the loss of a husband—only of the fact that the poet rendered herself immortal and helped bring honor to other *women*—echoing Gambara's urging in her 1532 poem that other women build a monument to honor Colonna. By 1628, it seems, Turina views Colonna as exemplary not due to what she did for her husband but due to what she did for herself and for the widowed poets who came after.

It bears reflecting on what these poems can tell us about the way in which women writers of the early modern period may have perceived their role models—not just as poets to emulate but as poets to surpass. One thing that is evident from the poems by Battiferra, Matraini, and Turina written in imitation of "Scrivo sol per sfogar l'interna doglia" is a desire to eclipse Colonna—to beat her at her own game. This is markedly different from the way in which Colonna herself interacted with women writers contemporary to her. It also goes against what has been commonly assumed in scholarship about the way women writers generally engaged with their forebears. This is most famously identified in the 1979 classic of feminist literary criticism, Sandra Gilbert and Susan Gubar's *The Madwoman in the Attic*, which argues that Harold Bloom's theory of the "anxiety of influence," in which the (male) author must "engage in heroic warfare with his 'precursor,'" is "intensely (even exclusively) male, and necessarily patriarchal."[67] *Madwoman* distinguishes the anxieties of the woman writer from those of the man, declaring that a woman cannot fit within the male literary canon Bloom identifies and its resulting Oedipal anxieties. Women writers, Gilbert and Gubar argue, do not view themselves as being in competition with their foremothers because they have no foremothers to be in competition *with*. Forty-some years after the publication of Gilbert and Gubar's seminal text, the study of European women writers, whether the women of nineteenth-century England or those of sixteenth-century Italy, is in a very different place. The literary landscape is now flooded with foremothers, and we can see that women writers did not always play entirely nice with their role models. The anxiety of Colonna's influence is palpable in the poems of her descendants. Thanks to the extraordinary body of scholarship that now makes up the field of Colonna studies, it is clear that Colonna not only provided an early model for women Petrarchists to imitate but was a literary "mother" many of them hoped to outdo.

CHAPTER SIX

"Widowhood for Its Own Sake"

Widows in Two Dialogues of the Counter-Reformation

This concluding chapter considers an innovative perspective on widowhood that we see in the closing decades of the sixteenth century: widows who defend the inherent value of widowed life as speakers in dialogue. The works under consideration in this chapter, Bernardo Trotto's *Dialoghi del matrimonio e vita vedovile* (Turin, 1578) and Moderata Fonte's *Il merito delle donne* (Venice, 1600), are, in superficial ways, an odd couple. Trotto's is a male-authored "quasi-documentary" dialogue featuring historical figures in a mixed-gender conversation in Turin, which the author claims occurred at the end of the Italian Wars in 1559.[1] It has also often been categorized as straightforward conduct literature alongside the treatises aimed at widows published in the same period.[2] Fonte's female-authored dialogue, on the other hand, presents a fictional *brigata* of elite Venetian women in the last decade of the century and has received substantial scholarly attention in the past few decades as an important and highly literary proto-feminist text.[3] The two works are linked, however, by the conversations' hostesses—both young and eloquent widows who count themselves lucky to have experienced "la vita vedovile per se stessa" (perhaps best translated as "widowed life for its own sake"). In both dialogues, we see the widow—Trotto's Ippolita and Fonte's Leonora—rhapsodize about the inherent value and delight they have experienced firsthand in widowed life. Though neither dialogue's author could boast the lived experience of widowhood, unlike the widowed poets under consideration in the previous chapter, both offer a distinct—and distinctly similar—voice for young, liberated widows. It is a voice that is very different from the mournful one of the *rime vedovili* explored in the last chapter—a joyous one instead, facing outward to the broader world.

In the following pages, I first analyze Trotto's dialogue within the broader conversation over widowhood and remarriage in Italy in the 1560s and 1570s. Trotto's dialogue presents far more radical ideas around widowhood and marriage than has been recognized, which sets it apart from the other male-authored texts on the subject in the same period. It also shows that a new kind of widowed voice emerges in the wake of the widowhood poetry by Colonna and others as well as the broader cultural discourse on widowhood over the course of the sixteenth century. I then turn to Moderata Fonte's dialogue and the similarities between the widowed speakers in each text. The two dialogues show that for young, wealthy widows at the end of the sixteenth century, widowhood could be experienced as a stage in which one could enjoy a life of liberty otherwise unattainable as a woman in the period.

Context: The Counter-Reformation, Widows, and Remarriage

Trotto's dialogue was published at the height of a newly revived debate over widows and remarriage in the Counter-Reformation Italy of the 1570s. The Church's official position was that widows should not remarry, following the long-standing view of patristics from Paul to Jerome and Augustine. This was reinforced by the reaffirmation of marriage as a sacrament at the twenty-fourth session of the Council of Trent in 1563 and an increased emphasis on *amore maritale*, or the love that existed *within* the constraints of marriage—specifically, the first (and ideally only) marriage between a man and a woman.[4] The standard assertion in texts not just by Church fathers but by sixteenth-century clerics and philosophers was that widows were of greatest use to the community when they remained widowed after their first husbands' deaths, modeling themselves on Anna and Judith, "armed" with their powerful prayers and devotions. This was at odds with the view of many families as well as civic authorities, who considered young widows a valuable economic asset to be deployed through strategic and advantageous remarriage.[5]

Trotto's text was published in an environment thickly populated by treatises and conduct literature in part responding to this debate, most authored by men of the Church advocating against remarriage; the 1570s saw a swath of books published on ideals of widowhood.[6] Of particular relevance are the cleric Orazio Fusco's *La vedova del Fusco* (Rome, 1570), the jurist Giulio Cesare Cabei's *Ornamenti della gentil donna vedova* (Venice, 1574), and finally, in 1575, the Veronese cardinal Agostino Valier's *Instruttione della vera et perfetta viduità*, published in Venice as part of his larger *Istituto di ogni stato lodevole delle donne cristiane* and also as a standalone resource for widows in 1577.[7] Trotto's dialogue, first printed in Turin the year after Valier's, borrows elements from all three of its predecessors. His significant shift in genre from conduct literature to dialogue, however, allows for two female voices to weigh in on the subject.

The three texts by Fusco, Cabei, and Valier, while diverse in their argument and reasoning, all come to the same, unsurprising conclusion: with very few exceptions, young widows should never remarry.[8] This consensus is also signaled by the choice of dedicatees. Fusco's text is dedicated to the noblewoman Clelia Salamona Oliva, who was left with a small child at the age of twenty-one when her husband died in the Siege of Mirandola in 1551 and never remarried;[9] Cabei's is dedicated to the influential widow

Ginevra Salviati de' Baglioni, who raised her son on her own after her husband's death; and Valier's is dedicated to the Venetian Adriana Pisani Contarini, who was widowed at thirty-two and devoted the rest of her life to the Church rather than take another husband.[10] All the dedicatees are thus *young* widows, who were of most concern to Church authorities as a group of unattached women to be managed following their husbands' deaths, and we also see among them young mothers who were left with the task of protecting and raising their children.

The three authors approach the subject differently, however, and it is worth a brief consideration of their diverse strategies. Fusco's *La vedova,* the most unusual and radical of the three, argues against the mainstream misogynistic belief that women are by nature dangerous and sinful, asserting that they are, to the contrary, naturally born perfect. It is, according to Fusco, their lifelong exposure to men—first their fathers and then their husbands—that corrupts them and is the root cause of any bad behavior on their part: "Nasce la fanciulla in grembo alla natura maestra de tutte le cose, e nel suo nascimento comincia a ricever torto dal proprio padre, dal quale non è lietamente ricevuta ne vista, come se bambino nascesse, ma dove si fanno allegrezze, feste, e giuochi, con suoni, e canti nella natività del maschio" (A girl develops in the womb as a master of all things naturally, but from her birth begins to receive wrongs from her father, by whom she is not happily received or regarded, whereas when a boy is born, happiness, celebration, and games are conducted, and songs accompany the birth of the male child).[11] Women are further wronged as they grow up, Fusco continues, when their fathers imprison them either in the convent or in marriage to unworthy men. It is only those lucky enough to be widowed who can finally realize their true and "excellent" selves: no longer subject to church, father, or husband, they can transform, becoming "come ucello che nell'aer vola" (like a bird who can fly in the sky).[12]

La vedova's unusual argument at first comes across as rather protofeminist—even, as Helena Sanson observes, sharing some of the later sentiments expressed by Venetian writers like Lucrezia Marinella, Moderata Fonte, and Arcangela Tarabotti.[13] Some have as a result questioned whether the author was actually Orazio Fusco or instead the widowed female publisher of the text, Lucrezia Dorico.[14] In her detailed study of the work, Sanson puts that alluring theory to bed and furthermore points out that the "seemingly female 'voice' encapsulated in the text becomes even more intriguing if the author is indeed a man of the Church, and therefore actually familiar with Latin and . . . other misogynistic patristic sources on women."[15] Her point here is an important one: that these ideas are articulated in a male-authored text suggests a broader diffusion of protofeminist views than we might think, twenty-some years before Fonte and Marinella's texts were printed. Despite the radical nature of his main argument, however, Fusco does not push his theory to a more liberatory conclusion or encourage women to do anything particularly daring or revolutionary during their widowhoods. Once released from the oppressive state of matrimony, his ideal widow, in a familiar turn, should live as Anna of Phanuel did, dedicating her time to God alone. The truly radical kernel of his argument is focused on fathers, who should take better care of their daughters as children and young women; widows are expected, as always, to behave in a chaste, prudent, and exemplary manner—and not remarry.

In *Ornamenti della gentil donna vedova* (1574), the Venetian jurist and poet Giulio Cesare Cabei urges young women, especially mothers, to remain widowed and care for their children alone. As Valier will reiterate in his treatise a few years later, Cabei argues that widows must bury all earthly pleasure alongside their husband. Notably, he underscores the importance of making public and visible this sacrifice: "deve mostrar al mondo d'aver sepolto nel monumento del marito ogni piacere, ogni diletto, ogni pensiero contrario alla honestà" (she must show the world that she has buried all pleasures and thoughts antithetical to virtue in her husband's tomb).[16]

Cabei's stress on this *public* performance of widowhood—a widow must not only *be* virtuous, in his view, but demonstrate it to the outside world—certainly resonates with what we have seen throughout this broader study. In particular, it recalls the way the widowed poets in chapter 5 may well have used their publicly directed displays of grief as a kind of protective shield against pressures to remarry from male relatives and others. Cabei's advice, too, may serve in part to instruct widows (and their sympathizers) how to protect themselves from pressure to remarry.[17] The true danger to a widow, he suggests, comes not from being alone and unprotected but from remarrying and thus putting one's own beloved children at risk. If a young widow with children remarries and has additional children with her second husband, he asks, which children will she love more?[18] He warns that this collision of first and second families can result in "una domestica guerra" (a domestic war) in which the children of the first husband are pitted against those of the second.[19] The widowed speaker Ippolita will echo these concerns and this phrasing in Trotto's *Dialoghi*; as she argues against remarriage, the childless Scaravelli says that a widow who brings children into a second marriage risks provoking such a "domestica guerra," as I discuss below.

The final treatise of the 1570s to which I draw our attention is Agostino Valier's *Della vera et perfetta viduità*, the second section of his influential *Instituzione d'ogni stato lodevole delle donne cristiane* (1577).[20] Valier's focus is on the spiritual conduct of widows and their utility as advocates on behalf of their city. He, too, is most interested in younger widows with many years of life ahead of them during which, if they are "saved" from remarriage, they can be counted on to act as emissaries for the Church. Valier's motivations are perhaps the most transparent of the three treatise-writers. He is eager to harness widows as a kind of cavalry, a group who offer the Counter-Reformation Church a resource of unique potential—a captive, devout workforce of praying women who, unlike nuns, lived *within* the community rather than apart from it. Like Cabei, Valier views widows as having to a degree died themselves alongside their husbands, "having buried in their husbands' tomb all the pleasures of this wretched world, and exchanged human pleasures for the pleasures of angels, prayers and tears."[21]

His target group, young widows of the noble class, were women with time on their hands, funds to spare, and no men in need of tending: ideal candidates to serve the Church not only as ambassadors to the beyond but as emissaries to other societal groups with neither the time nor the inclination to engage as regularly in devotional practice.

While Valier prescribes that widows practice their own devotions in private, away from the temptations and distractions of the "volgo" or crowd, he urges them to consider themselves crucial agents battling on behalf of their wider community, like Judith and Anna of Phanuel. Widows should be "maestre," or "teachers," who "teach with their lives, and instruct both households and neighborhoods, and even the city itself" how to conduct oneself as a servant of God.[22] Returning to the exemplary figure of the "vedova gloriosa" Judith, Valier reminds widows that their actions can have major consequences for their city, just as hers did. His choice of Judith is emblematic of how widows were viewed by many in the Counter-Reformation Church as a group that could be activated and called upon to act on the Church's behalf. Indeed, while Valier urges widows to pray in a solitary manner, he grants them a far more community-driven role than Cabei or Fusco does. By drawing attention to widows' great responsibility of spiritual teaching and prayer, Valier's text works to institutionalize the private act of widowly devotion as a crucial component of a spiritually healthy society.

In his *Dialoghi*, Bernardo Trotto incorporates elements from Fusco, Cabei, and Valier but comes to a decidedly different conclusion than theirs: remarriage is the right, even the noble, choice for young widows. His perspective is based in part, of course, on his role as a civic servant rather than a cleric, at a court that saw marriage as a central component of its power-building strategy. In presenting his argument, however, he articulates radical ideas around widowhood, remarriage, and the power dynamics between the sexes. This is especially interesting given the characters who serve as the agents of their delivery. The dialogue form allows Trotto to include not one but two female voices, including Ippolita, an eloquent and vivacious young woman who argues extensively for the inherent value in widowed life, even as she herself has conceded to marry a second time.

Trotto's *Dialoghi del matrimonio e vita vedovile*

When Trotto first published his dialogue in 1578, he claimed to have written it nearly twenty years earlier in the days following the signing of the Treaty of Cateau-Cambrésis of 1559, which, as we saw in chapter 4, ended a sixty-five-year struggle between France and Spain for control of the Italian peninsula. One of the many concessions made in the treaty by the French king, Henry II, was the restoration of Piedmont to Emanuele Filiberto, Duke of Savoy, the nephew of Charles V and a longtime ally of Spain. Henry made sure to keep a foothold in Savoy, however, by way of a series of strategic political marriages: in the most high-profile, his sister Marguerite de France was married to Duke Emanuele himself and Henry's daughter Elisabeth to King Philip II of Spain. During a joust to celebrate the signing of the treaty, Henry II received a fatal poke in the eye with a sword and died soon thereafter, leaving Catherine de' Medici a widow and a dominating power over the French court.

Trotto's *Dialoghi del matrimonio e vita vedovile* (henceforth *Dialoghi*, 1578, reprinted in 1583 with additional material) considers another marital alliance brokered between France and the Duchy of Savoy in 1559, that of a less high-profile but nevertheless remarkable Italian widow who made her way to France, offering us a rare glimpse into the relationship between the two courts and the powerful roles widows at all levels of courtly influence could play in them. The widow in question is Ippolita Scaravelli (ca. 1530–after 1601), a historical figure who was widowed as a young and eligible woman in Turin and was remarried to the Frenchman Jean de Chastellier, Duke de Milieu, an advisor to the French king stationed in Savoy. At the opening of the *Dialoghi*, the young and newly remarried Ippolita, seated in the cool of her garden on a hot summer day, declares that despite her grief following her first husband's death, she found widowhood itself to be an unexpectedly joyful stage of life.[23] "Purtroppo," she recounts, "era io contenta dello stato mio, e di quella bellissima vita scarca d'ogni travaglio; e più godea l'animo mio tal hor col cibo di varie opere, che io desiderosa, e solitaria leggeva" (Alas, I was happy with my state, and with that most beautiful life, free of all worry. And what's more, my soul enjoyed the sustenance of the many works which I desired to read alone; *Dialoghi*, 6).[24] Though Ippolita admits that this pleasurable life of freedom and solitary contemplation came at the cost of her first husband, she is still determined to demonstrate the wonders of "la vita vedovile per se stessa" to her guests. She defends widowed life as one that should be recognized as an important formative experience and life stage for a young woman, one she is reluctant to abandon.

Her primary interlocutor, the older, married Barbara d'Annebault, objects to Ippolita's rosy view of widowed life from the beginning of the dialogue, asking pointedly, "A che fine il Creator nostro ci ha dato questa morbidezza delle carni, la tenerezza del cuore, la facilità della mente, e la soavità dell'animo?" (For what purpose did our Creator give us this softness of flesh, this tenderness of heart, this facility of mind, and sweetness of spirit?; *Dialoghi*, 8). God has bestowed these lush qualities on women, she insists, to be enjoyed in marriage, not to be guarded jealously through living alone (or, though left unsaid, to be enjoyed by lusty suitors with a predilection for merry widows). "La vita vedovile," in Barbara's view, is a life "più misera, più dura, più aspera" than that of a married woman—more wretched, tough, and sterile (8). Their male interlocutor, the studious Astemio, who acts as an unofficial moderator throughout the dialogue, initially seems more inclined to side with Ippolita. She thanks him warmly during her speech for being one of her few acquaintances to refrain from criticizing her for enjoying her widowhood, and he observes early on that widows are generally viewed as a valuable part of society (11). By the time their lively conversation has come to a close, however, Ippolita has surrendered to her new reality as a wife: after asking Astemio to instruct her on the virtues of married life, the young woman falls silent, and we do not hear her voice again. The *Dialoghi*'s second day is populated exclusively with male voices, including Astemio's; the door to the radical potential of widowed life has been firmly closed.

We can only guess as to whether Ippolita's mind was actually changed on the subject, but her remarriage to Jean de Chastellier, Duc de Milieu (1529–1580) was a clear boon for her community in Turin. Trotto describes de Chastellier at the beginning of the dialogue in laudatory terms that indicate his political importance in Piedmont: "per sua prudenza, e valore inalzato ad altissimi gradi, e molto stimato fra quelli signori francesi, che in Piemonte erano al servitio del grande Re Henrico secondo" (due to his prudence, and valor, [he] was raised to the highest offices, and was greatly esteemed among those French Lords who were in Piedmont in the service of the great King Henry II; *Dialoghi*, 10). The dialogue itself is dedicated to Ippolita, now the Dame de Milieu, and the tone suggests a long and close relationship between writer and dedicatee: "All'ultimo Signora Hippolita," Trotto writes, "avete pur ritrovato soave, e dolce questo giogo maritale, che già si noioso, e grave lo stimavate; e ben sempre diss'io, che non saresti lungamente in pensiero di rimaner vedova" (In the end, Signora Hippolita, you have rediscovered that the marital yoke, which you once found so tedious and unpleasant, is soft and sweet; and I certainly always said that you would not remain a widow for long; 1). Like the *Cortegiano* before it, Trotto's dialogue is presented as a look back on an earlier time, taking place in the festive days around the couple's marriage in 1559.[25] By the time the dialogue was first published in 1578, the pair had been married for twenty years and were settled in France. In 1580, the duke died and Ippolita became a widow for the second time and would remain one for the rest of her life; though she was a young childless woman when her first husband, the Turin senator Bartolomeo Pettiti, died of unknown causes (most likely between 1555 and 1557), she was the mother of five children when de Chastellier was killed during the Wars of Religion at the Siège de La Mure in November 1580. She was thus not just an older widow, with the potential to become a Pauline *vere vidua*, but also the widow of an illustrious military hero, like Colonna or Gambara before her.

Trotto's *Dialoghi* offers rare insight into court life in Turin under Duke Emanuele Filiberto (1528–1580), in addition to boasting perhaps the most interesting philosophical debate on widowhood of the late sixteenth century.[26] In the second edition of 1583, numerous sonnets have been added at both the beginning and the end of the dialogue praising Trotto for his work—including one by Stefano Guazzo, author of the influential dialogue *La civil conversazione*—reflecting *Dialoghi*'s success after it was first published in 1578. The text was written during a twenty-year span of intense creative production at Emanuele Filiberto's court following the Treaty of Cateau-Cambrésis in 1559.[27] Granted rulership of the Duchy of Savoy, Filiberto—nephew of Carlo V, ally to Philip II of Spain, and newly married to Henry II's sister Marguerite—was well aware of the important political role his court could play in the continuing power struggle between France and Spain.[28] Keen to establish his court as a cultural center on par with Urbino and Ferrara, he commissioned a number of literary works that were published in the two decades after his triumphant return to Turin.[29] Torquato Tasso was among the many illustrious cultural figures to pass through the court, welcomed by Filiberto in 1578.[30]

The outpouring of Italian-language works also helped to establish Italian as the official language for Turin and Piedmont. Turin become the capital of the Duchy in 1563 (coincidentally, the same year marriage was reaffirmed as a sacrament in Trent), at which point legal texts and other documents began to be translated from French to Italian. This linguistic conversion played a role in the broader political project to reestablish the Savoy court's legitimacy in the wake of the French occupation, in which the experimentation and dialectical nature of Trotto's *Dialoghi* would have been very welcome—as well as the positive representation of a Piedmontese woman who married an advisor to the French king.

Trotto, a lawyer by training, was one of Filiberto's favored writers and thinkers. He was made a senator in 1551, held numerous important appointments in Piedmontese politics over the course of his career, and was named a lecturer in law ("primo lettore ordinario") at the university in 1561. While his Latin dialogue of 1572 and the two versions of *Dialoghi* from 1578 and 1583 are his only known single-authored published works, he also coauthored various legal treatises. The *Dialoghi* are clearly the crown jewel of his long career, despite his performed humility about their literary value. In the dialogue's *proemio,* he refers to them somewhat disparagingly, as "queste giovenili raccolte" (this youthful collection of observations; iii), situating them as immature writings not worthy of his later prestigious legal career. The description of the dialogue as an immature and inconsequential vernacular work is itself hard to take seriously, as is his claim that he wrote it in 1559 and only brushed it off in 1578 for publication. These humble protestations are further undermined by his reminder that marriage has a solemn role in the governance of any Republic: "le regole matrimoniali sono anco utilissime leggi, e necessario quanto altre, al governo della Repubblica" (marital rules are also most useful laws, and as necessary as any others, to the governance of the Republic; ix). Publishing the dialogue in 1578, with Ippolita a firmly established French noblewoman who had helped maintain the alliance between the French and Savoy courts for nearly twenty years, bolsters his message of marriage as a critical component of successful governance. From the first lines of the *proemio,* Trotto ties Ippolita's 1559 remarriage to the broader peace that descended on Piedmont and Savoy that year, characterized by good weather, celebrations, and the more high-profile marriages that were brokered by the treaty, those of Filiberto and Marguerite, and Philip II of Spain and Elisabeth, Henry II and Catherine de' Medici's daughter. Trotto moves swiftly from these celebrated royal weddings to Ippolita's; her remarriage, he asserts, has ramifications not only for her family's fortunes but for those of the entire duchy (vii).

The following discussion of the dialogue goes into some detail; this is important in understanding the resonances between *Dialoghi* and the later, far more famous dialogue by Fonte as well as the broader cultural conversation on widowhood in the last decades of the sixteenth century. The *Dialoghi* can be classified as what Virginia Cox has termed "quasi-documentary" dialogue: like the *Cortegiano,* one in which the author purports to recall a conversation that took place between historical figures.[31] Book I of Trotto's work distinguishes itself further within this micro-genre by representing the voices of two historical *women* opining on the value of different marital states *for* women, a major departure from the other published texts on widowhood in the period.[32] Trotto begins the first book of the dialogue by bringing us into the *locus amoenus* of the garden at Ippolita's private residence, where she has lived during her first marriage and her widowhood and which she will soon leave for the world of the French court. The idyllic and isolated space offers a refuge not just from the midday heat but also from the burning political climate one imagines just outside her home's walls.[33] Her primary interlocutor and first visitor is a woman who also has vested interests in the political stability of the newly independent Piedmont: Barbara d'Annebault, whose father Claude d'Annebault (1492–1552) was an important French military officer and governor of Piedmont when it was under French rule and whose husband, Gerolamo Porporato (1517–1581), was president of Turin's parliament.[34] We encounter her in Trotto's dialogue as she insists on the superiority of remarriage to widowhood, a happily married woman who believes that widowhood is the worst thing that could ever befall a woman and should be rectified as quickly as possible.[35] Just as she is preparing to explain to Ippolita why the married life is better than widowhood and Ippolita is preparing to argue the opposite, they are joined by a second visitor, the "pensoso" (pensive) Astemio, most likely a stand-in for the author, and they welcome him to take part in their conversation.[36]

Barbara is the first to argue her case fully and begins by declaring from the outset that the loss of a husband is the worst thing that could ever befall a wife.[37] Women are nothing without men, she says, and men nothing without women: "siano ogn'uno per se stesso l'huomo, e la donna cosa debole, e imperfetta?" (are not both men and women on their own weak and imperfect things?; *Dialoghi*, 5). It is marriage, she argues, that allows both men and women to reach their full potential. Not only humans, she continues, but all creatures benefit from marriage, for it is through coupledom that one procreates and creates a "nest" of one's own (6). Barbara contrasts birds and all manner of other, coupled animals tending peacefully to their nests with the fate of the lonely widow, who must protect herself, like a female sheep without her ram—or her shepherd—from the clutches of "lupi rapaci" (rapacious wolves; 8) who wish to do her harm. "Like the hare," widows must sleep with one eye open, always on alert against predators (8). The threat of violence, sexual and otherwise, from these "rapacious wolves" cuts through the protected locus amoenus of Ippolita's garden, returning the speakers and readers to the realities of post-treaty Turin for a moment. In Barbara's view, Ippolita needs a male protector to shield her from the violence to which widows are especially vulnerable; that her subsequent remarriage is to a political and martially powerful foreigner underscores that this much-feared violence can be as political as it is sexual. Just as Ippolita needs a male protector herself, so might the city of Turin need the benevolent French protection of men like de Chastellier, even after Piedmont's independence.[38]

Barbara suggests that remarriage is crucial not only for widows themselves but for the larger civic good. The exempla she chooses to cite are different from the standard pantheon we have seen used by Boccaccio and his imitators to praise widows—Dido, Judith, Artemisia—and her argument is very different from theirs as well. One noteworthy example she employs is Gorgo, the queen of Sparta; lifting from Plutarch with some liberal variations, Barbara recounts the words of Gorgo's husband Leonidas before he left for the Battle of Thermopylae: "io ti raccommando che ti rimariti con qualche huomo da bene, e che facci figliuoli . . . voglio che conosci, che anco dopo morte desidero il tuo bene; e voglio darti questo utilissimo consiglio, che non resti smarrita, sterile, e calamitosa vedovella" (I insist that you remarry to some good man, and that you have children . . . I want you to know that even after my death, I want the best for you; and I want to give you this precious advice, that you must not remain a hapless, sterile, and calamitous little widow; *Dialoghi*, 12). Leonidas's advice is briefer in Plutarch and far less detailed; simply, "Marry a good man, and bear good children."[39] Barbara's embellishment seems to be pointedly aimed at Ippolita. Like Gorgo, she is too young to remain a widow forever, and she has not yet fulfilled her civic duty as a wife, which is to bear children and perpetuate her family's bloodline: "Non è egli di tutte le creature commune, e naturale il desiderio di perpetuarsi nei secoli a venire?" (Is it not common and natural for all creatures to want to perpetuate themselves for the centuries to come?; 6). Barbara wants her, quite literally, out of her widow's weeds and in bed with a new husband, reproducing, as soon as possible. Her urgency reaches an almost absurd level as she finishes her monologue: "Squarcia quei panni oscuri, e corri a novo letto" (Tear off those dark clothes, and run to your new [marriage] bed; 12).[40]

Ippolita has, of course, done what Barbara wishes. In the days leading up to the dialogue's action, she became a wife once more, and during her second marriage to de Chastellier she would bear at least five children. And yet in her response to her friend, she presents a subtle and complex defense of widowed life, in which she argues for its value passionately before conceding that she herself must give it up. Her initial argument, similar to Fusco's, is that women do best on their own and that widowhood is therefore the "most blessed" life (*Dialoghi*, 4). She then shifts in tone, falling more in line with Cabei, Valier, and other Counter-Reformation thinkers who insist women must remain faithful to their first husbands, before discussing the ideal of widowhood as one in which one can engage in both spiritual and intellectual development of the highest kind. At the end of Ippolita's speech, she acknowledges to her friends that she knows she is, alas, too young to stay widowed and that she must return, at least temporarily, to the mundane world of marriage.

Trotto notes from the beginning of the dialogue that Ippolita was renowned for her eloquence: "di facondia non cede a donna alcuna, ne a molti uomini dell'età nostra" (in elegance of expression she was the lesser of no woman, nor of many men of our day; *Dialoghi*, ii). Her defense of women and widowhood, furthermore, is endowed with a double authority due to her experience as a widow and her ultimate choice to remarry; indeed, that Ippolita has acted according to her family's wishes and married again sets her up as all the more exemplary. She thus serves as an effective spokesperson for the worth of women within the dialogue, as she argues eloquently against broader misogynist narratives of women as weak and incapable of fending for themselves. She takes issue with Barbara's assertion that women are like lost sheep without their shepherd and defends them as far stronger than her friend: "Voi dite . . . che noi siamo morbide, e molli, e di corpo debole, e come pecorelle humane abbiamo bisogno di pastori, che ci guardino dai lupi, ma questo non può già dirsi di tutte le donne, essendovene molte di robustissime, e gagliarde membra" (You say . . . that we are soft, and flaccid, and have weak bodies, and like little human sheep we are in need of shepherds who will protect us from wolves, but this cannot be said of all women, as there are many who are made of stronger stuff than that; *Dialoghi*, 19). "La vita vedovile," she argues, must be understood not just as a tragedy that befalls a woman after her husband's death but instead as a state all its own: "vorremo solamente considerare la vita vedovile per se stessa, ci parrà in vero cosa beatissima" (if we are only able to consider the widowed life on its own terms, we will see that it is in truth a most blessed thing; 4).[41]

Considered apart from its generally tragic connotations—namely, the death of a husband—in Ippolita's eyes widowhood emerges as an otherwise-impossible state of autonomy in the life of a woman. It is men who benefit from marriage, Ippolita asserts, not women; as proof of this, she reminds her interlocutors of the apocryphal story of Calpurnia warning Julius Caesar of his impending assassination; if he had only believed her and stayed home, she says, he would have lived (*Dialoghi*, 30–31). Women, on the other hand, are subject to "infinite suffering" caused by the men they must put up with in marriage. This is an opinion echoed vigorously by Leonora in Fonte's *Il merito delle donne*: " a woman, when she is segregated from male contact, has something divine about her and can achieve miracles. . . . That certainly isn't the case with men, because it is only when a man has taken a wife that he reaches the peak of happiness, honor, and greatness."[42]

Though Ippolita speaks rhapsodically about the prelapsarian relationship between Adam and Eve, she argues against the value of the institution of marriage as she finds it, which has corrupted the original ideals embodied in the Bible. Adam and Eve, she says, should not be viewed as "married" in the same sense as citizens of her own contemporary world: "e veramente quella prima compagnia di Adamo e Eva, non era come il nostro matrimonio, benche voi le vogliate dar si duro nome; ma era una sola contentezza d'ambidui" (and truly, that first coupling of Adam and Eve, it was not like *our* marriage, even if you give it such a harsh name; it was rather the joyful, private union of two people; *Dialoghi*, 27). She thus makes a sophisticated distinction between the emotional connection between two people ("una sola contentezza d'ambidui") and those more cynical dimensions of contemporary marriage. Unlike that idyllic first coupling, marriage is no longer a safe space for women but rather a "prison" in which men are the jailers and women the captives. She returns to Barbara's idyllic descriptions of woodlands creatures, but in her version the birds and beasts are not happily coupled but rather trapped: "Qual ucello mai, o qual selvaggia fiera fu si crudele contra se stessa, che volesse ritornar alla rete, e al laccio, onde una volta fosse stata sciolta?" (What bird or proud beast would ever be so cruel to herself that she would willingly return to the net, and the trap, when she has already been freed once?; 45).

We see her tone progressively shift through the course of the dialogue to mimic the more conventional concerns articulated by Cabei and Valier, as she moves from strident criticism of the state of contemporary marriage, to familiar praise of legendary widows who stay loyal to the memory of their dead husbands. She reminds Barbara that there have been many successful female rulers who were fueled in part by their devotion to their husband's memory. She cites the example of Isis, who, after Osiris's death, was able to conceive a child with her husband's dead body, as well as Artemisia, Dido, and Judith. Judith, she notes, could become the liberator of her people only because she was not burdened with the duties of a second marriage (*Dialoghi*, 47). Contrary to widows who are given the opportunity to live this kind of glorious life, she continues, the unfortunate women who must remarry encounter a host of problems. Men who marry widows are never in love with them, but only after their money. Why else, she asks, would they choose an "already tainted" widow (50) over a virgin—an unexpectedly misogynist line in an otherwise quite protofeminist speech, if not necessarily a protofeminist dialogue. Indeed, she warns, before you know it, you'll be dead and your dowry will be in their hand.[43]

Remarriage here is presented not only as distasteful and disloyal but just as downright dangerous as Barbara suggests widowhood is—a widow's second husband is characterized not as the shepherd but as the true rapacious wolf from whom she needs protection. As Ippolita lists the numerous pitfalls associated with remarriage for widows, she echoes Cabei's warning of the "domestica guerra" and "battaglia segreta" that can ensue from a widow with children remarrying, quoting his 1574 treatise nearly verbatim (45). To the citizens of a city recovering from a long period of occupation and war, the idea of war within the domestic sphere would seem a great threat to the stability of the state itself.

Despite her litany of warnings against untrustworthy men, Ippolita says she does not want Barbara to think that she is "an enemy to all men" (*Dialoghi*, 46). In the only brief mention of the man who has made her a widow, she insists that she did love her "dolce primo marito," and she will learn to love her second husband as well, albeit with "gran fatica": "quale che si fosse il mio primo signore, e consorte, sempre l'ho con tanto affetto amato, che con gran fatica posso ancor col nove amore del secondo" (Just as I always loved my first lord and consort with great feeling, with great effort I will be able to love the second; 46). She puts a twist on Cabei and Valier's dreary insistence that widows should consider themselves "buried" along with their husbands as well as Barbara's earlier assertion that it is not yet time for Ippolita to be "buried in black garments" (12). It is, rather, *re*married women who are buried alive, or "sepolta nella carne"—forced to serve many different lords, on Heaven and on earth, and try to nourish their souls while they "prostituir le membra" (prostitute their bodies; 51–52) to a new husband. For Ippolita, to be a widow is to exist in an exalted and fulfilling spiritual and intellectual world; it is remarriage that serves as a widow's burial. Her ideal widow is Jerome's beloved Paula, who was able to devote her time to contemplation and intellectual discussion with men, much as Ippolita was able to in her relationship with Astemio (52).

Barbara, struck by Ippolita's rhetorical bravado, comments that she must have been granted divine help, for no young person could understand the complexities of the widowed state so well. Ippolita thanks her and says that she feels fortunate to have experienced the exalted state of widowhood, if only for a little while. She is well equipped for remarriage, armed with the knowledge she has gained from her first marriage and her widowhood. It is, however, a shame that so many young women are thrown into marriages with no experience at all—positing widowhood itself as a kind of training ground for a successful second marriage.

Trotto's dialogue offers us a version of Ippolita who presents a radical new idea of widowhood as a privileged space of liberty and intellectual riches, while also ventriloquizing many widespread Counter-Reformation beliefs about the evils of remarriage. While Trotto may well have borrowed from Fusco's treatise proclaiming widowhood the ideal state for women, to place such an argument in the mouth of a widow herself has no precedent. That the historical Ippolita was a woman in a high-profile marriage lends the character's argument a specific legitimacy, even if she ultimately surrenders and remarries.

Ippolita's Second Widowhood

In addition to serving as widowed muse to Trotto, Ippolita inspired poets at the French court of Catherine de' Medici after she was widowed a second time when Jean de Chastellier died heroically in 1580 at the Siège de la Mure during the Wars of Religion. Flaminio de Birague honored her "knowledge and wisdom" and Jacques de Romieu praised her in his *Mélanges* of 1584.[44] The most significant French work dedicated to Ippolita was by de Romieu's sister, Marie de Romieu (ca. 1556–1598), who wrote at least eight poems in her honor after Chastellier's death. De Romieu's *Les premières oeuvres poétiques* was published in 1581 and included the verse *Discours que l'excellence de la femme surpasse celle de l'homme* (Discourse on how the excellence of women surpasses that of men), ostensibly written in response to a misogynist tract by her brother.[45] Ippolita, who offered countless examples of widowed women to emulate in Trotto's dialogue, is here offered as an example herself. De Romieu depicts her as a romantic, exotic character; she imagines the Italian widow, of a "peuple estrange," as a woodland nymph in the forests of the Chastellier estate in one poem and in another as Juno, the goddess of marriage, with the three graces (her three daughters, Françoise, Marie, and Renée). De Romieu urges nymph-Ippolita to leave her worldly worries behind her at the court after her husband's death and return to where she belongs, among "la compagnie divine" (the divine company) of satyrs, fauns, and other creatures of the pastoral imaginary.[46] In a shift from her representation in Trotto's dialogue as a young woman focused on family and city, these poems cast Ippolita as a leader, a heroic widow who serves as exemplum for other women after her husband's death. The poems suggest that Ippolita has perhaps reached the state of ideal widowhood she spoke of so wistfully and eloquently in Trotto's dialogue: now that she has achieved her status as a widow with children, whose husband died honorably, she can devote herself to a life of the mind, and cast aside all worldly concerns.

Ippolita did not, as far as we know, take de Romieu's advice and trade Paris for the glories of pastoral life. During her second widowhood, she became even more ensconced in the world of the French court, as one of Catherine de' Medici's ladies-in-waiting. In addition to her three daughters, she had at least two sons, Guy and Gabriel Chastellier; a document listed in the Archives Nationales de Paris identifies Ippolita, Guy, and Gabriel as present at La Queue-en-Brie, just southwest of Paris, on September 26, 1584, as Guy sends his brother home to Piedmont to inspect their land holdings there.[47] The document suggests that Ippolita took an active interest in her sons' political activities in her native Piedmont and perhaps served as advisor to them.[48]

It also bears considering whether de Romieu's insistence that Ippolita leave the court after her husband's death and take up a less political, calmer country life may have been connected to the Italian widow then dominating the French court, the queen Catherine de' Medici herself. Despite holding remarkable power, the "wicked Italian queen" was also widely reviled in France in the 1570s and 1580s, especially after the Saint Bartholomew's Day Massacre.[49] With a reputation as politically ruthless, an Italian importer of Machiavellian scheming into the French court, Catherine was frequently depicted in widow's habit in negative contemporary visual representations. De Romieu ends her *Discours* with praise of Catherine; the poet's verses to Ippolita are third from the end, separated from those to Catherine only by those for Marguerite de Valois.

Ippolita became a widow for the second time in the markedly different political and social environment of France, which was carrying on its own legal debate on remarriage and widows' rights at the time. In 1560, a year after Ippolita was remarried and Catherine de' Medici was widowed, Catherine's eldest son, the newly crowned King Francis II, issued an edict placing limits on what "a widow with children could give a second husband in marriage."[50] Much like in Italy, French lawmakers were concerned that widows with children would turn their dowries over to their second husbands, leaving children from first marriages penniless and vulnerable. There was also anxiety, and occasional astonishment, over just how well some women took to widowhood. The court writer and gossip Brantôme observed that the widows of Catherine's court did not seem particularly interested in remarriage, instead finding their greatest power in their widowhood, once they had been "freed" from the bonds of matrimony.[51] Brantôme paints a picture of the widows at the French court that suggests the young Turinese widow we meet in Trotto's dialogue did end up, twenty-some years later and a country away, in an environment where widows dared to enjoy their independence.

Ippolita's Afterlife: Leonora in Moderata Fonte's *Il merito delle donne*

Although Scaravelli only found a world in which women were able to enjoy a liberated widowhood after her move to France, the portrayal of Ippolita in Trotto's dialogue may well have inspired a character in a subsequent Italian dialogue that has received more extensive critical attention. In Moderata Fonte's *Il merito delle donne* (written in 1592 and published posthumously in 1600), the young, widowed hostess Leonora is vivacious, eloquent, and downright thrilled to be free of the bonds of matrimony.[52] She speaks openly about the rich, free, and pleasurable intellectual life that widowhood can offer; unlike Ippolita, she has no new husband, nor does she want one.

The political and geographical context of Fonte's dialogue—Venice in the last decade of the sixteenth century—is significantly different from that of Trotto's, set in Turin just after the end of the Italian Wars. As Cox has argued, Fonte's dialogue was written in a moment when "vast numbers of upper-class woman in Italy were finding themselves deprived of their traditional career of marriage . . . this was a development whose importance can scarcely be exaggerated in a society that offered no real alternative to women of this class . . . a whole class of women—and precisely those most likely to be readers and writers—were finding their status and identity under threat." Just as Trotto's dialogue represents a Turin in transition from an occupied city to the new seat of an independent court, Fonte's "reflects the social realities of an economy in transition," with women's role in society at the center of that transition.[53] It is also a dialogue with no identifiable historical characters, written by a female author rather than a male one.

The similarities between the depictions of the widows who star in Trotto and Fonte's very different dialogues, however, are striking. *Il merito delle donne* presents a group of women animatedly discussing and debating the various life stages of a woman and the "worth of women" over two days, along with related matters scientific, historical, and cultural. Instead of two women and a male interlocutor, Fonte offers us seven women who create a space without men in which they are free to talk openly, and among them represent all the imaginable life stages of an upper-class woman: "alcune nobili e valorose donne di età e stato diferenti, ma di sangue e costumi conformi, gentili, virtuose e di elevato ingegno, le quali, percioché molto si confacevano insieme, avendo tra loro contratto una cara e discreta amicizia" (A group of noble and spirited women, all from the best-known and most respected families of the city, who, despite their great differences in age and marital status, were so united by breeding and taste that a tender bond of friendship had formed between them).[54] In addition to Leonora, the young widowed hostess, we are introduced to the older widow Adriana, who is elected queen and directs their conversation; the newlywed Helena; Cornelia, a married women; Corinna, a *dimesse* whose antagonism to marriage rivals that of Leonora; the not-yet-married Virginia; and an older married woman, Lucrezia. Adriana divides the women into two opposing groups to argue the pros and cons of marriage, with Leonora, Corinna, and Cornelia arguing against, and the others arguing in favor. While Fonte devotes much more time in the dialogue to Leonora than to Adriana, it is worth noting that the elected ruler of the newly formed community is also a widow, a kind of dowager regent—a category of ruler the Venetian Republic never had.

The young Leonora is one of the more compelling and charismatic speakers: "era una discretissima giovene e (benché vedova, ricca e bella fosse) non avea più animo di maritarsi" (a sensible young woman, who, though young, rich, and a widow, no longer had any inclination to marry).[55] Like Ippolita in Trotto's piece, she is the hostess for the days' discussion, her home itself a symbol of her full liberation from patriarchal society and her entry into an alternate matrilineal one. In the opening pages of the dialogue, she welcomes her friends into her magnificent garden at the palazzo she has recently inherited from an aunt who lived in Padua, who was herself by choice unmarried and who has died recently: "Ella, essendo fanciulla, non volse mai maritarsi e così vivendo con buona facoltà che l'avolo mio le lasciò, fece ridur . . . il giardino a questa bellezza che voi vedete e insieme vi fè fabricar questa bella fontana con queste figure tutto a suo proposito e secondo la sua opinione che aveva contra il sesso virile" (This aunt, from the time she was a girl, was resolved never to marry and so, on the good income she inherited from my grandfather . . . she transformed this garden into the beautiful state in which you see it now; and at the same time she had this fountain built, with these figures, as a statement of the way in which she intended to live her life and of the views she held against the male sex).[56] The figures she refers to in her aunt's elaborate fountain are allegorical representations of Chastity, Solitude, Liberty, Naïveté, Falsehood, and Cruelty. Each figure has a device of symbolic significance: Solitude's is the phoenix, "a dinotar che ella si compiacque di viver sola; e da per sé visse, morì e rinacque sola con la fama delle sue buone opere" (to show that my aunt enjoyed living alone and that she lived on her own terms and, after death, was reborn in the fame she gained from her good works). Liberty's is "il quale libero e solo illustrando se stesso comparte la sua luce a tutto l'universo" (the sun, which stands free and alone, giving light to itself and sharing its light with the whole universe).[57]

The two devices, while certainly popular in the Renaissance overall, will also be familiar to readers of Colonna's verse; as we have seen, Colonna compares herself to the phoenix in "Mentre la nave mia," as entirely unique and different from the "schiera" of examples of wives and widows she considered emulating. Colonna also described her husband D'Avalos as her "sun" or "Sole" throughout her widowed verse, an appellation that became so iconic we even see her "Sole" referenced in rime vedovili in imitation of hers, such as in the incipit of Matraini's "Quanto l'alta Colonna il suo gran Sole," or in the body of Turina's madrigal "Porti, Vittoria, il vanto" ("con rime alte e famose / adornandone il ciel del tuo bel Sole" [with sublime, famous verses, adorning heaven with your fair Sun]).[58] That Leonora's aunt chose to make the Sun the device representative of her own "Liberty" suggests a kind of protofeminist reappropriation of the male-gendered Sun, which had also stood in for the most famous husband in sixteenth-century lyric poetry.[59]

Beyond the fountain itself, the garden Leonora has inherited from her aunt, which Adriana declares a "paradiso," is truly edenic: lush, ripe, and filled with plants and fruit, in stark contrast with the "sterility" of widowed life Barbara described in Trotto's dialogue.[60] Leonora is delighted by the material glory of her new home, but even more so by the liberty she has found in her widowhood. Unlike Ippolita, she does not seem at all resigned to the possibility of remarriage: "Che io mi viva in riposo e che io senta una somma felicità nel ritrovarmi senza, considerando quanto sia bella cosa la libertà" (I derive the greatest happiness from living in peace, without a man. For we all know what a marvelous thing freedom is).[61]

Adriana plays a role similar to that played by Barbara in Trotto's dialogue. She is an advocate for marriage for all the young ladies of the piece, including Leonora, and comments that it is a shame that Leonora has not yet remarried: "è peccato, che voi non vi rimaritate, essendo così giovene e così bella" (it's a pity that you don't think of remarrying . . . young and lovely as you are).[62] Leonora's response is spirited and extreme: she would rather drown than remarry and go back to a life of "servitù e pene" (servitude and suffering). Why, she asks Adriana, would she return to such a life when she has just "uscita" (escaped)?[63] Her words recall Ippolita's description of marriage as a "prison," her rhetorical question an echo of Ippolita's, when she asks her interlocutors what bird or wild beast would possibly ever return to a hunter's net voluntarily. But Leonora does not surrender, as Ippolita does, to the secular expectation of remarriage for young widows, nor is she interested in living her life as a vere vidua might and as her fellow citizen Valier had urged his readers. Instead, we see her put up an extraordinary fight throughout the dialogue, engaging in more than one hypothetical battle. Asked by Lucrezia what emblem she would carry into battle, Leonora responds "'Porterei sopra l'elmo la Fenice'" ("I'd wear an image of the phoenix on my helmet").[64] We have already seen the device of the phoenix in her aunt's fountain; Elena remarks that she would also be imitating Ariosto's great woman warrior Marfisa in *Orlando furioso,* who sported the image of a phoenix and was famously determined to live "senza consorte."

Marfisa is "an appropriate point of reference for Leonora," Cox observes, "as one of the very few examples in literature of the period of a female character consistently resistant to marriage for other than religious reasons."[65] When we think about Leonora not only as a woman resistant to marriage but specifically as a resistant *widow,* the comparison becomes even more interesting. She is averse to remarriage not because of grief for her husband nor due to a desire for a chaste life. Nor, in fact, is she much interested in civic engagement in the broader sense, outside the small utopian community she and her friends have formed in her aunt's beautiful house. She wants to remain widowed, and thus unattached, simply because it is how she is happiest.

What might it mean that Leonora—a widow who views marriage with disdain and is against her own remarriage at all costs—is the creation of an author who was, by the accounts we have, a happily married woman? It may suggest something about the elasticity of widowhood as both an identity category and a female ideal in literature by the end of the sixteenth century. As we have seen, the disconsolate widow had long been a figure that male poets ventriloquized with impunity, a useful way to capture a community's collective mourning after loss. At the same time, while the poets of rime vedovili discussed in chapter 5 demonstrate how widowed writers could cultivate an authorial identity predicated on their membership in a club with very specific rules, we also see widowed writers who quite purposefully did *not* dwell on their widowhoods in print. The most prominent example of this is Veronica Gambara, who, after a brief foray into poems lamenting the loss of her husband, articulated her desire to move on to different topics; while the famed noblewoman Isabella d'Este was a widow for the last twenty years of her life, this is not what she was known or celebrated for, either in her lifetime or afterward.[66]

A little more than twenty years apart, Trotto and Fonte respectively presented Ippolita and Leonora as young widows unequivocally happy in their widowhoods. By the end of Trotto's dialogue, Ippolita has relented to the arguments in favor of the married life. Moreover, Trotto's readers know from the outset of the dialogue that she has remarried; her words in praise of "la vita vedovile per se stessa" (widowhood for its own sake) can therefore be taken to be relatively unthreatening to the mainstream societal view in favor of remarriage in sixteenth-century Turin. But Fonte offers us a very different ending. The widowed Adriana's last act before she relinquishes her role as queen is to ask Leonora to consider changing her mind about marriage, "poiché ancora è così giovanetta, procuri anch'essa di trovarsi una degna e graziosa compagnia, con la qual vive e mora consolatamente e non porga occasione a maldicenti di ragionar di lei cosa, che non si deve" (since she's still such a slip of a girl . . . to try to seek out a worthy and charming companion for herself, with whom she can lead a long and happy life—if only to avoid the risk of giving occasion for malicious gossip and slander).[67] Adriana's attempt at persuasion chimes with her precursor, Barbara, the older, once-widowed, and now remarried interlocutor in Trotto's dialogue. Both women are depicted as wanting their young, widowed friends to be happy, to find a companion with whom they can live "consolatamente" rather than as "sconsolate." But Leonora is far from a "sconsolata"; she is much happier as a widow than she ever was as a wife. Her laughing response to Adriana's entreaty—"Prima veggiamo accasata Virginia [the young, unmarried woman of the piece], che è fanciulla e tra tanto vi penserò sopra, e forse che mi disporrò ad accettare il vostro consiglio con quelli saggi e santi ricordi che voi mi avete dati" (Well, let's see Virginia married first since it's her first time. And, in the meantime, I'll think it over, and who knows? Perhaps eventually I'll come round to accepting your counsel, along with all the sound and sensible advice you have given me)—can be read in two ways.[68] Either Leonora intends to use her friend Virginia as a distraction, or she is admitting that as a young, beautiful, and rich widow, she may need to remarry at some point herself, to serve her family and her city. But for now, unlike Ippolita, she is able to remain alone and free in her private garden, enjoying the pleasures of "la vita vedovile per se stessa."

Epilogue

There was an extraordinary diversity in the ways widows were represented in late medieval and Renaissance texts and in how widowed writers represented themselves. The widow in Italian literature can be understood as a kind of "hybrid figure"—part allegory, part "real" woman; part male, part female.[1] She is thus a character imbued with meaning before she ever opens her mouth. If we consider only some of the different modes of widowhood examined in this book, not just one emotional community but several emerge: the merry widows, the sacred visionaries, the consolatory icons, the mourning widow-poets, the widows in search of liberty. Each of these groups share, as Barbara Rosenwein articulates, "the same or very similar norms and values about emotional behavior," but there remains a great variety of perspectives among the groups over the fundamentals of widow's work.[2] Does one grieve in public, for all to see, or retreat from the world to mourn alone? Should a widow devote her life to the memory of her husband, or should she push past into a broader civic or spiritual role? Is it the task of the widowed writer to focus on that experience, or can she move into different genres, different topics, different emotions?

Cities and Women

The cities of the late Middle Ages and Renaissance were not neutral spaces for widows to navigate. Instead, the dangers were often multiple: external enemies faced by all citizens in common; familial pressures to remarry and risk losing one's children; local governments legislating public expressions of grief, and even mourning attire. In her discussion of Christine de Pizan's city building, Marilynn Desmond observes that the France in which Christine constructed the urban utopia of *The Book of the City of*

Ladies was dedicated to the fortification of its cities to defend against English incursions. In the same period, there was an active debate over rightful succession to the French throne, which focused on whether the English king Edward III had a legitimate claim through his maternal line (it was ruled that he did not). Edward's claim, Desmond notes, "resulted in a proliferation of statements concerning the place of the female in the construction of royal lineage."[3] The purpose of de Pizan's construction project was not only to defend women's reputations, providing shelter against the misogynist vitriol of Matheolus and others, but to offer citizenship, legitimacy, and an alternative genealogy to women—and to women rulers.[4] It thus also becomes a commemorative project, a textual mausoleum in which the accomplishments of female leaders are memorialized—where Dido, for one, can be celebrated as a city builder in perpetuity, even though she was not able to enjoy Carthage for very long while she lived. Desmond makes the connection between Dido and Christine explicit:

> As a woman of wit and agency, a widow who constructs a city, Dido effectively figures Christine's textual construction of her authorial self. Not only does Christine's representation of herself as a woman who becomes a man upon her husband's death . . . replicate the tradition of Dido putting aside her female nature in order to go into exile, but the standard statement that Dido is a virago resonates powerfully with the fact that Jean Gerson labeled Christine "virilis ilia femina" and "ilia virago" during the Rose debate. In addition, Christine's emphasis upon her role as the builder of a textual city . . . invites a comparison between Christine the author and Dido the city builder.[5]

Christine and Dido had a further quality in common: their status as foreigners. Always present in the Dido narrative is her identity as a woman from somewhere else: a refugee from Phoenicia in Africa, a foreign queen who distracts Aeneas from his imperial task of founding Rome. Aligning herself with the foreign virago Dido through the act of city building, the Italian-born Christine not only appropriates a model of "manly" widowhood for herself but inserts herself into a transhistorical lineage of widowed rulers immune to the legitimacy debates of fifteenth-century France.

Two Seventeenth-Century Versions of Judith

This is worth keeping in mind as we consider the so-called *tutrici*, a unique example of co-rulership by two widows in Florence two centuries later. Christine de Lorraine (1565–1637, widowed 1609) and her daughter-in-law Maria Maddalena d'Austria (1589–1631, widowed 1621), ruled together from 1621 to 1628 after the death of Cosimo II de' Medici, Grand Duke of Tuscany (1590–1621)—Christine's son and Maria Maddalena's husband. His son with Maria Maddalena, Ferdinando II, became grand duke at the tender age of ten; until he reached his majority in 1628, his grandmother and mother ruled together, as had been specifically stipulated by Cosimo's will. The terms of the will were precise, "restrict[ing] foreign influence over the city and prevent[ing]

Cosimo's male relatives from gaining political influence and subverting the legitimate line of succession."[6] There was thus a seven-year period when the powerful Medici duchy was ruled not by one but by two *foreign* widows, the French-born Christine and the Austrian-born Maria Maddalena, with "opposing political positions and national loyalties."[7] Christine had trained for widowed leadership at the knee of her grandmother, the powerful widowed regent Catherine de' Medici, who died in 1589, shortly after negotiating the match between her French granddaughter and her Italian relative Ferdinando.[8] By the time of the tutrici, Christine had already been a widow for twelve years and had established herself as an important religious patron in Florence; Galileo wrote his famous *Lettera a Madama Cristina di Lorena, granduchessa di Toscana* attempting to reconcile Church doctrine and Copernicanism in June 1615. Maria Maddalena had an even more impressive family pedigree, as a Habsburg princess; her brother was the Holy Roman Emperor Ferdinand II, who reigned from 1619 to 1637.[9]

Until somewhat recently, scholarship on the years the two widows ruled together painted a laughably clichéd picture of the court as the ultimate in Counter-Reformation sterility.[10] In one representative example, Angelo Solerti dismissed the court in this way: "non si parlò d'altro che di messe, di vespri, di sermoni religiosi sotto l'austera e bigotta granduchessa Maria Maddalena, reggente" (No one spoke of anything but masses, vespers, and religious sermons under the austere and sanctimonious Grand Duchess and regent Maria Maddalena).[11] Scholars such as Maria Galli Stampino and Kelley Harness have since disproven this prejudiced assumption, with Galli Stampino observing that a combination of "post-unification anti-clericalism" and "misogynistic prejudice" led to scholarly dismissal of the two widowed regents as nothing more than dull, pious women with little interest in the cultivation of cultural innovation.[12] While Solerti was not wrong that the two women were both heavily invested in religious orthodoxy, the reign of the tutrici was still a period of cultural richness in Florence, with both widows active as patrons.[13] Worthy of special consideration is the opera *La Giuditta* with libretto by Andrea Salvadori, commissioned by Maria Maddalena and performed in 1626 for the brief visit of Cardinal Francesco Barberini after brokering peace between France and Spain with the Treaty of Monzon.[14] As we saw in chapter 3, Judith was a familiar character in Florence, a figure who was appropriated in the city both by the Medici and by their enemies to represent the victory of liberty over tyranny as early as the fifteenth century. There was a significant difference, however, between the symbolism imposed upon Donatello's 1460 statue and an embodied Judith on a stage in front of the two widowed coregents, singing Salvadori's libretto, set to music by the court composer Marco da Gagliano. "Unlike the political implications of Judith imagery in fifteenth- and sixteenth-century Florence," Harness astutely observes, "in 1626 actual female rulers presided over the city, with the effect that Judith could act as the allegorical representation not only of Florence, but of its regents."[15]

We cannot know, of course, whether, when Maria Maddalena commissioned the opera, she would have been aware that an earlier widow in the Medici family, mother to a powerful Medici leader, had also made Judith her own. Lucrezia Tornabuoni's sacred narrative of the Judith story was never published, although it is preserved in an elaborate manuscript in the Biblioteca Nazionale Centrale in Florence.[16] Jane Tylus has shown that Tornabuoni's writings "enjoyed far wider currency in her own day than in ours"; not only were they read by illustrious contemporaries such as Angelo Poliziano, Luigi Pulci, and the burlesque poet Bernardo Bellincioni, they were praised as late as the sixteenth and seventeenth centuries.[17] It is certainly possible that either or both Christine and Maria Maddalena had read Tornabuoni's work or at least had some notion of its existence. The choice of subject matter performed in front of the Barberini cardinal, however, ultimately proved too audacious for Maria Maddalena. Fearful that he would interpret the opera as a threatening message from the Medici widows regarding territorial tensions between Florence and his uncle, Pope Urban VIII, she "asked her secretary of state to convince the pope that the opera did not refer to the Barberini family—an extraordinary example," Harness observes, "of what a modern-day political commentator might term 'damage control.'"[18]

The bold Judith was a woman on the mind of many a Renaissance widow, however, even if she proved a little too audacious for some. In the archive in Città di Castello that contains Francesca Turina's writings, published and unpublished, there is a brief sonnet titled "A Santa Giuditta" that did not make it into her 1595 or 1628 volumes. Perhaps it was written after, or perhaps it simply did not make the cut; she was a prolific poet. The poem dedicated to Judith is found in a group of a dozen handwritten sonnets, all addressed to popular saints, including Mary Magdalene, Catherine of Siena, Teresa of Avila, and Filippo Neri. Unlike her published sonnets to Francesca Romana in the 1628 *Rime*, Turina does not specifically identify Judith as a widow in the poem, but it offers a great amount of detail from Judith's story in fourteen lines.

A Santa Giuditta
Generosa virago, honesta, e bella,
splendor del sesso feminile, e gloria
che formasti di te si degna historia
c'honore d'ogni secolo t'appella;
Adorna andasti sol con vile ancella
nel campo, onde portasti alta vittoria
finch'ebro il Duce, absorta ogni memoria
non ode, in grembo al sono, e non favella.
Troncasti ardita la superba testa
d'Holoferne, e furtiva la portasti,
Dio ringratiando, a mezza notte in fretta
et, offrendola a' tuoi, ne fer gran festa
e la Giudea co 'l tuo valor salvasti
qual t'haver Dio per si grand opra.

(Generous, virtuous and beautiful virago, splendor and glory of the female sex, whose story is so heroic that in every age you are spoken of with honor! Alone, you entered the enemy camp, dressed in your finest, with your humble maidser-

> vant, and left having secured a lofty victory over the drunken commander who, lost in his dreams in the depths of sleep, could hear nothing, and said nothing. Daring, you cut off the proud head of Holofernes, and furtive, you quickly carried it [away] in the middle of the night, and, thanking God, offered it to your people, who celebrated it greatly. So you saved Judea with your valor, just as God blessed you for your great deed.)[19]

It is by no means Turina's most masterful poem and is probably a draft; the incipit's description of Judith—"generosa virago, honesta, e bella"—is generic enough that it could apply to nearly any exemplary widow. There is a boldness to the poem's language, however, that is particularly noticeable in contrast to Maria Maddalena's "damage control" after the performance of *La Giuditta* or Tornabuoni's careful use of the term "vedovetta" to describe Judith—"a diminutive," Tylus observes, "that perhaps takes away from the virile acts Judith will go on to perform."[20] Instead, Judith is a "virago" here, a manly woman; we see no apology or cushion in Turina's sonnet to Judith, only a surfeit of words that unapologetically celebrate the virility, valor, and violence she demonstrated by killing Holofernes to save her people before retreating back to her life of widowed isolation.

The tale of the "little widow" Judith was one of many widow stories told and retold, by authorial voices both widowed and not, to construct different communities, craft different lineages, and further different goals. As we have seen, Turina was a poet concerned with securing her own place in lineages, poetic and otherwise, and was careful to align herself with widows who had triumphed in ways she hoped to as well. It is thus little wonder that she tried her hand at an interpretation of the Judith story, adding the Hebrew widow to her own personal widow city.

Notes

Introduction

1. "Adont vers moy vint ma maistresse, / Qui a plusieurs la joye estrece, / Si me toucha par tout le corps . . . Je m'esveillay et fu le cas / Tel qu'incontinent et sanz doubte / Transmuee me senti toute. / Mes membres senti trop plus fors / Qu'ainçois et cil grant desconfors / Et le plour, ou adés estoie, / Auques remis . . . Vray homme fus devenu." *Le livre de la mutacion de fortune par Christine de Pisan*, ed. Suzanne Solente (Paris: Picard, 1959–1966), ll. 1335–1342; translation in Christine de Pizan, *The Book of the Mutability of Fortune*, ed. and trans. Geri L. Smith (Toronto: Iter, 2017), 47.

2. Leah DeVun, *The Shape of Sex: Nonbinary Gender from Genesis to the Renaissance* (New York: Columbia University Press, 2021), 5.

3. Blake Gutt, "Transgender Mutation and the Canon: Christine de Pizan's *Livre de La Mutacion de Fortune*," *Postmedieval* 11, no. 4 (2020): 451–458, 455. On the interpretive benefits and risks of applying a trans or gender-fluid lens to premodern figures, see especially the introduction to *Trans Historical: Gender Plurality before the Modern*, ed. Greta LaFleur, Masha Raskolnikov, and Anna Kłosowska (Ithaca, NY: Cornell University Press, 2021), 1–24.

4. Gutt makes the important choice to refer to the narrator Christine of the *Mutacion* with he/him pronouns and to the author Christine with she/her pronouns. Gutt, "Transgender Mutation and the Canon," 454. Miranda Griffin and Robert Mills do this as well. Griffin explains, "I shall follow [Mills's] example, taking Christine the narrator at his word; after all, he insists he is a man to this day," in "Fortune's Touch: Reading Transformation in Christine de Pizan's Mutacion de Fortune," in *Ovidian Transversions: "Iphis and Ianthe," 1300–1650*, ed. Valerie Traub, Patricia Badir, and Peggy McCracken (Edinburgh: Edinburgh University Press, 2019), 100; Robert Mills, *Seeing Sodomy in the Middle Ages* (Chicago: University of Chicago Press, 2015), esp. 121–127.

5. See Marilynn Desmond, *Reading Dido: Gender, Textuality, and the Medieval Aeneid* (Minneapolis: University of Minnesota Press, 1994), esp. 195–196.

6. While I generally view it as best practice to refer to early modern women writers exclusively by their last names, as we do with male writers, I choose to alternate between Christine and de Pizan throughout, as so many feminist scholars of the author have done before me, because Christine herself often referred to herself by her first name.

7. See Kevin Brownlee, "Widowhood, Sexuality, and Gender in Christine de Pizan," *Romanic Review* 86, no. 2 (1995): 339–353.

8. Allison M. Levy, *Re-membering Masculinity in Early Modern Florence: Widowed Bodies, Mourning, and Portraiture* (Burlington, VT: Ashgate, 2006), 65. On the hermaphrodite in premodern discourse, see DeVun, *Shape of Sex*, esp. 163–169.

9. Sara M. Adler, "Vittoria Colonna: Michelangelo's Perfect Muse," *Italica* 92, no. 1 (2015): 5–32, 5. Abigail Brundin suggests that Michelangelo's description highlights the "essentially non-gendered nature of their interaction" in *Vittoria Colonna and the Spiritual Poetics of the Italian Reformation* (Burlington, VT: Ashgate, 2008), 24.

10. Irene Zanini-Cordi, *Donne sciolte: abbandono ed identità femminile nella letteratura italiana* (Ravenna: Longo, 2008), 75, translation my own.

11. On the patroness par excellence, Isabella d'Este, who was widowed in 1519, see Lisa K. Regan, "Ariosto's Threshold Patron: Isabella d'Este in the 'Orlando Furioso,'" *MLN* 120, no. 1 (2005): 50–69. On widow patrons in general, see Carolyn Valone, "Women on the Quirinal Hill: Patronage in Rome, 1560–1630," *Art Bulletin* 76, no. 1 (1994): 129–146 and "Roman Matrons as Patrons: Various Views of the Cloister Wall," in *The Crannied Wall: Women, Religion and the Arts in Early Modern Europe*, ed. Craig Monson (Ann Arbor: University of Michigan Press, 1992), 49–72.

12. The most recent and extensive scholarly works on widowhood and conduct literature are important studies by Paolo Pucci and Helena Sanson; see esp. Pucci, *Tra ideale e reale. La vedova (in)dipendente nella trattatistica e nei carteggi italiani* (sec. XV–XVII) (Rome: Edizioni di storia e letteratura, 2024) and Sanson, "Widowhood and Conduct in Late Sixteenth-Century Italy: The 'Unusual' Case of *La vedova del Fusco* (1570)," *The Italianist* 35, no. 1 (2015): 1–26, and "Conduct for the Real Widow: Giulio Cesare Cabei's *Ornamenti Della Gentildonna Vedova* (1574)," in *Conduct Literature for and about Women in Italy, 1470–1900: Prescribing and Describing Life*, ed. Helena Sanson and Francesco Lucioli (Paris: Classiques Garnier, 2016), 41–61. See also Girolamo Savonarola, *A Guide to Righteous Living and Other Works*, ed. and trans. Konrad Eisenbichler (Toronto: University of Toronto Press, 2003), and Paolo Pucci, "Finalmente libera, ma non per molto: la vedova nella trattatistica italiana del xvi secolo," *Rivista Di Studi Italiani* 33, no. 1 (2015): 187–214.

13. See esp. Margaret Alexiou, *The Ritual Lament in Greek Tradition* (Cambridge, MA: Harvard University Press, 1974).

14. All English translations of the Bible throughout this study come from the Douay-Rheims version. Richard Challoner and Michael Tweedale, *The Holy Bible: Douay-Rheims Version: The Old Testament First Published by the English College at Douay, A.D. 1609, and the New Testament First Published by the English College at Rheims, A.D. 1582* (London: Baronius Press, 2008).

15. See Katherine Clark Walter, "Purgatory, Punishment, and the Discourse of Holy Widowhood in the High and Later Middle Ages," *Journal of the History of Sexuality* 16, no. 2 (2007): 169–203, for a discussion of Jerome's classification of virgins, widows, and wives into a tripartite structure, three groups of "harvesters who respectively reaped the 'centesimus et sexagesimus et tricesimus fructus' (the hundred-, sixty-, and thirtyfold fruit)" (170).

16. Katherine Clark Walter, *The Profession of Widowhood: Widows, Pastoral Care, and Medieval Models of Holiness* (Washington, DC: Catholic University of America Press, 2018), 25.

17. Jerome, *The Sacred Writings of Saint Jerome*, ed. Philipp Schaff (Altenmünster, Germany: Jazzybee Verlag, 2012), 12.5.

18. Augustine, Letter 130, in *Letters*, trans. Sister Wilfrid Parsons (Washington, DC: Catholic University of America Press, 1951), 289.

19. Augustine had a personal connection to widowhood that informed his perspective and through which he informed the world of the importance of widows: his mother Monica, who became an important patron saint of widows. See Levy, *Re-membering Masculinity*, 43–46.

20. See esp. Unn Falkeid and Anna Wainwright, eds., *The Legacy of Birgitta of Sweden: Women, Politics and Reform in Renaissance Italy* (Leiden: Brill, 2023).

21. Analyzing the manner in which Colonna's promoters described her in the 1540s, Abigail Brundin writes in *Vittoria Colonna* that their descriptions often seem close "to that of a nun . . . her pious image was seemingly absorbed and accepted whole-heartedly by her reading public, to the extent that sixteenth-century published editions of the sonnets sometimes carried woodcut images of [Colonna] dressed in a plain habit and kneeling before a crucifix in prayer" (24).

22. Clark Walter, *Profession of Widowhood*, and Levy, *Re-membering Masculinity*. Edited volumes on widowhood in medieval and early modern Europe include Sandra Cavallo and Lyndan Warner, eds., *Widowhood in Medieval and Early Modern Europe* (New York: Routledge, 1999); Catherine E. King, ed., *Renaissance Women Patrons: Wives and Widows in Italy c. 1300–c. 1550* (New York: Manchester University Press, 2004); Louise Mirrer, ed., *Upon My Husband's Death: Widows in the Literature and Histories of Medieval Europe* (Ann Arbor: University of Michigan Press, 1992); and Allison M. Levy, ed., *Widowhood and Visual Culture in Early Modern Europe* (Burlington, VT: Ashgate, 2003).

23. Carol Lansing, *Passion and Order: Restraint of Grief in the Medieval Italian Communes* (Ithaca, NY: Cornell University Press, 2008); Juliana Schiesari, *The Gendering of Melancholia: Feminism, Psychoanalysis, and the Symbolics of Loss in Renaissance Literature* (Ithaca, NY: Cornell University Press, 1992); Sharon T. Strocchia, "Funerals and the Politics of Gender in Early Renaissance Florence," in *Refiguring Woman: Perspectives on Gender and the Italian Renaissance*, ed. Marilyn Migiel and Juliana Schiesari (Ithaca, NY: Cornell University Press, 1991), 155–168; and Strocchia, *Death and Ritual in Renaissance Florence* (Baltimore: Johns Hopkins University Press, 1992).

24. While scholarship on this subject is now vast, see especially Brundin, *Vittoria Colonna*; Virginia Cox, *Women's Writing in Italy, 1400–1650* (Baltimore: Johns Hopkins University Press, 2008); Cox, *The Prodigious Muse: Women's Writing in Counter-Reformation Italy* (Baltimore: Johns Hopkins University Press, 2011); Giovanna Rabitti, "Vittoria Colonna as Role Model for Cinquecento Women Poets," in *Women in Italian Renaissance Culture and Society*, ed. Letizia Panizza (Oxford: European Humanities Research Association, 2000), 478–497; Diana Robin, *Publishing Women: Salons, the Presses, and the Counter-Reformation in Sixteenth-Century Italy* (Chicago: University of Chicago Press, 2007); Sarah Gwyneth Ross, *The Birth of Feminism: Woman as Intellect in Renaissance Italy and England* (Cambridge, MA: Harvard University Press, 2009); Jane Tylus, *Reclaiming Catherine of Siena: Literacy, Literature, and the Signs of Others* (Chicago: University of Chicago Press, 2009); and Elissa B. Weaver, *Convent Theatre in Early Modern Italy: Spiritual Fun and Learning for Women* (Cambridge: Cambridge University Press, 2007).

25. Barbara H. Rosenwein, *Generations of Feeling: A History of Emotions, 600–1700* (Cambridge: Cambridge University Press, 2016), 25.

26. Giulia Calvi, "Widows, the State, and the Guardianship of Children in Early Modern Tuscany," in *Widowhood in Medieval and Modern Europe*, ed. Sandra Cavallo and Lyndan Warner (New York: Routledge, 1999), 209–219, 209.

27. Isabelle Chabot, "Widowhood and Poverty in Late Medieval Florence," *Continuity and Change* 3, no. 2 (1988): 291–311.

28. Stanley Chojnacki, *Women and Men in Renaissance Venice: Twelve Essays on Patrician Society* (Baltimore: Johns Hopkins University Press, 2002), 95.

29. Christiane Klapisch-Zuber, "The 'Cruel Mother': Maternity, Widowhood, and Dowry in Florence in the Fourteenth and Fifteenth Centuries" in *Women, Family, and Ritual in Renaissance Italy* (Chicago: University of Chicago Press, 1985), 117–131, 118.

30. Klapisch-Zuber, "'Cruel Mother,'" 119.

31. David Herlihy and Christiane Klapisch-Zuber, *Tuscans and Their Families: A Study of the Florentine Catasto of 1427* (New Haven, CT: Yale University Press, 1985), 216–217.

32. Herlihy and Klapisch-Zuber, *Tuscans and Their Families*, 207–211.

33. Chojnacki, *Women and Men*, 100; Monica Chojnacka, *Working Women of Early Modern Venice* (Baltimore: Johns Hopkins University Press, 2001), 16.

34. Chojnacki, *Women and Men*, 96.

35. See Chabot, "Widowhood and Poverty"; Nicholas Terpstra, *Cultures of Charity: Women, Politics, and the Reform of Poor Relief in Renaissance Italy* (Cambridge, MA: Harvard University Press, 2013); and Chojnacka, *Working Women*.

36. See Terpstra, *Cultures of Charity*, 20.

37. Richard Trexler, "A Widow's Asylum of the Renaissance: The Orbatello of Florence," in *Dependence in Context in Renaissance Florence* (Binghamton, NY: Medieval and Renaissance Text and Studies, 1994), 415–448, 417.

38. Chojnacka, *Working Women*, 111.

39. Chojnacka points to the case of a late sixteenth-century Cremonese widow who moved between four different Venetian neighborhoods over the course of a ten-year period. Chojnacka, *Working Women*, 112.

40. Terpstra, *Cultures of Charity*, esp. 55–59.

41. Chabot, "Widowhood and Poverty," 293.

42. Lucrezia Tornabuoni, *Lettere*, ed. Patrizia Salvadori (Florence: Olschki, 1993).

43. Caroline Murphy, *Lavinia Fontana: A Painter and Her Patrons in Sixteenth-Century Bologna* (New Haven, CT: Yale University Press, 2003), 138.

44. Terpstra, *Cultures of Charity*, 212.

45. Valone, "Women on the Quirinal Hill"; and Nicholas A. Eckstein, "The Widows' Might: Women's Identity and Devotion in the Brancacci Chapel," *Oxford Art Journal* 28, no. 1 (2005): 101–118.

46. See Sarah Kay, "The Didactic Space: The City in Christine de Pizan, Augustine, and Irigaray," in *Text und Kultur: Mittelalterliche Literatur 1150–1450*, ed. Ursula Peters (Stuttgart: J.B. Metzler, 2001), 438–466.

47. Johannes van Oort, *Jerusalem and Babylon: A Study into Augustine's* City of God *and the Sources of His Doctrine of the Two Cities* (New York: Brill, 2015), 107. On the varied meanings encompassed in Augustine's *civitas*, see esp. 102–112.

48. Desmond, *Reading Dido*, 207.

49. Kay, "Didactic Space," 448. See Christine de Pizan, *Le livre de la cité des dames*, ed. and trans. Éric Hicks and Thérèse Moreau (Paris: Stock/Moyen Âge, 1986).

50. Desmond, *Reading Dido*, 209–211.

51. David Herlihy, *Mapping Households in Medieval Italy* (Washington, DC: Catholic University of America Press, 1972), 14.

52. Murphy, *Lavinia Fontana*, 94. See also Ann Crabb's discussion of Alessandra Strozzi in relationship to her sons during their exile from Florence in *The Strozzi of Florence: Widowhood and Family Solidarity in the Renaissance* (Ann Arbor: University of Michigan Press, 2000).

53. Cristelle Louise Baskins, "Trecento Rome: The Poetics and Politics of Widowhood," in Levy, *Widowhood and Visual Culture*, 197–209, and Unn Falkeid, *The Avignon Papacy Contested: An Intellectual History from Dante to Catherine of Siena* (Cambridge, MA: Harvard University Press, 2017).

54. Dante, *Purgatorio* VI.76–78, 112–114, in *The Divine Comedy of Dante Alighieri*, vol. 2: *Purgatorio*, ed. Ronald L. Martinez, trans. Robert M. Durling (New York: Oxford University Press, 2003). See Natalia Costa-Zalessow, "The Personification of Italy from Dante through the Trecento," *Italica* 68, no. 3 (1991): 316–331.

55. Of particular note is Vespasiano da Bisticci's *Lamento d'Italia per la presa d'Otranto fatta dai Turchi nel 1480*, published in Florence in 1480. See Anna Wainwright, "Widows, Lament, and Ottoman Anxieties in Quattrocento Florence," in *Gendering the Renaissance*, ed. Meredith K. Ray and Lynn Lara Westwater (Newark: University of Delaware Press, 2023), 23–43.

56. Strocchia, *Death and Ritual in Renaissance Florence*, 10–12.

57. Juan Luis Vives, *The Education of a Christian Woman: A Sixteenth-Century Manual*, trans. Charles Fantazzi (Chicago: University of Chicago Press, 2007), 433.

58. Jacobus, *The Golden Legend: Readings on the Saints*, trans. William Granger Ryan (Princeton, NJ: Princeton University Press, 2012), 122.

59. Vives, *Education of a Christian Woman*, 436.

60. Savonarola, *Guide to Righteous Living*.

61. Levy, *Re-membering Masculinity*, 79.

62. See especially Cox, *Women's Writing in Italy* and *Prodigious Muse*; Robin, *Publishing Women*; and Ross, *Birth of Feminism*.

63. Of particular note, two edited volumes on Colonna have come out within the past decade: Abigail Brundin, Tatiana Crivelli, and Maria Serena Sapegno, eds., *A Companion to Vittoria Colonna* (Leiden: Brill, 2016), and Virginia Cox and Shannon McHugh, eds., *Vittoria Colonna: Poetry, Religion, Art, Impact* (Amsterdam: Amsterdam University Press, 2021).

64. Virginia Cox, "Women Writers and the Canon in Sixteenth-Century Italy," in *Strong Voices, Weak History: Early Women Writers and Canons in England, France, and*

Italy, ed. Pamela Jones Benson and Victoria Kirkham (Ann Arbor: University of Michigan Press, 2005), 14–31, 17.

65. See Maria Serena Sapegno, "La costruzione di un Io Lirico al femminile nella poesia di Vittoria Colonna," *Versants* 46 (2003): 15–37, 17, and Tatiana Crivelli, "The Print Tradition of Vittoria Colonna's *Rime*," in Brundin, Crivelli, and Sapegno, *Companion to Vittoria Colonna*, 69–139, 122n24.

Chapter 1 Dante, Petrarch, and the Ethics of Widowhood

1. Gendered lament and its uses in community ritual has, of course, an even more expansive history. See esp. Alexiou, *Ritual Lament in Greek Tradition*.

2. See especially Baskins, "Trecento Rome," and Falkeid, *Avignon Papacy Contested*, esp. 95–120.

3. Olivia Holmes observes, "For Dante, terrestrial Rome prefigures celestial Jerusalem, but it also recalls whorish Babylon . . . the two cities—one pointing downward, and the other upward—are superimposed, and can easily be mistaken for one another." *Dante's Two Beloveds: Ethics and Erotics in the "Divine Comedy"* (New Haven, CT: Yale University Press, 2008), 127. On Lamentations in Dante, see Ronald L. Martinez, "Dante between Hope and Despair: The Tradition of Lamentations in the *Divine Comedy*," *Logos* 5, no. 3 (2002): 45–76.

4. *Purgatorio*, VI.112–114. Translation by Robert M. Durling in Dante Alighieri, *The Divine Comedy*, vol. 2: *Purgatorio*, trans. Robert M. Durling, ed. Ronald L. Martinez (New York: Oxford University Press, 2003). Further citations appear parenthetically with the abbreviation *Purg.*

5. Baskins, "Trecento Rome."

6. Baskins, "Trecento Rome."

7. Baskins, "Trecento Rome," 201.

8. This second image, Baskins notes, was most likely directed at the church's patrons, the powerful Colonna family, who stood in opposition to Cola's rebellion. Baskins, "Trecento Rome," 201. See also Ronald G. Musto, *Apocalypse in Rome: Cola Di Rienzo and the Politics of the New Age* (Berkeley: University of California Press, 2003), 111–112.

9. On this, see Falkeid, *Avignon Papacy Contested*, esp. 100–101.

10. Lansing, *Passion and Order*, 154.

11. See, for example, Lansing, *Passion and Order*, 63.

12. Baskins, "Trecento Rome," 198.

13. Strocchia, *Death and Ritual in Renaissance Florence*, 10. On Fra Remigio de' Girolami's sermon on the distinctions between various mourning verbs and gestures, see Lansing, *Passion and Order*, 56.

14. Francesco Petrarca, *Rerum senilium* liber XIIII, trans. Benjamin Kohl, in *The Earthly Republic: Italian Humanists on Government and Society*, ed. Benjamin G. Kohl and Ronald Witt (Philadelphia: University of Pennsylvania Press, 1997.

15. Strocchia, *Death and Ritual in Renaissance Florence*, esp. 10–15.

16. For tears as external evidence of the authenticity of a person's feelings within, see Lyn Blanchfield, "The Sincere Body: The Performance of Weeping and Emotion in Late

Medieval Italian Sermons," *Quidditas* 20 (1999): 117–135. This may also have been linked to the long tradition of professional female mourners. Boncompagno da Signa's *Rhetorica antiqua* (1215) surveyed historical and cross-cultural mourning practices and pointed to, among other examples, the use in ancient Rome of professional female mourners hired for funerals, which continued into the *computatrices* tradition in Rome as well as in the Italian South. See Lansing, *Passion and Order*, 63–64.

17. Diane Owen Hughes, "Mourning Rites, Memory, and Civilization in Premodern Italy," in *Riti e rituali nelle società medievali*, ed. Jacques Chiffoleau, Lauro Martines, and Agostino Paravicini Bagliani (Spoleto: Centro Italiano di Studi sull'Alto Medioevo, 1994), 33.

18. Strocchia, *Death and Ritual in Renaissance Florence*, 10–12.

19. See esp. Lansing, *Passion and Order*, 53–55. Lansing hypothesizes that there may have been a generally incredulous reaction if "the court would fine a new widow . . . for her show of sorrow at her husband's funeral" (55).

20. Hughes, "Mourning Rites," 31, and Schiesari, *Gendering of Melancholia*, 163.

21. Lansing, *Passion and Order*, 55.

22. Dante Alighieri, *Vita nuova*, ed. Michele Barbi (Florence: Bemporard, 1932); all translations by Andrew Frisardi, exclusive to the Digital Dante Project, https://digitaldante.columbia.edu/text/library/la-vita-nuova-frisardi/, unless otherwise noted. Further citations appear parenthetically.

23. On this see esp. Holmes, *Dante's Two Beloveds*, 140.

24. See esp. Ronald L. Martinez, "Mourning Beatrice: The Rhetoric of Threnody in the *Vita nuova*," *MLN* 113, no. 1 (1998): 1–29, and "Dante Between Hope and Despair," 49.

25. On the fate of this other letter, see esp. Holmes, *Dante's Two Beloveds*, 140.

26. Jelena Todorovic, *Dante and the Dynamics of Textual Exchange: Authorship, Manuscript Culture, and the Making of the "Vita Nova"* (New York: Fordham University Press, 2016).

27. Nancy J. Vickers, "Widowed Words: Dante, Petrarch, and the Metaphors of Mourning," in *Discourses of Authority in Medieval and Renaissance Literature*, ed. Kevin Brownlee and Walter Stephens (Hanover, NH: University Press of New England, 1989), 97.

28. "Cattivella" is also the adjective used to lament the fate of the wicked widow Elena in Boccaccio's *Decameron* VIII.7, the tale of the scholar and the widow (VIII.7.13). See Teodolinda Barolini, "The Scholar and the Widow: Corrupt Appetite and Moral Failure in Society's Intellectual Elite (VIII.7)," in *The Decameron Eighth Day in Perspective*, ed. William Robins (Toronto: University of Toronto Press, 2020): 148–189, 167.

29. Holmes, *Dante's Two Beloveds*, 142.

30. Holmes, *Dante's Two Beloveds*, 144.

31. Teodolinda Barolini, *Dante's Lyric Poetry: Poems of Youth and of the "Vita nuova" (1283–1292)*, trans. Richard Lansing and Andrew Frisardi (Toronto: University of Toronto Press, 2014), 196.

32. Martinez, "Mourning Beatrice," 11.

33. On the history of *sfogare*, see Tylus, *Reclaiming Catherine of Siena*, 212–213.

34. The adjective perhaps most associated with widows in the Italian tradition is "sconsolata" or "inconsolable," as I will discuss in the next chapter.

35. On the significance of this instance of direct discourse to the entire project of the *Commedia*, see Barolini, *Dante's Lyric Poetry*, 249. See also Teodolinda Barolini, "Errancy: A Brief History of Dante's *Ferm Voler*," in *The Oxford Handbook of Dante*, ed. Manuele Gragnolati, Elena Lombardi, and Francesca Southerden (Oxford: Oxford University Press, 2021), 568.

36. Barolini suggests that in the sonnet "I' vegno 'l giorno atte 'nfinite volte," Cavalcanti expresses impatience with Dante's depression after Beatrice's death. Barolini, *Dante's Lyric Poetry*, 250.

37. Barolini, "Errancy," 567. My argument in this chapter has been much influenced and expanded by Teodolinda Barolini's tracing of the ethical code defined in "L'amaro lagrimar che voi faceste" by the caveat "se non per morte," and I thank her for our rich discussions on the subject over the years.

38. Vickers, "Widowed Words," 99.

39. All translations of the *RVF* are from Francesco Petrarch, *Petrarch's Lyric Poems: The Rime Sparse and Other Lyrics*, trans. Robert M. Durling (Cambridge, MA: Harvard University Press, 2005).

40. Vickers, "Widowed Words," 107.

41. This is not the only instance when Petrarch uses these words. As I discuss in greater detail in chapter 4, in Petrarch's Triumph of Death, the figure of Death is described as "una donna involta in veste negra," who threatens the "brigata allegra" led by Laura marching in from the Triumph of Chastity. For Petrarch, a widowed woman—or poem—draped in black mourning clothes is thus not necessarily a productive or even a neutral presence in poetry but can be construed as dangerous, a threat to love and to life.

42. See Holmes, *Dante's Two Beloveds*, 122, on Semiramis as the first sinner we meet in *Inferno*.

43. All citations and translations from *Inferno* are from *The Divine Comedy of Dante Alighieri*, vol. 1: *Inferno*, trans. Robert M. Durling, ed. Ronald L. Martinez (Oxford: Oxford University Press, 1996). Further citations appear parenthetically.

44. "A vizio di lussuria fu sì rotta / che libito fé licito in sua legge, / per tórre il biasmo in che era condotta. / Ell'è Semiramìs, di cui si legge / che succedette a Nino e fu sua sposa: / tenne la terra che 'l Soldan corregge" (So broken was she to the vice of lust that in her laws she made licit whatever pleased, to lift from herself the blame she had incurred. She is Semiramis, of whom we read that she succeeded Ninus and was his wife: she ruled the lands the Sultan governs now; *Inferno* V.55–60).

45. On adultery and incest, see Mary Douglas, *Purity and Danger: An Analysis of Concepts of Pollution and Taboo* (New York: Routledge, 2015), esp. 67. See also Leviticus 18:6–20, esp. 18:6–7: "None of you shall approach to any that is near of kin to him, to uncover their nakedness. . . . The nakedness of thy father, or the nakedness of thy mother, shalt thou not uncover: she is thy mother; thou shalt not uncover her nakedness."

46. Barolini observes that in his harsh treatment of Dido, "Dante does not lodge any criticism that he does not lodge against himself." Barolini, "Errancy," 578.

47. Jacques Le Goff, *The Birth of Purgatory* (Chicago: University of Chicago Press, 1991).

48. Barbara Newman, *From Virile Woman to WomanChrist: Studies in Medieval Religion and Literature* (Philadelphia: University of Pennsylvania Press, 1995), 111.

49. See Clark Walter, "Purgatory," 177–178.

50. Le Goff, *Birth of Purgatory*, 350–351.

51. Clark Walter, "Purgatory," 173–175..

52. Le Goff, *Birth of Purgatory*, 73.

53. Barolini ties Dante's ethical stance originating in "L'amaro lagrimar" to Dante's encounter with Nino Visconti in "Errancy," 576–577.

54. Deborah Parker, "Ideology and Cultural Practice: The Case of Dante's Treatment of Beatrice d'Este," *Dante Studies* 111 (1993): 131–147, 135; Sara E. Díaz, "'Dietro a lo sposo, sì la sposa piace': Marriage in Dante's *Commedia*" (PhD diss., New York University, 2012), 152.

55. Thomas Kuehn, *Law, Family, and Women: Toward a Legal Anthropology of Renaissance Italy* (Chicago: University of Chicago Press, 1994), 199.

56. On Dante's use of "bende" to connote gendered dress, see Teodolinda Barolini, "'Sotto Benda': The Women of Dante's Canzone 'Doglia Mi Reca' in the Light of Cecco d'Ascoli," *Dante Studies, with the Annual Report of the Dante Society* no. 123 (2005): 83–88.

57. Díaz, "'Dietro a lo sposo,'" 154.

58. The choice to translate "pianger dirotto" as "broken weeping" by Durling here is subtle; "broken" should be understood not as "interrupted" but as related to a broken emotional state. The phrase "pianger dirotto" is sometimes translated more loosely, as "flooding tears" (Hollander) or "overflowing tears" (Longfellow), which allows for a somewhat more readily understood image; Durling's use of broken, however, allows English readers of the poem to see the connection between Nella's "pianger dirotto" and the earlier pejorative descriptions of Semiramis as a widow who is broken or "rotta," and Dido as a widow who "broke faith" or "ruppe fede" with her husband's memory.

59. See Fabian Alfie, *Dante's Tenzone with Forese Donati: The Reprehension of Vice* (Toronto: University of Toronto Press, 2011); Danielle Callegari, "Grey Partridge and Middle-Aged Mutton: The Social Value of Food in the Tenzone with Forese Donati," *Dante Studies* 133, no. 1 (2015): 177–190.

60. See especially Díaz, "'Dietro a Lo Sposo,'" 167–175, for a discussion of Forese's conjugal debt and fragile masculinity. As Díaz points out, there is no hint in the *tenzone* that Nella seeks pleasure elsewhere. See also Grace Delmolino, "The Economics of Conjugal Debt from Gratian's *Decretum* to *Decameron* 2.10: Boccaccio, Canon Law, and the Loss of Interest in Sex," in *Reconsidering Boccaccio: Medieval Contexts and Global Intertexts*, ed. Olivia Holmes and Dana E. Stewart (Toronto: University of Toronto Press, 2018), 133–163, on conjugal debt in the Middle Ages.

61. Le Goff, *Birth of Purgatory*, 13.

62. In the *Golden Legend*, one of many versions of the story with which Dante and his readers would have been familiar, the widow's son has been, rather neatly, killed by Trajan's son. Baskins, "Trecento Rome," 152.

63. Barolini observes that the use of direct discourse in general "is a way of creating the illusion of reality in a text"; in *Purgatorio* X, Dante "constructs the dialogue between Trajan and the widow, rendered in direct discourse, to lend the illusion of a fourth dimension to the sculpted reliefs on the terrace of pride." Teodolinda Barolini, "The Making of a Lyric Sequence: Time and Narrative in Petrarch's *Rerum vulgarium fragmenta*," in *Dante*

and the Origins of Italian Literary Culture (New York: Fordham University Press, 2006), 193–223, 216.

64. See Nancy Vickers's analysis of Trajan and the widow, "Seeing Is Believing: Gregory, Trajan, and Dante's Art," *Dante Studies* 101 (1983): 67–85. Vickers suggests that Dante is thinking of Trajan's Column, which tells a story through images in a similarly filmic progression, but that Gregory would have been looking at a different relief altogether.

65. This citation and translation come from *The Divine Comedy of Dante Alighieri*, vol. 3: *Paradiso*, trans. Robert M. Durling, ed. Ronald L. Martinez (Oxford: Oxford University Press, 2011).

66. Petrarch used a similar diminutive—"vedovetta"—in the *Trionfi* to describe the Hebrew widow Judith, which Lucrezia Tornabuoni would appropriate for her fifteenth-century sacred narrative on the subject, discussed in chapter 3.

Chapter 2 Boccaccio's Many Merry Widows

1. A section of this chapter will appear in *The Decameron Second Day in Perspective*, ed. Victoria Kirkham (Toronto: University of Toronto Press, forthcoming).

2. The focus in this chapter is on Boccaccio's vernacular works; for a discussion of widowed exempla in *De claris mulieribus*, see chapter 4.

3. On misogyny in *Il corbaccio*, see Millicent Marcus, "Misogyny as Misreading: A Gloss on *Decameron* VIII.7," *Stanford Italian Review* 4, no. 1 (1984): 23–40, and Regina Psaki, "Women Make All Things Lose Their Power: Women's Knowledge, Men's Fear in the *Decameron* and the *Corbaccio*," *Heliotropia* 1, no. 1 (2003): 1–13.

4. On Elena, see esp. Barolini, "Scholar and the Widow," and Robert M. Durling, "A Long Day in The Sun: *Decameron* 8.7," in *Shakespeare's "Rough Magic": Renaissance Essays in Honor of C. L. Barber*, ed. Peter Erickson (Newark: University of Delaware Press, 1985), 269–275.

5. On exemplary widows in *De claris mulieribus*, see Stephen Kolsky, *The Ghost of Boccaccio: Writings on Famous Women in Renaissance Italy* (Turnhout: Brepols, 2005), 63–89.

6. Giovanni Boccaccio, *Filocolo* IV, 51–55, in *Tutte le opere*, 10 vols., ed. Vittore Branca et al. (Milan: Mondadori, 1964–1994). See Gur Zak, "Boccaccio's *Filocolo* and the Polyphony of Consolation," *Mediaevalia* 42, no. 1 (2021): 187–225, 202, for this conversation in the context of consolation in the *Filocolo*.

7. Rebecca West describes the novella as a "road story" and the widow as living in a space "betwixt and between"; see her important reading of the tale, "*Decameron* II, 2: A Dream Trip," *Italian Quarterly* 37, no. 143–146 (2000): 127–142.

8. Sergio Zatti, "Il mercante sulla ruota: la seconda giornata," in *Introduzione al Decameron*, ed. Michelangelo Picone and Margherita Mesirca (Florence: Franco Cesati Editore, 2004), 79–98, 79.

9. Zatti identifies Rinaldo as one of a "triptych" of merchants in Day II, along with Landolfo and Andreuccio, representative of "il solitario protagonismo mercantile" or the solitary merchant as protagonist-hero, Zatti, "Il mercante sulla ruota," 82–83.

10. Vittore Branca suggests that it is probably the same Marchese d'Azzo; see Giovanni Boccaccio, *Decameron* in *Tutte le opere*, vol. 4, ed. Vittore Branca (Milan: Mondadori, 1976), 100n6. See also West, "Dream Trip," 138.

11. *Decameron* is cited from Boccaccio, *Decameron* in *Tutte le opere*. All translations are from Giovanni Boccaccio, *The Decameron*, trans. G. H. McWilliam (New York: Penguin, 1975), unless otherwise noted. Further citations appear parenthetically.

12. On Boccaccio's attention to travel in the beginning of the story, see esp. West, "Dream Trip," 128–129.

13. On Rinaldo's straightforward understanding of faith and piety, see Gary Cestaro, "Rinaldo D'Asti: Drama of the Signifié," *Carte Italiane* 7, no. 1 (1986): 14–27, esp. 18.

14. Branca in Boccaccio, *Decameron*, in *Tutte le opere*, 102n1.

15. Translation my own. McWilliam translates this as "depressed and miserable," but it is important to recognize the pointedly mournful nature of the original: "dolente e isconsolato."

16. Jacobus, "Saint Julian," in *Golden Legend*, 126–131.

17. Branca notes that the only other comparison of a human's sounds to those of a stork is in *Decameron* VIII.7, the tale of the scholar and the widow, when the widow Elena will not allow Rinieri inside despite his being nearly frozen to death (VIII.7.39). Barolini also notes this in "Scholar and the Widow."

18. 1 Timothy 5: 10. See also Donald Wayne Riddle, "Early Christian Hospitality: A Factor in the Gospel Transmission," *Journal of Biblical Literature* 57, no. 2 (1938): 141–154. As Riddle points out, widows were also viewed as figures in need of charity and hospitality themselves, along with orphans and the poor.

19. In 1 Corinthians, Paul says that while it is better to stay unmarried, those widows "who do not contain themselves" sexually should remarry, "for it is better to marry than to burn" (1 Corinthians 7:9).

20. Giovanni Boccaccio, *The Decameron*, trans. Wayne A. Rebhorn (New York: Norton, 2013), 873n1.

21. Cavallo and Warner, *Widowhood in Medieval and Early Modern Europe*, 7.

22. Klapisch-Zuber, *Women, Family, and Ritual*, 119.

23. Clark Walter, "Purgatory," 177–178.

24. See Klapisch-Zuber, *Women, Family and Ritual*, esp. 124, for mistrust of Florentine widows.

25. Teodolinda Barolini, "Boccaccio's Philosophy of Consolation: The Place of the Other in Life's Transactions," in *Boccaccio 1313–2013*, ed. Francesco Ciabattoni, Elsa Filosa, and Kristina Olson (Ravenna: Longo Editore, 2013), 89–105, 90.

26. Translation my own.

27. There are echoes of this nostalgia for the widowed life in the vivacious young widow Ippolita in Bernardo Trotti's *Dialoghi del matrimonio e la vita vedovile*, which I discuss in chapter 6.

28. Barolini, "Scholar and the Widow," 151.

29. Barolini, "Boccaccio's Philosophy of Consolation," 95.

30. Heather M. Arden, "Grief, Widowhood, and Women's Sexuality in Medieval French Literature," in Mirrer, *Upon My Husband's Death*, 306. See also Alfonso D'Agostino, *La matrona d'Efeso e la vedova consolata: Il personaggio della vedova nella letteratura medievale* (Milan: CUEM, 2019).

31. Strocchia, *Death and Ritual in Renaissance Florence*, and Hughes, "Mourning Rites."

32. Ronald L. Martinez suggests that Boccaccio probably began to write the *Decameron* in 1349 and had it "substantially complete" by 1351 but continued revising until at least 1372. Martinez, "Also Known as 'Prencipe Galeotto' (*Decameron*)," in *Boccaccio: A Critical Guide to the Complete Works*, ed. Victoria Kirkham, Michael Sherberg, and Janet Smarr (Chicago: University of Chicago Press, 2013), 23–40, 24. See chapter 1 of this book for an extended discussion of Florentine legislation around women's mourning practices.

33. Zatti, "Il mercante sulla ruota," 84.

34. Elissa Weaver, "Fashion and Fortune in the *Decameron*," in *Boccaccio 1313–2013*, ed. Francesco Ciabattoni, Elsa Filosa, and Kristina Olson (Ravenna: Longo Editore, 2015), 71–86, 76.

35. Weaver observes "Boccaccio's use of clothes in his *novelle* reflects the high social and economic value of dress in the Tuscan mercantile world and the importance of social hierarchy, of class distinctions." Weaver, "Fashion and Fortune," 75. This passing mention of *cintolini* has outsized historical importance in the history of fashion, representing the earliest known reference to garters in European literature. James Robinson Planché, *A Cyclopaedia of Costume or Dictionary of Dress, Including Notices of Contemporaneous Fashions on the Continent: The Dictionary*. (London: Chatto and Windus, 1876), 198. See also Katherine Lester and Bess Viola Oerke, *Accessories of Dress: An Illustrated Encyclopedia* (North Chelmsford, MA: Courier, 2013), 303.

36. Weaver, "Fashion and Fortune," 77.

37. On "donna" versus "femmina," see Giuliano Bonfante, "Femmina e donna," in *Studia philologica et literaria in honorem L. Spitzer*, ed. A. G. Hatcher and C. L. Selig (Bern: Francke Verlag, 1958), 77–109, as well as Vittorio Russo, "Perorazioni d'amore da parte di 'donne' e 'femmine' nel *Decamerone*," in *Con le Muse in Parnaso* (Naples: Bibliopolis, 1983), 88–107.

38. Louise Mirrer describes widows as "an ambiguous human sign." Mirrer, *Upon My Husband's Death*.

39. On "concupiscibile" in the *Decameron*, see Quondam, "Le cose (e le parole) del mondo," in Giovanni Boccaccio, *Decameron*, ed. Amedeo Quondam, Maurizio Fiorilla, and Giancarlo Alfano (Milan: BUR Rizzoli, 2013), 1669–1815.

40. David Wallace, *Giovanni Boccaccio, Decameron* (Cambridge: Cambridge University Press, 1991), 53.

41. Multiple scholars have pointed to Tancredi's reaction, much like that of a jilted lover, as the most concerning part of the tale. See Wallace, *Giovanni Boccaccio*, 54–55, for a discussion.

42. This also calls to mind Trecento mourning practices, in which women were encouraged to grieve at home rather than in the streets, where they might instigate a vendetta or violence. See Strocchia, *Death and Ritual in Renaissance Florence*, esp. 10–13.

43. Carla Bozzolo, "Il 'Decameron' come fonte del 'Livre de la cité des dames' di Christine de Pisan," in *Miscellanea di studi e ricerche sul Quattrocento francese*, ed. Simone Franco (Turin: Giappichelli, 1967), 4.

44. See Patricia Phillippy, "Establishing Authority: Boccaccio's *De Claris Mulieribus* and Christine de Pizan's *Le Livre de La Cité des Dames*," *Romanic Review* 77, no. 3 (1986): 167–194, 168, 174.

45. See Marcus, "Misogyny as Misreading," 28–29, on Rinieri's Parisian education.

46. Dante refers to his widowed canzone "Li occhi dolenti" as "questa cattivella canzone" in *Vita nuova*. Barolini points out that Rinieri is also described as "cattivello" when "his love turns to hate." Barolini, "Scholar and the Widow," 167.

47. Barolini, "Scholar and the Widow," 154.

48. Justin Steinberg has recently argued that the scholar views his punishment of Elena as on behalf of the "entire republic of scholars" and is thus a form of "sovereign justice," or an excessive level of punishment like that meted out to the schismatics in *Inferno* 28. Steinberg, *Law and Mimesis in Boccaccio's* Decameron: *Realism on Trial* (Cambridge: Cambridge University Press, 2023), 88.

49. Barolini points to the fact that Elena represents a "relatively new social construct: the widow whose money and agency are also connected to an urban rather than a feudal setting." Barolini, "Scholar and the Widow," 164.

50. Psaki, "Women Make All Things Lose Their Power," 113–114.

51. Barolini, "Scholar and the Widow," 159, 189. "Like Boccaccio himself," she suggests, "and like the great poets with whom Boccaccio identifies in the Introduction to Day Four, a learned man must remain in touch with *umanità* and *compassione*." Indeed, Barolini points to the possibility that this convincing perspective on the tale has perhaps been unexplored due to the tendency of critics to "identif[y] with the scholar." Barolini, "Scholar and the Widow," 152n11.

52. For the scholarly debate over the date of the work's composition, see Robert Hollander, *Boccaccio's Last Fiction: "Il Corbaccio"* (Philadelphia: University of Pennsylvania Press, 1998), 5.

53. Marcus, "Misogyny as Misreading," 38.

54. Marilyn Migiel, *A Rhetoric of the Decameron* (Toronto: University of Toronto Press, 2003), 177.

55. Hollander, *Boccaccio's Last Fiction*, 68. In a suggestive reading, Michaela Paasche Grudin returns to the association between allegorical widowhood and the Avignon Papacy, which I discussed in the previous chapter, but inverts the standard model: in the *Corbaccio*, she suggests, the widow represents not the city of Rome, abandoned and disconsolate, but the papal curia. M. P. Grudin, "Making War on the Widow: Boccaccio's *Il Corbaccio* and Florentine Liberty," *Viator* 38, no. 2 (2007): 127–158.

56. Sara E. Díaz, "Authority and Misogamy in Boccaccio's *Trattatello in laude di Dante*," in Holmes and Stewart, *Reconsidering Boccaccio*, 164–188, 175.

57. Hollander observes that the *Corbaccio*'s "evident and frequent recourse to the texts of Dante serves to underline its difference from rather than its dependence upon the moral strategies of the Dantean original." Hollander, *Boccaccio's Last Fiction*, 2.

58. Giovanni Boccaccio, *Il corbaccio*, ed. P. G. Ricci (Turin: Einaudi, 1977). All translations my own.

59. This particular deception brings to mind the misogynist diatribe of Giannozzo in Leon Battista Alberti's *I libri della famiglia*, in which he proudly recounts how he instructed his young wife to avoid the use of all makeup. See Carla Freccero, "Talking Commodities: Woman in a Renaissance Text," *Rethinking Marxism* 3, no. 4 (September 1990): 238–250.

60. Boccaccio, *Il corbaccio*, 64.

61. See Strocchia, *Death and Ritual in Renaissance Florence*, 149.

62. Boccaccio, *Il corbaccio*, 65.

63. Isabelle Chabot, "Lineage Strategies and the Control of Widows in Renaissance Florence," in Cavallo and Warner, *Widowhood in Medieval and Modern Europe*, 127–144, 130.

64. Calvi, "Widows, the State, and the Guardianship of Children," 209.

65. Her desire to live in a "casetta, vedova, e sola" is also an interesting precursor to the sixteenth-century widow Vittoria Trissino Frattina, who insisted that her family build her a small cell or *celletta* in their courtyard in which for her to live and pray alone, as a Dominican tertiary. See Adriana Chemello, "Oltre il recinto," in *Oltrecanone: Per una cartografia della scrittura femminile*, ed. Annamaria Crispino (Rome: Manifestolibri, 2003), 34–50.

66. Clark Walter, *Profession of Widowhood*, 334.

67. Boccaccio, *Il corbaccio*, 83.

Chapter 3 Sacred Role Models from Judith and Anna to Birgitta of Sweden

1. For Turina's bibliography, see Francesca Turrini Bufalini, *Rime spirituali sopra i misteri del santissimo rosario*, in *Letteratura italiana antica* 6, ed. Paolo Bà (2005), 153–220, and Francesca Turini Bufalini, *Autobiographical Poems: A Bilingual Edition*, ed. Natalia Costa-Zalessow, trans. Joan E. Borrelli with Natalia Costa-Zalessow (New York: Bordighera Press, 2009). Turina is styled variously as Francesca Turina, Francesca Turini Bufalini, and Francesca Turrini Bufalini; I use "Turina" to refer to her throughout this study.

2. Francesca Turrini Bufalini, *Le Rime* (1628), in Bà, *Letteratura italiana antica* 11 (2010), 149.

3. Turrini Bufalini, *Le Rime*, 257. Translation my own.

4. Francesca Canepuccia, "How to Become a Prophetess: Strategies for Authorizing a Prophetic Mission in the Works of Francesca Romana" (PhD diss., University of Oslo, 2022).

5. On women visionaries and authorship, see esp. Barbara Newman, "What Did It Mean to Say 'I Saw'? The Clash between Theory and Practice in Medieval Visionary Culture," *Speculum* 80, no. 1 (2005): 1–43, and Dyan Elliott, *Proving Woman: Female Spirituality and Inquisitional Culture in the Later Middle Ages* (Princeton, NJ: Princeton University Press, 2004).

6. Elena Ciletti, "Patriarchal Ideology in the Renaissance Iconography of Judith," in Migiel and Schiesari, *Refiguring Women*, 38.

7. See Ciletti, "Patriarchal Ideology," 35–70.

8. Elena Ciletti and Henrike Lähnemann, "Judith in the Christian Tradition," in *The Sword of Judith: Judith Studies across the Disciplines*, ed. Kevin R. Brine, Elena Ciletti, and Henrike Lähnemann (Cambridge: Open Book, 2010), 41–65, 44–45.

9. See Carey A. Moore, *Judith: A New Translation with Introduction and Commentary* (New York: Doubleday, 1985), 38–49.

10. Ciletti, "Patriarchal Ideology," 42.

11. On the influence of Judith outside of Italy, see Brine, Ciletti, and Lähnemann, *Sword of Judith*.

12. Ciletti and Lähnemann, "Judith in the Christian Tradition," 28. See also David Marsh, "Judith in Baroque Oratorio," in Brine, Ciletti, and Lähnemann, *Sword of Judith*, 385–396.

13. In her poem praising Joan of Arc, Christine de Pizan compares the French heroine to the biblical widow. Benjamin Cornford, "Christine de Pizan's *Ditie de Jehanne d'Arc*: Poetry and Propaganda at the Court of Charles VII," *Parergon* 17, no. 2 (2000): 75–106.

14. For an analysis of Judith in Florentine art, see Roger J. Crum, "Judith between the Private and Public Realms in Renaissance Florence," in Brine, Ciletti, and Lähnemann, *Sword of Judith*, 291–306, esp. 293–294.

15. Levy, *Re-membering Masculinity*, 67.

16. Sarah Blake McHam, "Donatello's Bronze *David* and *Judith* as Metaphors of Medici Rule in Florence," *Art Bulletin* 83, no. 1 (2001): 32–47, 32.

17. The inscription reads, "Regna cadunt luxu surgent virtutibus urbes caesa vides humili colla superba manu" (Kingdoms fall through luxury, cities rise through virtues; behold the neck of pride severed by the hand of humility); see Roger J. Crum, "Severing the Neck of Pride: Donatello's Judith and Holofernes and the Recollection of Albizzi Shame in Medicean Florence," *Artibus et Historiae* 22 (2001): 23–29.

18. Mary D. Garrard, *Artemisia Gentileschi and Feminism in Early Modern Europe* (Chicago: University of Chicago Press, 2020), 133, 136–137.

19. Levy, *Re-membering Masculinity*, 67.

20. Garrard, *Artemisia Gentileschi and Feminism*, 137.

21. The full text of Tornabuoni's Judith narrative as well as an excellent translation can be found in Jane Tylus, *Sacred Narratives: Lucrezia Tornabuoni de' Medici* (Chicago: University of Chicago Press, 2001), 118–162. Tylus points out that Luigi Pulci uses the same "vedovetta" to refer to Judith in his 1478 epic *Morgante* (a work dedicated to Tornabuoni) and that the word "perhaps takes away from the virile act Judith will go on to perform" (120).

22. Judith herself is less of a presence in this Florentine retelling of her story than in other versions, and Tylus argues that Tornabuoni's poem "can be said to speak more about the pride and reckless ambition of kings than about the faithfulness of a Hebrew woman." Tylus, *Sacred Narratives*, 121.

23. Gerry Milligan, "Unlikely Heroines in Lucrezia Tornabuoni's 'Judith' and 'Esther,'" *Italica* 88, no. 4 (2011): 538–564, 542.

24. Tornabuoni, *Lettere*, 2:81. All translations my own.

25. Tornabuoni, *Lettere*, 2:87.

26. Tornabuoni, *Lettere*, 2:149.

27. Tornabuoni, *Lettere*, 2:147.

28. On Tornabuoni's patronage and influence in Florence before and after her husband's death, see especially K.J.P. Lowe, "A Matter of Piety or of Family Tradition and Custom? The Religious Patronage of Piero de' Medici and Lucrezia Tornabuoni," in *Piero de' Medici "il Gottoso" (1416–1469): Kunst im Dienste der Mediceer*, ed. Andreas Beyer and Bruce Boucher (Berlin: Akademie Verlag, 1993), 55–69, and Natalie Tomas, *The Medici Women: Gender and Power in Renaissance Florence* (Aldershot: Ashgate, 2003).

29. See Garrard, *Artemisia Gentileschi and Feminism*, 127.

30. Sarah Harris, "Letting (H)Anna Speak: An Intertextual Reading of the New Testament Prophetess (Luke 2.36–38)," *Feminist Theology* 27, no. 1 (September 2018): 60–74, 63.

31. Clark Walter, *Profession of Widowhood*, 171.

32. Simeon's praise is known as the *Nunc dimittis*, from the opening line "Nunc dimittis servum tuum, Domine," or "Now thou dost dismiss thy servant, O Lord" (Luke 2:29).

33. See esp. Andrés García Serrano, "Anna's Characterization in Luke 2:36–38: A Case of Conceptual Allusion?," *Catholic Biblical Quarterly* 76, no. 3 (2014): 464–480, and Harris, "Letting (H)anna Speak."

34. Serrano, "Anna's Characterization in Luke 2:36–38," 472.

35. Harris, "Letting (H)anna Speak," 63.

36. Letter LIV in Jerome, *Sacred Writings*, 16.

37. San Bernardino da Siena, *Le prediche volgari inedite. Firenze 1424, 1425-Siena 1425*, ed. P. Dionizio Pacetti (Siena: Catagalli, 2012), 249–250. Translation my own.

38. Girolamo Savonarola, *Book of the Life of the Widow*, in *Guide to Righteous Living*, 211–212.

39. *La vedove svecese* is a 1648 biography of Birgitta of Sweden by Girolamo Alle. Girolamo Alle, *La vedova svecese cioe' la vita di santa Brigida* (Bologna: Carlo Zenero, 1648).

40. See Falkeid, *Avignon Papacy Contested*, esp. 121–145, on Birgitta's contributions to the debate on the Avignon Papacy.

41. On Birgitta's role in the broader debate over the Avignon Papacy, see esp. Falkeid, *Avignon Papacy Contested*, and Claire Sahlin, *Birgitta of Sweden and the Voice of Prophecy* (Woodbridge: Boydell & Brewer, 2001). On her political philosophy, see Falkeid, "The Political Discourse of Birgitta of Sweden," in *A Companion to Birgitta of Sweden and Her Legacy in the Later Middle Ages*, ed. Maria Oen (Leiden: Brill, 2019), 80–102.

42. Renate Blumenfeld-Kosinski, *Poets, Saints, and Visionaries of the Great Schism, 1378–1417* (University Park: Pennsylvania State University Press, 2004), 7.

43. See esp. Ben-Aryeh Debby, "Reshaping Birgitta of Sweden in Tuscan Art and Sermons," in Oen, *Companion to Birgitta of Sweden*, 223–246.

44. See Thomas Luongo, "God's Words, or Birgitta's? Birgitta of Sweden as Author," in Oen, *Companion to Birgitta of Sweden*, 25–52.

45. On Birgitta's family pedigree, see esp. Sahlin, *Birgitta of Sweden*, 14.

46. On the disputed dates of Ulf's death, see Marguerite T. Harris and Albert Tyle Kezel, *Birgitta of Sweden: Life and Selected Writings* (New York: Paulist Press, 1989), 77n32.

47. Harris and Kezel, *Birgitta of Sweden*, 77–78.

48. See Maria H. Oen, "Birgitta Birgersdotter and the *Liber celestis revelacionum*," in Oen, *Companion to Birgitta of Sweden*, 1–24.

49. Sahlin, *Birgitta of Sweden*, 17.

50. "Go to Rome, where the streets are paved with gold and reddened with the blood of saints . . . you shall stay there in Rome until you see the supreme pontiff and the emperor there at the same time in Rome, and to them you shall announce my words." Harris and Kezel, *Birgitta of Sweden*, 92.

51. Birgitta had received a vision when still living in Sweden that she would die in "a glorious place, in Rome." See Harris and Kezel, *Birgitta of Sweden*, 84.

52. See esp. Anna Fredriksson, "Challenging and Championing St. Birgitta's *Revelations* at the Councils of Constance and Basel," in Oen, *Companion to Birgitta of Sweden*, 103–131.

53. See Brian Richardson, "Birgitta and Pseudo-Birgitta: Textual Circulation and Perceptions of the Saint," in Falkeid and Wainwright, *Legacy of Birgitta of Sweden*, 35–55.

54. See Falkeid, *Avignon Papacy Contested*, esp. 130–133.

55. *Revelations* IV.78, in Birgitta of Sweden, *The Revelations of St Birgitta of Sweden*, ed. Bridget Morris, trans. Denis Searby (Oxford: Oxford University Press, 2008), 2:149.

56. *Revelations* IV.78, in Birgitta of Sweden, *Revelations*, 2:150.

57. Falkeid, *Avignon Papacy Contested*, 133.

58. Roger H. Ellis, "The Swedish Woman, the Widow, the Pilgrim and the Prophetess: Images of St. Bridget in the Canonization Sermon to Pope Boniface IX," in *Santa Brigida, profeta dei tempi nuovi* (Rome: Libreria Editrice Vaticana, 1993), 93–150.

59. See esp. Ellis, "Swedish Woman."

60. Alphonso of Jaen, "The Hermit's Letter to Kings," in Birgitta of Sweden, *Revelations*, 4:17.

61. See Fredriksson, "Challenging and Championing."

62. Alphonso of Jaen, "Hermit's Letter to Kings," 16.

63. Birgitta of Sweden, *Revelations* II.18 in Birgitta of Sweden, *Revelations*, 1:221.

64. Birgitta of Sweden, *Revelations* II.18, 1:221.

65. See, for example, Catherine of Siena's letter CCXXXIII to Pope Gregory XI, in which she is "la vostra indegna e miserabile figlioula" (your unworthy and wretched daughter).

66. As I discuss in chapter 4, Vittoria Colonna also compares herself to a phoenix in one of her most complex widowhood poems, the canzone "Mentre la nave mia," in which she shuffles through a variety of classical role models before deciding that she is role model enough herself. See esp. Virginia Cox, "The Exemplary Vittoria Colonna," in Brundin, Crivelli, and Sapegno, *Companion to Vittoria Colonna*, 467–501; see also Unn Falkeid, "'The Most Illustrious and Divine of All the Sibyls': Saint Birgitta in the Prophetic Visions of Tommaso Campanella and Queen Cristina of Sweden," in Falkeid and Wainwright, *Legacy of Birgitta of Sweden*, 277–307.

67. See Sahlin, *Birgitta of Sweden*; Maria H. Oen and Unn Falkeid, eds., *Sanctity and Female Authorship: Birgitta of Sweden and Catherine of Siena* (New York: Routledge, 2019), and Falkeid and Wainwright, *Legacy of Birgitta of Sweden*.

68. Birgitta of Sweden, Extravagantes 56, in Birgitta of Sweden, *Revelations*, 4:276.

69. Birgitta of Sweden, Extravagantes 56, 4:276.

70. Birgitta of Sweden, Extravagantes 56, 4:276.

71. Clark Walter, "Purgatory," 169.

72. See Le Goff, *Birth of Purgatory*, 25.

73. *Revelations* IV.60, in Birgitta of Sweden, *Revelations*, 2:40.

74. *Revelations* IV.61, in Birgitta of Sweden, *Revelations*, 2:40.

75. *Revelations* VII.14, in Birgitta of Sweden, *Revelations*, 3:32.

76. *Revelations* VII.14, 3:32.

77. From Enrico Garavelli's introduction to Lodovico Domenichi, *Vita di santa Brigida e santa Caterina di Svezia*, ed. Enrico Garavelli (Manziana: Vecchiarelli, 2016).

78. For analysis of Birgitta's influence on Francesca, see Alessandra Bartolomei Romagnoli, "Brigida di Svezia e la reinvenzione della Storia Sacra: il cammino la terra la visione," in *Predicatori, mercanti, pellegrini. L'Occidente medievale e lo sguardo letterario sull'Altro tra l'Europa e il Levante*, ed. Giuseppe Mascherpa and Giovanni Strinna (Mantua: Universitas Studiorum, 2018), 189–217, and Canepuccia, "How to Become a Prophetess."

79. Translation from Romanesco in *Santa Francesca Romana. Edizione critica dei trattati latini di Giovanni Mattiotti*, ed. Alessandra Bartolomei Romagnoli (Vatican City: Libreria Editrice Vaticana, 1994).

80. Arnold Esch, *Tre sante ed il loro ambiente sociale a Roma: S. Francesca romana, S. Brigida di Svezia e S. Caterina da Siena* (Rome: Roma nel Rinscimento, 2001).

81. On Cybo, see esp. Robin, *Publishing Women*, 100–104.

82. Clara Stella, "A Lineage of Apocalyptic Queens: The Portrayal of Birgitta of Sweden in Domenica Narducci's Sermon to Caterina Cibo (1533)," in Falkeid and Wainwright, *Legacy of Birgitta of Sweden*, 107–128, 126.

83. Domenica Narducci, *I sermoni di Domenica da Paradiso. Studi e testo critico*, ed. Rita Librandi and Adriana Valerio (Florence: Sismel, 1999), 128.

84. Narducci, *I sermoni di Domenica da Paradiso*, 129.

85. See Stella, "Lineage of Apocalyptic Queens," 116; Domenica Narducci, *Domenica da Paradiso. Scritti spirituali*, 2 vols., ed. Gerardo Antignani (Poggibonsi: Edizioni Tipolito Arti Grafiche Nencini, 1984–1985), 1:91–254; and Adriana Valerio, "Le lettere di Domenica da Paradiso tra Bibbia e Profezia," *Hagiographica* 6 (1999): 235–256, 237, Letter XXIV.

86. Narducci, *I sermoni di Domenica da Paradiso*, 138.

87. Narducci, *I sermoni di Domenica da Paradiso*, 138–139.

88. Robin, *Publishing Women*, 245, and Ramie Targoff, *Renaissance Woman: The Life of Vittoria Colonna* (New York: Farrar, Straus & Giroux, 2018), 121–122.

89. Robin, *Publishing Women*, 245.

90. On Birgitta's potential influence on Colonna, see Unn Falkeid, "'*Magistra apostolorum*.' The Virgin Mary in Birgitta of Sweden and Vittoria Colonna," in Cox and McHugh, *Vittoria Colonna: Poetry, Religion, Art, Impact*, 75–94.

91. Pier Mattei Paluzzi, *Vita della Beata Ludovica Albertoni* (Rome: Corvo, 1672), 152.

92. Rome's population is estimated to have been cut in half during the year of the Sack. Judith Hook, *The Sack of Rome: 1527*, 2nd ed. (New York: Palgrave Macmillan, 2004), 177–180.

93. Paluzzi, *Vita*, 154–155.

94. Paluzzi, *Vita*, 155.

95. A mass at the chapel celebrating the event was attended by numerous local and foreign luminaries, including the expatriate Queen Christina of Sweden. The sculpture was completed by Bernini in his old age and is considered one of his finest pieces; scholars tend to believe that at a time when he was relegating much of the physical labor of his art to his apprentices, his hand played a prominent role in the completion of the statue. See esp.

Shelley Karen Perlove, *Bernini and the Idealization of Death: The Blessed Ludovica Albertoni and the Altieri Chapel* (University Park: Pennsylvania State University Press, 1995).

96. See Falkeid and Wainwright, "Introduction," in Falkeid and Wainwright, *Legacy of Birgitta of Sweden*, 1–33.

97. On *pinzochere*, see Anna Benvenuti Papi, "Mendicant Friars and Female 'pinzochere' in Tuscany: From Social Marginality to Models of Sanctity," in *Women and Religion in Medieval and Renaissance Italy*, ed. Daniel Bornstein and Roberto Rusconi, trans. Margery J. Schneider (Chicago: University of Chicago Press, 1996), 85–106.

98. Paluzzi, *Vita*, 147.

99. See Anna Esposito, "St. Francesca and the Female Religious Communities of Fifteenth-Century Rome," in Bornstein and Rusconi, *Women and Religion in Medieval and Renaissance Italy*, 197–218.

100. See Simon Ditchfield, "Thinking with Saints: Sanctity and Society in the Early Modern World," *Critical Inquiry* 35, no. 3 (2009): 552–584.

101. Falkeid and Wainwright, "Introduction."

Chapter 4 Dido, Death, and Exemplarity

1. See Gerry Milligan, "The Politics of Effeminacy in 'Il Cortegiano,'" *Italica* 83, no. 3/4 (2006): 345–366 and "Masculinity and Machiavelli," in *Seeking Real Truths: Multidisciplinary Perspectives on Machiavelli*, ed. Patricia Vilches and Gerald Seaman (Leiden: Brill, 2007), 149–172.

2. On Colonna as "ur-widow," see esp. Virginia Cox, "The Exemplary Vittoria Colonna," in Brundin, Crivelli, and Sapegno, *Companion to Vittoria Colonna*, 467–502.

3. Cicero, *Tusculanae Disputationes*, book III, section XXXI, paragraph 75.

4. Christine de Pizan, *Le livre de la cité des dames*, ed. and trans. Éric Hicks and Thérèse Moreau (Paris: Stock/Moyen Âge, 1986), 151.

5. Caria was also home to the fountain Salmacis, featured in Ovid's *Metamorphoses*, which was rumored to make anyone who drank from its waters effeminate, as well as the name of the nymph who resided there and whose prayer to the gods allowed her to become one with Hermaphroditus. Ovid, *Metamorphoses* IV, trans. Rolfe Humphries (Bloomington: Indiana University Press, 1960), esp. ll. 284–287. See also Luc Brisson, *Sexual Ambivalence: Androgyny and Hermaphroditism in Graeco-Roman Antiquity* (Berkeley: University of California Press, 2002), 51–54.

6. Giovanni Boccaccio, *De claris mulieribus*, trans. Virginia Brown (Cambridge, MA: Harvard University Press, 2003), 233; de Pizan, *Cité des dames*, 84.

7. Ludovico Ariosto, *Orlando furioso*, ed. Lanfranco Caretti (Turin: Einaudi, 1992), 37.8.

8. On the possibility that the Sebastiano portrait is of Colonna as Artemisia, see Monica Bianco, "Per la datazione di un sonetto di Vittoria Colonna (e di un probabile ritratto della poetessa ad opera di Sebastiano del Piombo," *Italique* 11 (2008): 92–107, and Cox, "Exemplary Vittoria Colonna."

9. See Sheila ffolliott, "Catherine de' Medici as Artemisia: Figuring the Powerful Widow," in *Rewriting the Renaissance: The Discourses of Sexual Difference in Early Modern Europe*, ed. Margaret Ferguson, Maureen Quilligan, and Nancy Vickers (Chicago: University of Chicago

Press, 1986), 241. On Catherine de' Medici's influence on Italian literature during her regency, see Gerry Milligan, *Moral Combat: Women, Gender, and War in Italian Renaissance Literature* (Toronto: University of Toronto Press, 2018), 198.

10. On female biography, see Kolsky, *Ghost of Boccaccio*, and Valerie Hoagland, "Unstable Exemplarity: The Politics of Female Biography in Early Modern Italy" (PhD diss., New York University, 2016).

11. See esp. Ditchfield, "Thinking with Saints," 579.

12. Timothy Hampton, *Writing from History: The Rhetoric of Exemplarity in Renaissance Literature* (Ithaca, NY: Cornell University Press, 1990), 3.

13. Kay, "Didactic Space," 440.

14. Cox, "Exemplary Vittoria Colonna," 471.

15. For a review of the scholarship on the social history of Italian widowhood, see the introduction to this book.

16. The Penelope story is deftly adapted by Giambattista Cini in his 1569 comedy *La vedova*, which was performed at the Palazzo Vecchio in Florence when Archduke Carl of Austria visited Cosimo I. See Allison Levy's important analysis of the play and the stage set in the broader context of widowhood in sixteenth-century Florence in *Re-membering Masculinity*, 59–93.

17. See my discussion, for example, of the Widow of Ephesus in chapter 2.

18. On the widespread popularity of the volume in the Renaissance, see Cox, *Women's Writing in Italy*, 636.

19. See Cox, *Women's Writing in Italy*, 25–26, and Hoagland, "Unstable Exemplarity," 117–118.

20. Cox, *Women's Writing in Italy*, 26.

21. For a precious, cross-referenced list of the women who appear in numerous female biographies from Boccaccio to Betussi, see the appendices to Hoagland, "Unstable Exemplarity," 264–301.

22. Desmond, *Reading Dido*; James Simpson, "Subjects of Triumph and Literary History: Dido and Petrarch in Petrarch's *Africa* and *Trionfi*," *Journal of Medieval and Early Modern Studies* 35, no. 3 (2005): 489–508; Barolini, "Errancy," and "Dante and Francesca Da Rimini: Realpolitik, Romance, Gender," *Speculum* 75, no. 1 (2000): 1–28; and John Watkins, *The Specter of Dido: Spenser and Virgilian Epic* (New Haven, CT: Yale University Press, 1995).

23. The oldest account is in Timaeus of Tauromenium, the fullest account in Justin. See Desmond, *Reading Dido*, 23–73.

24. Desmond, *Reading Dido*, 78. Desmond has pointed out that Augustine's interpretation of the *Aeneid* in *City of God* erases Dido completely. On the question of Dido's ethnicity, see esp. Joyce Green MacDonald, *Women and Race in Early Modern Texts* (Cambridge: Cambridge University Press, 2002), 69–72.

25. In the sixteenth century, Dido tragedy plays mostly adhering to the Virgilian version of her story were popular. Mary E. Smith has shown, however, that sixteenth-century Italian playwrights including Pazzi, Giraldi-Cinthio, and Dolce all combined elements of the two versions of the Dido story in their tragedies, a move later adopted by Christopher Marlowe in his English-language version. Smith, "Marlowe and Italian Dido Drama," *Italica* 53, no. 2 (1976): 223–235.

26. See Simpson, "Subjects of Triumph and Literary History," 492.

27. "Ut quai studio castitatis ac servandae viduitatis extinctam sciret." Translation from Desmond, *Reading Dido*, 23.

28. Boccaccio, *De claris mulieribus*, 174–175: "Adveniente Enea troiano numquam viso, mori potius quam infringendam fore castimoniam rate."

29. "Dido quorum subsidio confidebat, cui exuli frater unicus erat hostis? Nonne et Didoni procatores fuere plurimi? Imo, et ipsa Dido eratne saxea aut lignea magis quam hodierne sint? Non equidem. Ergo mente saltem valens, cuius non arbitrabatur posse viribus evitare illecebras, moriens, ea via qua potuit evitavit." Boccaccio, *De claris mulieribus*, 177.

30. Remarkably, this suggests that it is better for Christian widows to kill themselves than to marry again: remarriage is *worse* than the grievous sin of suicide. Boccaccio calls it "wicked" that Paul's advice—that it is better to remarry than to burn with desire—be used for such ill purposes: "nec putetnt, dum lacrimas dederint et pullas assumpserint vestes, defuncto peregisse omnia. In finem usque servandus est amor, si adimplere velint viduitatis officium" (Let [widows] not think that by mourning and dressing in black they have executed all the duties owed to the dead. Love must be maintained to the end if they want to fulfill the obligations of widowhood). Boccaccio, *De claris mulieribus*, 181.

31. Triumph of Chastity, ll. 10–12, in Francesco Petrarca, *Trionfi, Rime Estravaganti, Codice degli Abbozzi*, ed. Vinicio Pacca and Laura Paolino (Milan: Mondadori, 1996). All translations my own except otherwise noted. Further citations appear parenthetically.

32. It also recalls the "popol tutto" of *RVF*'s proemial sonnet, "Voi ch'ascoltate"; Petrarch has a long-standing prejudice against what we might term "groupthink."

33. Dennis Dutschke, "Petrarch's Triumphal and Cheerful ('Allegra') Judith (Triumphys Cupidinis III, 52–57)," *Nuova Rivista Di Letteratura Italiana* 1, no. 1 (1998): 41.

34. Eugenio Refini, "Con Bel Parlar. Il Fascino Ambiguo di Giuditta Figura Eloquentiae tra Petrarca e Possevino," in *Le donne della Bibbia. La Bibbia delle donne. Teatro, letteratura e vita, Atti del XV Convegno Internazionale di Studio*, ed. Camos Gorris Rosanna (Fasano: Schena Editore, 2012), 279.

35. Refini, "Con Bel Parlar," 276.

36. I translate "onestate" here as "loyalty and honor." In Petrarch, and in the Capasso poem to follow, we see "honestate" as a virtue tied to a widow's chastity and loyalty to her husband's memory.

37. Desmond, *Reading Dido*, 200.

38. Desmond, *Reading Dido*, 216. For Kevin Brownlee, Christine "may be seen as a Dido made good in the literary sphere—a Dido, that is, who becomes not a traffic victim of erotic passion on the stage of political history, but rather, a female Virgil, a poet who recounts *historia*." Brownlee, "The Image of History in Christine de Pizan's *Livre de la Mutacion de Fortune*," in "Contexts: Style and Values in Medieval Art and Literature," special issue, *Yale French Studies* (1991): 50.

39. Desmond, *Reading Dido*, 31.

40. Desmond, *Reading Dido*, 196.

41. For the medieval and Renaissance humanist schoolboys soaked in Virgil and in exempla, Desmond argued, "Dido—in her colonized and gendered identity—figure[d] difference writ large." *Reading Dido*, 7.

42. Virgil, *The Aeneid of Virgil*, trans. Allen Mandelbaum (New York: Bantam Books, 1971), 82. As Kevin Brownlee has noted, Christine de Pizan includes a similar Dido-esque declaration in *La vision*: "n'oubliant ma foy et bonne amour promise a lui, deliberay en sain propos de jamaiz autre n'avoir" (III.6) (mindful of my vow and the good love promised him, I decided in a sound deliberation never to take another [husband]; 111). Brownlee, "Widowhood, Sexuality, and Gender," 343.

43. Molly Martin deftly analyzes Gambara's choice of the passage from the *Aeneid* in "Veronica Gambara: Widowhood, Poetry, and Power in Italian Renaissance Court Culture" (PhD diss., New York University, 2007), 39–43.

44. Cox, *Women's Writing in Italy*, 67–68.

45. Molly M. Martin, "Critical Introduction," in *Veronica Gambara, Complete Poems: A Bilingual Edition*, ed. and trans. Paola Ugolini and Molly M. Martin (Toronto: Iter, 2014), 11.

46. See Melissa Swain, "Spousal Sovereignty: The Ruling Couple and Its Representations in Quattrocento Italy, with Special Reference to Federico de Montefeltro (1422–1482) and Battista Sforza (c. 1446–1472)" (PhD diss., New York University, 2016), for a comprehensive discussion of the massive grief project undertaken by Federico da Montefeltro, Colonna's maternal grandfather, when Battista died.

47. On Colonna's involvement in the Salt Wars, see esp. Robin, *Publishing Women*, 42–79, and Targoff, *Renaissance Woman*, 208–225.

48. Cox, *Women's Writing in Italy*, 68.

49. Jessica Goethals, "Representing the Sack of Rome and Its Aftermath: 1527–1540" (PhD diss., New York University, 2012), 31–32.

50. Carlo Dionisotti, *Scritti sul Bembo*, ed. Claudio Vela (Turin: Einaudi, 2002), 117–122.

51. See Cox, *Women's Writing in Italy*, 66, and Goethals, "Representing the Sack of Rome," 342.

52. Cox points to "how large a place within the poetic cult of Colonna . . . was given to her exemplary stoicism in the face of adverse fortune, emblematized by her device of a rock at sea standing firm against the ferocious battering of the waves." *Women's Writing in Italy*, 63.

53. See Cox, "Exemplary Vittoria Colonna," 467–470, on Colonna in female biography in her own lifetime and after.

54. Giuseppe Betussi, *Libro di messer Gio. Boccaccio delle donne illustri, tradotto per m[esser] Giuseppe Betussi, con una additione fatta dal medesimo delle donne famose dal tempo di m[esser] Giovanni fino a i giorni nostri e alcune altre state per inanzi* (Venice: Comin di Trino di Monferrato, 1545), 214r.

55. Lodovico Dolce, *Dialogo della institutione delle donne* (Venice: Giolito de Ferrari, 1547), 168–169.

56. Dolce, *Dialogo*, 178.

57. Martin, "Critical Introduction," 18.

58. Ginevra was Vittoria Colonna's great-aunt through Colonna's mother, Agnese di Montefeltro. Arienti also authored *Trattato della pudicizia* (1487), a text written shortly after his own wife's death in defense of his sister-in-law Smiralda Argenteo, a recent widow, and her right to remarry. Arienti's defense of his sister-in-law's right to remarry can be viewed

within this larger political argument for "chaste" or "moral" remarriage. On this, see Kolsky, *Ghost of Boccaccio*, 69–80.

59. "Ma voi, illustrissima regina, che così accerba giovinetta in mezo al regno di Venere, circondata da tante delitie regali, fragile per il sesso feminile, vedovella all'hora all'hora lasciata ch'assai più lode porta alla continentia che se verginella fosse stata, poché non v'è alcuno di così sciocho parere che non dica che sia maggior laude astenersi dal piacer incominciato a gustare ch'il sprezzar il non gustato" (But you, most illustrious queen, who came of age in Venus's realm, surrounded by so many royal delights, and vulnerable to them due to your female sex, are now a widow, abandoned; and you bring much greater praise to the continent than if you had been a virgin, for there is no one so foolish as to say that it is not more virtuous to abstain from pleasure you have already tasted, than to scorn it untasted). Antonio Colbertaldo, *Storia di Caterina Corner regina di Cipro: La prima biografia*, ed. Daria Perocco (Padova: Libro, 2012), 151–152.

60. Colbertaldo, *Storia di Caterina Corner*, 151–152.

61. See Daria Perocco, "Caterina Cornaro: una corte, una regina e la creazione di un mito," *MLN* 129, no. 3 (2014): S35–S44.

62. See esp. Julia L. Hairston, "Skirting the Issue: Machiavelli's Caterina Sforza," *Renaissance Quarterly* 53, no. 3 (2000): 687–712.

63. Niccolò Machiavelli, *Discorsi sopra la prima Deca di Tito Livio*, ed. Mario Martelli (Florence: Sansoni, 1971), 289. On the complex origins of the story in the classical tradition, see esp. Hairston, "Skirting the Issue."

64. It is worth pointing out that after the events depicted here by Machiavelli, Sforza did bear another child, and one who would have a profound effect on the Italian Wars, the famed condottiere Giovanni delle Bande Nere (1498–1526). See John Freccero, "Medusa and the Madonna of Forlì: Political Sexuality in Machiavelli," in *In Dante's Wake*, ed. Danielle Callegari and Melissa Swain (New York: Fordham University Press, 2015), 118–130, and also Milligan, *Moral Combat*, 185.

65. See Milligan, *Moral Combat*, 179–180, and Christine Shaw and Michael Mallett, *The Italian Wars 1494–1559: War, State and Society in Early Modern Europe* (New York: Routledge, 2019), 19–20, on Caterina Sforza and the Italian Wars.

66. In Foresti's 1497 biography of Sforza, he praises "her wartime strategy during the invasion of Charles VIII in 1494, in which she made alliances with the Florentines, the pope, and King Ferdinand of Naples." Milligan, *Moral Combat*, 177–178.

67. Milligan, *Moral Combat*, 178.

68. "Muliebres lacrimas pro virili a se reiecit." Foresti describes her first as having been "totam noctes illam in lachrymis consumpsit" (consumed the whole night in tears), f. 160. Quoted in Milligan, *Moral Combat*, 276n67–68.

69. Joyce De Vries, "Casting Her Widowhood: Contemporary and Posthumous Portraits of Caterina Sforza," in Levy, *Widowhood and Visual Culture*, 93–108.

70. De Vries, "Casting Her Widowhood," 100.

71. "Franza e Spagna e Imperatore / m'àno tuta disolata!" "Lamento de' venetiani," in Antonio Medin and Ludovico Frati, eds., *Lamenti storici dei secoli XIV, XV, e XVI*, 3 vols. (Bologna: 1887–1894), 1:99. Quoted and translated in Goethals and Wainwright,

"Ventriloquizing Birgitta: The Saint's Prophetic Voice During the Italian Wars," in Falkeid and Wainwright, *Legacy of Birgitta of Sweden*, 164.

72. Milligan, *Moral Combat*, 181n79. Milligan notes that according to Pasolini, "the lament not only reflects the sentiments of Caterina found in her letters, it also reflects words that may have been uttered by her" (181n79).

73. Milligan, *Moral Combat*, 182.

74. Castiglione, papal nuncio to Charles V, published the dialogue only the year after the Sack of Rome and felt terrible guilt for not having foreseen or prevented the catastrophe itself. See esp. Goethals, "Representing the Sack of Rome," 82.

75. Letizia Panizza fully traces Camma's Renaissance fortunes in "Plutarch's Camma: A Greek Literary Heroine's Adventures in Renaissance Italy," in *Italy and the Classical Tradition: Language, Thought and Poetry 1300–1600*, ed. Carlo Caruso and Andrew Laird (London: Bloomsbury, 2013), 101–117.

76. Baldassare Castiglione, *Il cortegiano*, ed. Giulio Preti (Turin: Einaudi, 1965), 272. All translations my own.

77. Castiglione, *Il cortegiano*, 272.

78. Castiglione, *Il cortegiano*, 272. See Virginia Cox, "The Female Voice in Italian Renaissance Dialogue," *MLN* 128, no. 1 (2013): 53–78.

79. Castiglione, *Il cortegiano*, 1.

80. See esp. Diana Robin's comprehensive analysis of Costanza and her salon in *Publishing Women*, 1–78.

81. See Kenneth Gouwens, "Female Virtue and the Embodiment of Beauty: Vittoria Colonna in Paolo Giovio's Notable Men and Women," *Renaissance Quarterly* 68, no. 1 (2015): 33–97 and Jessica Goethals, "The Flowers of Italian Literature: Language, Imitation and Gender Debates in Paolo Giovio's Dialogus de Viris et Foeminis Aetate Nostra Florentibus," *Renaissance Studies* 29, no. 5 (2015): 749–771.

82. See Giosuè Capasso, "Triumphem Novem Viduarem," in *Le Farse; Il Trionfo; Il Lamento*, ed. Milena Montanile (Naples: Istituto nazionale di Studi sul Rinascimento meridionale, 1990), for a facsimile and transcription of the manuscript. Further citations appear parenthetically.

83. See Cristelle Louise Baskins, *Cassone Painting, Humanism, and Gender in Early Modern Italy* (Cambridge: Cambridge University Press, 1998).

84. De Vries, "Casting Her Widowhood," esp. 99–100.

85. The castle was taken over in 1494 from the Aragon family when Naples became an occupied city.

86. Jordan Lancaster, *In the Shadow of Vesuvius: A Cultural History of Naples* (London: I.B. Tauris, 2019), 25–27, and Francesco Torraca, *Studi di storia letteraria napoletana* (Naples: Vigo, 1884), 286.

87. He also labels them, strikingly, as a "concistoro," a term generally reserved for an ecclesiastic council of men; Dante describes the gods of Olympus as the "sommo consistoro" in *Purg.* IX, l. 24.

88. On the figure of Death represented visually as a woman, see Kristen Keach Muyo, "Boccaccio's Pisan Allegory of 'Death' in Petrarch's Triumphus Mortis," *California Italian Studies* 11, no. 1 (2022): 1–21.

89. All translations from Petrarch's *Triumphs* are my own.

90. She is also, it is worth noting, the catalyst for the extended conversation between Petrarch and Laura in the second *capitolo* of the Triumph of Death, an exchange in direct discourse much like the conversation between Dante and Beatrice within the poem "Li occhi dolenti."

91. For a discussion of Petrarch's letter, see chapter 1 in this book.

92. The term "consolatory icon" is from Cox, *Women's Writing in Italy*, 66, where she applies it specifically to Colonna.

93. Giovanna d'Aragona (1454–1517); Giovanna (1479–1518), widow of Ferdinando II/Ferrandino; Isabella d'Aragona (1470–1524), widow of Gian Galeazzo Sforza of Milan; Costanza d'Avalos (1460–1541), who ruled Ischia after the death of her husband Federico del Balzo (1455–1487, brother of Queen Isabella of Naples); Laura Sanseverino (married 1500; d. 1522), whose husband Innico II d'Avalos (1467–1503), Costanza's brother, was later praised by Ariosto in Canto 33 of *Orlando furioso* for his protection of Ischia; Ippolita d'Aragona (ca. 1468–after 1529); Beatrice Sanseverino (b. 1486), married to Roberto Orsini, count of Pacentro (1481–1502); Barbara Gonzaga (ca. 1482–1558); and Vittoria Cantelmo, countess of Terranova, widow of Galeotto Carafa.

94. On Costanza's escapades, see Robin, *Publishing Women*, 7–8.

95. On Medusa and Renaissance widows, see Freccero, "Medusa and the Madonna of Forlì."

96. On Campanile's *tempio* and the later *tempi* to Giovanna d'Aragona, see Robin, *Publishing Women*, 5, 102–123.

97. Transcription and translation in Virginia Cox, *Lyric Poetry by Women of the Italian Renaissance* (Baltimore: Johns Hopkins University Press, 2013), 141–144.

98. Cox, "Exemplary Vittoria Colonna," 501.

99. See Cox, *Lyric Poetry*, 141–144.

100. On Colonna's time at San Silvestro, see esp. Targoff, *Renaissance Woman*, 44–57.

101. Cox, *Lyric Poetry*, 273–274.

102. Martin, "Critical Introduction," 25–27.

103. On Terracina's publication history, see Amelia Papworth, "Pressure to Publish: Laura Terracina and Her Editors," *Early Modern Women* 12, no. 1 (2017): 3–24.

104. See Cox, *Women's Writing in Italy*, 80–85.

105. Laura Terracina, *Settime rime sovra tutte le donne vedove di questa nostra citta di Napoli titolate et non titolate* (Napoli: Mattio Cancer, 1561), 4.

106. This of course also recalls Christine de Pizan's building of the allegorical City of Ladies, with each exemplary woman from history and legend constituting a building block for the city.

107. Terracina, *Settime rime*, 56v, ll. 5 and 7.

108. See Robin, *Publishing Women*, 3–5, 111.

109. Terracina, *Settime rime*, 59r, ll. 11–12.

Chapter 5 Widowed Verse

1. On elegy more broadly, see Matthew Greenfield, "The Cultural Functions of Renaissance Elegy," *English Literary Renaissance* 28, no. 1 (Winter 1998): 75–94.

2. A section of this chapter first appeared as "Outdoing Colonna: Widowhood Poetry in the Late Cinquecento," in Cox and McHugh, *Vittoria Colonna: Poetry, Religion, Art, Impact*, 95–113. See Sapegno, "La costruzione di un Io lirico," 17, and Crivelli, "Print Tradition," 122n24. A handful of male poets, especially inspired by Colonna, might be included in this category as well. See Shannon McHugh, *Petrarch and the Making of Gender in Renaissance Italy* (Amsterdam: Amsterdam University Press, 2023), 221–254.

3. On women poets doing similar work of reappropriating the voice of the female mourner in poetry, see Schiesari, *Gendering of Melancholia*, 160–190.

4. Christine de Pizan, *Oeuvres poétiques de Christine de Pisan*, ed. Maurice Roy, 3 vols. (Paris: Firmin Didot, 1886–1896).

5. Brownlee, "Widowhood, Sexuality, and Gender," 340.

6. Brownlee, "Widowhood, Sexuality, and Gender," 340. On further ways that Christine brokered her authority as a woman writer in Paris, see Lori Walters, "The Figure of the *Seulette* in the Works of Christine de Pizan and Jean Gerson," in *Desireuse de plus avant enquerre*, ed. Liliane Dulac, Anne Paupert, Christine Reno, and Bernard Ribémont (Paris: Champion, 2008), 119–140.

7. Translation in *The Selected Writings of Christine de Pizan*, ed. and trans. Renate Blumenfeld-Kosinski (New York: Norton, 1997), 6–7.

8. Translation by Blumenfeld-Kosinski, *Selected Writings*, 6–7.

9. Walters, "Figure of the *Seulette*," 122–123.

10. Dante, *The Divine Comedy of Dante Alighieri*, vol. 1: *Inferno*, trans. Robert M. Durling, ed. Ronald L. Martinez (Oxford: Oxford University Press, 1996), XXVI.125. See John Freccero, "Shipwreck in the Prologue," in Callegari and Swain, eds., *In Dante's Wake*, 12–23.

11. See chapter 4 of this book, and Colonna translation from Cox, *Lyric Poetry*, 142.

12. Transcription and translation in Cox, *Lyric Poetry*, 134. Further citations appear parenthetically.

13. As Sapegno points out, the primary intertext for Colonna here is most likely *RVF* 293, which is also self-consciously about writing, and underlines Petrarch's intent in his poems mourning the death of Laura: he is not looking for fame, he says, but only to "sfogare il doloroso core," or "expiate his mournful heart." Maria Serena Sapegno, "The *Rime*: A Textual Conundrum?" in Brundin, Crivelli, and Sapegno, *Companion to Vittoria Colonna*, 140–194, 154.

14. Brundin, *Vittoria Colonna*, xi. On the development of Colonna's authorial voice in the proemial sonnet, see esp. Sapegno, "La costruzione di un Io lirico."

15. See Cox, *Lyric Poetry*, 134, for an audit of the poem's Petrarchan influences.

16. Cox, "Women Writers and the Canon," 17–19.

17. Ariosto, *Orlando furioso*, English translation from Ludovico Ariosto, *Orlando furioso*, trans. Guido Waldman (Oxford: Oxford University Press, 1998, 442.

18. Sapegno, "The *Rime*," 146, and Cox, *Women's Writing in Italy*, 114–115.

19. On the complex history of the *amorose* order, see esp. Crivelli, "Print Tradition," and Sapegno, "The *Rime*."

20. Sapegno, "The *Rime*," 142.

21. See esp. Giovanna Rabitti, "Vittoria Colonna, Bembo e Firenze: un caso di ricezione e qualche postilla," *Studi e problem di critica testuale* 44 (1992): 127–155; Cox, "Women

Writers and the Canon," 19–22, and *Lyric Poetry*, 146–148. Gambara's 1532 sonnet "O de la nostra etade unica gloria" and Colonna's response, "Di nuovo il cielo de l'antica gloria," were printed together in Vittoria Colonna's *Rime* of 1558, edited by Corso, *Tutte le rime . . . con l'espositione del signor Rinaldo Corso, nuouamente mandate in luce da Girolamo Ruscelli* (Venice: Giovanni Battista and Melchiorre Sessa, 1558), and in Lodovico Domenichi's 1559 anthology of poems by women writers, *Rime diverse d'alcune nobilissime et virtuosissime donne* (Lucca: Vincenzo Busdraghi, 1559). For a modern edition, see Cox, *Lyric Poetry*, 273–274. Martin argues, "Gambara's sonnet . . . helped fortify Colonna's 'monumental' status as the female Apollo of the era," in Ugolini and Martin, *Veronica Gambara, Complete Poems*, 15.

22. Cox, *Women's Writing in Italy*, 68.

23. Martin, "Critical Introduction," 4, 23.

24. Gambara, *Complete Poems*, 42.

25. Pietro Bembo, *Prose e rime*, ed. Carlo Dionisotti (Turin: UTET, 1960).

26. Translation in *Poems of Widowhood*, ed. Ramie Targoff, trans. Ramie Targoff and Troy Tower (Toronto: Iter, 2021) with small adjustments.

27. Gambara, *Complete Poems*, 42.

28. The last line of this sonnet mimics the first line of *RVF* 289, "L'alma mia fiamma oltre le belle bella." Translation Gambara, *Complete Poems*, 20–21.

29. Gambara, *Complete Poems*, 20–21, ll. 9–10.

30. Gambara, *Complete Poems*, 20–21, ll. 9, 12.

31. Martin, "Critical Introduction," 5.

32. See esp. Brundin, *Vittoria Colonna*; Cox, "Women Writers and the Canon," 76–81, and "Exemplary Vittoria Colonna"; Goethals, "Flowers of Italian Literature"; Diana Robin, "The Breasts of Vittoria Colonna," *California Italian Studies* 3, no. 1 (2012): 1–16.

33. Targoff, *Renaissance Woman*, esp. 11–18.

34. We now know her influence over this genre extends further still: see Tatiana Crivelli, "'She Showed the World a Beacon of Female Worth': Vittoria Colonna in Arcadia," in Cox and McHugh, *Vittoria Colonna: Poetry, Religion, Art, Impact*, 351–370, for a discussion of Colonna's importance for the Arcadia movement in the late seventeenth and eighteenth centuries. Of particular note is a widowhood sonnet by Prudenza Gabrielli Capizucchi (1654–1709), "Talor di mia magion la più romita," which shares remarkable resonances with the poets in this chapter (364–365).

35. The three women under consideration here do not represent the first instance of women being placed in clear competition with Colonna. Cox points to the conscious attempts following Colonna's death to locate her rightful successor, with, notably, male poets consciously setting up other women poets as sure to equal or even outdo her in rather audacious ways. Cox notes specifically the cases of Tullia d'Aragona (1510–1556)—who is described by Benedetto Arrighi in her *Rime* (1547) as "a pale predecessor 'moon' to d'Aragona's glorious 'sun'"—and of Laura Terracina (1519–1577), whom Francesco Ferosi described "as equal to the 'lofty Vittoria'" in her *Rime seconde* (1549). Cox, *Women's Writing in Italy*, 80–81.

36. See Graham Smith, "Bronzino's 'Portrait of Laura Battiferri," *Source: Notes in the History of Art* 15, no. 4 (1996): 30–38. On Battiferri's social status, see Victoria Kirkham, ed. and trans., *Laura Battiferra and Her Literary Circle, an Anthology: A Bilingual Edition* (Chicago: University of Chicago Press, 2006), 26.

37. See esp. Kirkham, *Laura Battiferra*, 26, and Rabitti, "Vittoria Colonna as Role Model," 488–491.

38. Kirkham brings these poems to light and offers an important analysis of their influence and innovation in *Laura Battiferra*, 192–199.

39. On Colonna's "fateful name" and the tradition of puns deriving from it, see Walter Cupperi, "'Il nome fatale di Vittoria': note su due medaglie della Marchesa di Pescara," in *Lo sguardo archeologico: i normalisti per Paul Zanker*, ed. F. De Angelis (Pisa: Editions of the Normale, 2007), 239–253. Colonna plays on "Vittoria" and "victory" often herself, as in the poem "A le vittorie tue, mio lume eterno."

40. Transcription and translation from Kirkham, *Laura Battiferra*, 193.

41. Cox, *Lyric Poetry*, 134, l. 3.

42. The *memoria-vittoria* rhyme in Battiferri's final tercet and the allusion to writing as a victory over death echo the second quatrain of Veronica Gambara's tribute sonnet to Colonna, "O de la nostra etade unica gloria," discussed in chapter 4.

43. See Chiara Matraini, *Selected Poetry and Prose: A Bilingual Edition*, ed. and trans. E. MacLachlan, introduction by Giovanna Rabitti (Chicago: University of Chicago Press, 2008), esp. 1–10, for Matraini's detailed biography.

44. See esp. Gerry Milligan, "Proving Masculinity before God and Women: Laura Terracina and Chiara Matraini Writing War in the Renaissance," in *The Poetics of Masculinity in Early Modern Italy and Spain*, ed. Gerry Milligan and Jane Tylus (Toronto: University of Toronto Press, 2010), 185–212, on Matraini's oration on the art of war, and Shannon McHugh, "A Guided Tour of Heaven and Hell: The Otherworldly Journey in Chiara Matraini and Lucrezia Marinella," *Early Modern Women* 9, no. 1 (2014): 25–46, on the *Dialoghi spirituali*.

45. Cox, *Women's Writing in Italy*, 90.

46. Rabitti, introduction to Matraini, *Selected Poetry and Prose*, 5–6. Matraini is described as the "scelerata vedova" or "wicked widow" in the 1547 *Vita di Gherardo Sergiusti*, published in Lucca, coincidentally, the same year as Colonna's death.

47. Cox, *Lyric Poetry*, 396.

48. See Cox, *Lyric Poetry*, 149, for a discussion of Matraini's Colonnesque *cento*, and Matraini, *Selected Poetry and Prose*, 143, for a version of "Alto mio sol." Rabitti points to the influence of Colonna on Matraini's entire oeuvre, both her widowed verse and her late life spiritual turn, in Rabitti, "Vittoria Colonna as Role Model."

49. Chiara Matraini, "Quanto l'alta Colonna il suo gran sole," MS Vatican City, Biblioteca Apostolica Vaticana, Vat. Lat. 5225, cited by Rabitti in the introduction to *Selected Poetry and Prose*, xv. Rabitti suggests the sonnet may have been written to mark Colonna's death in 1547, although it is curious that it would not have made it into her 1555 edition in that case. Cristina Acucella suggests it was more likely written between the first and second edition of Matraini's *Rime*. Cristina Acucella, "Cambi Di Progetto: Vittoria Colonna, modello e antimodello nei proemi di Chiara Matraini," in *L'Italianistica oggi: ricerca e didattica*, ed. Beatrice Alfonzetti, Teresa Cancro, Valeria Di Iasio, and Ester Petrobon (Rome: Adi Editore, 2017), 8.

50. Transcription and translation in Cox, *Lyric Poetry*, 150.

51. Happily, Turina is receiving greater attention of late, notably with the excellent essays in *Francesca Turini Bufalini e la "Letteratura di Genere,"* ed. John Butcher (Città di Castello: Biblioteca del Centro Studi "Mario Pancrazi," 2018). On Turina's life and works, see Francesca Turrini Bufalini, *Rime spirituali sopra i misteri del santissimo rosario*, in Bà, *Letteratura italiana antica* 6 (2005), 153–220; Turini Bufalini, *Autobiographical Poems*; Cox, *Prodigious Muse*, most saliently 80–84; and poems translated and analyzed in Cox, *Lyric Poetry*. See also Ilaria Rossini, "La voce della vedova. Temi e motivi da Giovanni Boccaccio a Francesca Turini Bufalini," in *Francesca Turini Bufalini e la "Letteratura di Genere,"* 191–196.

52. See esp. David Herlihy, *The Family in Renaissance Italy* (St. Charles, MO: Forum Press, 1974), 8, on the average age gaps between women and their husbands.

53. "Con le fatiche e col sangue," "con la sincerità dell'affetto, e con la devozione dell'inchiostro." Turrini Bufalini, *Rime spirituali*, 153. See Francesco Giusti, "Le circostanze del dolore. Il canzoniere di fine cinquecento di Francesca Turina Bufalini e i suoi modelli," *Rinascimento* 52 (2012): 251–290, for a discussion of Turina's strategic use of her grief in the dedicatory letter to the pope.

54. Transcription and translation in Cox, *Lyric Poetry*, 155.

55. Transcription and translation in Cox, *Lyric Poetry*, 152.

56. Cox, *Lyric Poetry*, 153. Matraini's can be found as poem 51 in Cox, *Lyric Poetry*, 147.

57. Cox, *Lyric Poetry*, 153.

58. This window into her heart also recalls the Renaissance conceit of the crystal heart; see Lina Bolzoni, *Il cuore di cristallo* (Turin: Giulio Einaudi, 2010).

59. On the visual representation of Death as a female figure and Petrarch's *Triumphs*, see Muyo, "Boccaccio's Pisan Allegory."

60. Turrini Bufalini, *Le Rime* (1628), 214. Cox observes that "while the capacity of portraits to evoke presence and their disconcerting unresponsiveness were established topoi, Turina vivifies them by having her poet 'madly' address the portrait directly, as though it were her living husband or ghost." See Cox, *Lyric Poetry*, 155. See also Simone Monti, "Widows, Poetry, and Portraits: Livia Spinola and Francesca Turina on the Portraits of Their Dead Husbands," in *Petrarch and Sixteenth-Century Italian Portraiture*, ed. Ilaria Bernocchi, Niccolò Morelli, and Federica Pich (Amsterdam: Amsterdam University Press, 2024), 43–61.

61. Turrini Bufalini, *Le Rime* (1628), 219.

62. A letter by Carlo Gualteruzzi suggests that Colonna had turned to spiritual verse by 1536, before her first poems were published in 1538. Ornella Moroni, *Carlo Gualteruzzi, 1500–1577 e i corrispondenti* (Vatican City: Biblioteca apostolica vaticana, 1984), 65.

63. For Turina's relationship with the Colonna family, see Igea Torrioli, *Francesca Turina Bufalini e la società colta tifernate nel sec. XVI* (Città di Castello: Grifani-Donati, 1940), 18, 26, 27, as well as Turrini Bufalini, *Rime spirituali*, 143–144.

64. Turrini Bufalini, *Le Rime* (1628), 149.

65. The younger Vittoria (1610–1675) would prove herself an impressive Colonna in her own right, as the famous Carmelite Chiara Maria della Passione, who became prioress of the convent of Regina Coeli in Trastevere after its founding by her sister Anna in 1654. See especially Fabrizio Nurra, *Chiara Maria della Passione, carmelitana scalza: un'eremita*

nel cuore di Trastevere (Rome: OCD, 2012) and Natalia Costa-Zalessow, "Francesca Turini Bufalini's Encomiastic Poems for Lucrezia Tomacelli Colonna," *Italica* 90, no. 3 (2013): 365–377.

66. "Quella alta Colonna / che coi suoi dotti e sì sonori carmi / immortalossi e onor rese a ogni donna." Turrini Bufalini, *Le Rime* (1628), 151.

67. See Susan Gubar and Sandra M. Gilbert, *The Madwoman in the Attic: The Woman Writer and the Nineteenth-Century Literary Imagination* (New Haven, CT: Yale University Press, 1978), esp. 47–48, and Harold Bloom, *The Anxiety of Influence: A Theory of Poetry* (Oxford: Oxford University Press, 1973).

Chapter 6 "Widowhood for Its Own Sake"

1. See Virginia Cox, *The Renaissance Dialogue: Literary Dialogue in Its Social and Political Contexts, Castiglione to Galileo* (Cambridge: Cambridge University Press, 1992), on quasi-documentary dialogue.

2. On this see esp. Sanson, "Widowhood and Conduct."

3. See esp. Caroline Castiglione, "Why Political Theory Is Women's Work: How Moderata Fonte Reclaimed Liberty for Women Inside and Outside Marriage," in *Challenging Women's Agency and Activism in Early Modernity*, ed. Merry Wiesner-Hanks and Andrea Pearson (Amsterdam: Amsterdam University Press, 2021), 141–162; Virginia Cox, "The Single Self: Feminist Thought and the Marriage Market in Early Modern Venice," *Renaissance Quarterly* 48, no. 3 (Autumn 1995): 513–581; Suzanne Magnanini, "Una selva luminosa: The Second Day of Moderata Fonte's *Il merito delle donne*," *Modern Philology* 101, no. 2 (2003): 278–296; and Meredith K. Ray, "Scientific Culture and the Renaissance *Querelle des Femme*," in *Daughters of Alchemy: Women and Scientific Culture in Early Modern Italy* (Cambridge, MA: Harvard University Press, 2015), 73–110.

4. Brian Richardson, "*Amore maritale*: Advice on Love and Marriage in the Second Half of the Cinquecento," in Panizza, *Women in Italian Renaissance Culture and Society*, 194–208, 199.

5. Richardson, "*Amore maritale*," 199–203.

6. For an expansive survey of conduct literature aimed at women in the early modern period, see Sanson and Lucioli, *Conduct Literature for and about Women in Italy*.

7. As discussed in previous chapters, conduct texts from earlier in the century addressed the subject of widowhood as well, including Juan Luis Vives's important *The Education of a Christian Woman*, first published in Italian in 1523, and Lodovico Dolce's *Della institutione delle donne* (1545), with the widowed Dorotea as main speaker (see Sanson, "Widowhood and Conduct"). Girolamo Savonarola's *The Book of the Life of the Widow*, published a century earlier in Florence in 1491, was republished eight times in Venice in the first half of the sixteenth century, the last time in 1547 in the early years of the Council of Trent. See Savonarola, *Guide to Righteous Living*.

8. A further text by Orazio Zarrabini, similar in argument to Cabei's, was published in 1586: *De lo stato verginale, maritale e vedovile. Libri tre*.

9. Sanson, "Widowhood and Conduct," 9.

10. Earlier in the century, Giovan Giorgio Trissino dedicated his 1524 *Epistola del Trissino de la vita, che dee tenere una donna vedova* to Margherita Pio Sanseverino, a widowed

noblewoman and friend of his who had lost her Neapolitan husband, Marco Antonio Sanseverino. Published as Margherita was entering the convent, the letter urges widows to conduct themselves as chaste, unobtrusive, and pious members of society. Trissino was a regular at Veronica Gambara's court in Coreggio.

11. Orazio Fusco, *La vedova del Fusco* (Rome: I Dorici, 1570), 3r.

12. Fusco, *La vedova*, 29, 36.

13. Sanson, "Widowhood and Conduct," 14.

14. Fusco, *La vedova*, 2r–2v.

15. Sanson, "Widowhood and Conduct," 3.

16. Cabei, *Ornamenti della gentil donna vedova* (Venice: Christoforo Zanetti, 1574), 30.

17. Cabei, *Ornamenti*, 20.

18. This is reminiscent of fifteenth-century Florentine concerns addressed by Klapisch-Zuber in her study "The Cruel Mother" on widows who were separated from their children upon remarriage. See the introduction to this book.

19. Cabei, *Ornamenti*, 21–22, translation my own.

20. His *Instituzione* is divided into three parts: the first section for *dimesse*, young unmarried women; the second for widows; and the third for married women. See the very good introduction by Francesco Lucioli, in Agostino Valier, *Instituzione d'ogni stato lodevole delle donne cristiane*, ed. Francesco Lucioli (Cambridge: Modern Humanities Research Association, 2015): 1–41. See Cox, "Single Self," for an examination of Valier's section on dimesse as it relates to Moderata Fonte's *Il merito delle donne*.

21. Lucioli, introduction to *Instituzione*, 4.

22. Valier, *Instituzione*, 133–135.

23. Bernardo Trotto, *Dialoghi del matrimonio e vita vedovile* (Turin: Francesco Dolce, 1578). A second edition was published by Niccolò Bevilacqua, also in Turin, in 1583. Trotto is referred to as Trotto and Trotti interchangeably in texts both Renaissance and modern; I have chosen to use Trotto throughout, and further citations appear parenthetically. Translations are my own.

24. The use of the adjective "desiderosa" (desirous) here is particularly suggestive, given the prominent societal anxiety about the widow as both a desiring subject and an object of desire.

25. Due to Trotto's many allusions to Castiglione's dialogue, *Dialoghi* was sometimes referred to as *Il cortegiano sabaudo*. See Maria Luisa Doglio and Mario Guglielminetti, "La letteratura a corte," in *Storia di Torino III: Dalla dominazione francese alla ricomposizione dello stato*, ed. Giuseppe Ricuperati (Turin: Einaudi, 1998), 599–672.

26. Doglio and Guglielminetti, "La letteratura a corte."

27. Trotto published an earlier dialogue in Latin, *Soluto matrimonio*, or "On the Dissolution of Marriage," in 1572, coauthored with Martino Cravotto. This dialogue certainly warrants further study, particularly in the context of the long legal history of marriage.

28. Only the Duchy of Savoy (composed of Piedmont and Savoy) and the Republic of Venice were given their independence in the agreement between Henry II of France and Philip II of Spain.

29. These included a number of works on marriage, including Giovanni Maria Bianchi Salassieri's *Orazione matrimoniale al serenissimo Emanuel Filiberto* (1560). Doglio and

Guglielminetti, "La letteratura a corte," 605. The importance of strategic marriage alliances continued in successive generations: in 1585, Filiberto's son Carlo Emanuele married Catherine of Austria, and the city prepared an elaborate triumphal entry for the couple that rivaled the Medici wedding triumphs. See Marta Gonzalez, "Pageantry and the Projection of Status: The Triumphal Entries of Catherine of Austria (1585) and Christine of France (1620) in Turin," *Mélanges de l'Ecole française de Rome. Italie et Méditerranée* 115, no. 1 (2003): 29–50.

30. See Doglio and Guglielminetti, "La letteratura a corte," for a comprehensive portrait of Filiberto's court.

31. Cox, "Female Voice in Italian Renaissance Dialogue," 54.

32. See Cox, "Female Voice in Italian Renaissance Dialogue"; see also Janet Levarie Smarr, *Joining the Conversation: Dialogues by Renaissance Women* (Ann Arbor: University of Michigan Press, 2005), for dialogues authored by women.

33. Cox points out that the form of dialogue itself allows the writer to present himself as "a careless and sociable creature, who has simply recorded the fruits of a pleasant afternoon's listening." Cox, *Renaissance Dialogue*, 42–43. Adriana Chemello has pointed to Leonora's garden in Fonte's dialogue as a location "apart from the 'public' space, which has always excluded honest women," and we see the same arrangement here. See Adriana Chemello, "La donna, il modello, l'immaginario: Moderata Fonte e Lucrezia Marinella," in *Nel cerchio della luna: figure di donna in alcuni testi del XVI secolo*, ed. Marina Zancan (Venice: Marsilio, 1983), 95–170 (147).

34. See Claudio Bertolotto, "I ritratti marmorei dei Porporato e di Manfredo Solaro," in *Arte e devozione nella chiesa B. V. Maria del Monte Carmelo al Colletto presso Pinerolo. Gli ex voto ritrovati (secc. XVI–XVII)*, ed. M. Marchiando Pacchiola (Pinerolo: Arti grafiche, 1994), 7–14.

35. The historical Barbara predeceased her husband, in 1571.

36. Astemio is the only character in the two-book dialogue who does not have a historical equivalent and is also the only character to appear in both Book I and Book II. Doglio and Guglielminetti hypothesize that Astemio may be "a proiezione d'autore" (a projection of the author) in Doglio and Guglielminetti, "La letteratura a corte," 616. The name itself may suggest that Astemio, or even Trotto himself, abstained from marriage. I have found no records that indicate Trotto himself ever married.

37. Trotto, *Dialoghi*, 3.

38. Trotto, *Dialoghi*, 9.

39. Plutarch, *Plutarch's Moralia*, 16 vols., ed. Frank Cole Babbitt (Cambridge, MA: Harvard University Press, 1969).

40. Trotto, *Dialoghi*, 12.

41. Trotto, *Dialoghi*, 4.

42. Trotto, *Dialoghi*, 41. Translation of Fonte in Moderata Fonte, *The Worth of Women: Wherein Is Clearly Revealed Their Nobility and Their Superiority to Men*, ed. and trans. Virginia Cox (Chicago: University of Chicago Press, 1997), 100.

43. Unlike in cities such as Florence and Venice, where women were given back their dowries after their husbands' deaths, widows in Turin did not have control over their dowries. Instead, the dowry went back to her family and then into the hands of a second hus-

band in the case of remarriage. Sandra Cavallo, "Proprietà o possesso? Composizione e controllo dei beni delle donne a Torino (1650–1710)," in *Le ricchezze delle donne: diritti patrimoniali e poteri familiari in Italia* (sec. XIII–XIX), ed. Giulia Calvi and Isabelle Chabot (Turin: Rosenberg & Sellier, 1998), 187–207.

44. Flaminio de Birague, *Les premières oeuvres poétiques* (1585), ed. Roland Guillot and Michel Clément (Geneva: Droz, 1998) and Anne R. Larsen, "Paradox and the Praise of Women: From Ortensio Lando and Charles Estienne to Marie de Romieu," *Sixteenth Century Journal* 28, no. 3 (1997): 761–762.

45. The discourse itself is a "feminist refashioning" in verse of Ortensio Lando's Paradox XXV, "Che la donna è di maggior eccellentia, che l'huomo," and Estienne's faithful French translation of Lando's piece. See Larsen, "Paradox and the Praise of Women."

46. Marie de Romieu, *Les premières oeuvres poétiques de Mademoiselle Marie de Romieu, Vivaroise: contenant un brief discours que l'excellence de la femme surpasse celle de l'homme, non moins recréatif que plein de beaux exemples . . .* (Paris: L. Breyer, 1581), 42.

47. Guy de Chastellier, the eldest son, had taken over his father's title and his diplomatic post in Piedmont, becoming "seigneur de Millieu, conseiller du Roi et général de ses finances en Piémont"; the document catalogue describes him as being "présent au château du Plessis-Saint-Antoine près la Queue-en-Brie: remise a son frère Gabriel Chastellier, de la pension que le Roi lui a donné, 'desirant faire un voyage en Italye pour apprandre le faict des armes et aultres bons exercices' en la presence d'Hyppolite Descaravelly, dame d'honneur de la Reine-mère, et de plusieurs témoins dont Pierre Herouard. 26 septembre 1584." Archives Nationales de France, Cote MC/ET/XIX/163. Despite the archivist's best efforts, this document has yet to be located. It is believed to have been misfiled at some point in a twentieth-century reorganization.

48. The Archives Nationales also contains Jean de Chastellier's will; he left much of his wealth to Guy Chastellier, his eldest son.

49. N. M. Sutherland, "Catherine de Medici: The Legend of the Wicked Italian Queen," *Sixteenth Century Journal* 9, no. 2 (July 1978): 45–56, 45.

50. Barbara B. Diefendorf, "Widowhood and Remarriage in Sixteenth-Century Paris," *Journal of Family History* 7, no. 4 (1982): 379–395, 379.

51. Pierre de Bourdeilles de Brantôme, André de Bourdeille, Louis Lacour, and Prosper Mérimée, *Oeuvres complètes de Pierre de Bourdeilles, abbé et seigneur de Branthôme* (Nendeln, Liechtenstein: Kraus Repr, 1977), 706–707.

52. All original quotations from Fonte are from Moderata Fonte, *Il merito delle donne: ove chiaramente si scuopre quanto siano elle degne e più perfette de gli uomini*, ed. Adriana Chemello (Milan: Eidos, 1988). All translations are from Fonte, *Worth of Women*. Cox also contextualizes Fonte's dialogue in terms of the Venetian marriage market in Cox, "Single Self."

53. Cox, "Single Self," 528–529.

54. Fonte, *Il merito delle donne*, 10, translation in Fonte, *Worth of Women*, 44.

55. Fonte, *Il merito delle donne*, 11, translation in Fonte, *Worth of Women*, 46.

56. Fonte, *Il merito delle donne*, 14, translation in Fonte, *Worth of Women*, 54.

57. Fonte, *Il merito delle donne*, 14, translation in Fonte, *Worth of Women*, 54.

58. Transcription and translation in Cox, *Lyric Poetry*, 155. See my extended discussion of these poems in chapter 5 of this book.

59. On D'Avalos as Colonna's "Sun," see esp. Sapegno, "La costruzione di un Io Lirico."

60. On the garden, see Cox, "Single Self," 567.

61. Fonte, *Il merito delle donne*, 11, translation in Fonte, *Worth of Women*, 47.

62. Fonte, *Il merito delle donne*, 14, translation in Fonte, *Worth of Women*, 53.

63. Fonte, *Il merito delle donne*, 14, translation in Fonte, *Worth of Women*, 53.

64. Fonte, *Il merito delle donne*, 85, translation in Fonte, *Worth of Women*, 230.

65. Cox in the notes to Fonte, *Worth of Women*, 230n191.

66. It is also useful to consider what Leonora's strenuous defense of widowhood and argument against remarriage can tell us about the historical debate over marriage. Contained in the 1563 reaffirmation of marriage by the Catholic Church was the idea that "a legitimate marriage was indissoluble" and essentially inescapable, a notion that, Caroline Castiglione argues, Fonte pushes back against in her dialogue. Castiglione, "Why Political Theory Is Women's Work," 146.

67. Fonte, *Il merito delle donne*, 97, translation in Fonte, *Worth of Women*, 259.

68. Fonte, *Il merito delle donne*, 97, translation in Fonte, *Worth of Women*, 259.

Epilogue

1. I borrow this term from Teodolinda Barolini, who discusses Beatrice as a "hybrid figure: a composite whose elements come both from the courtly tradition and the moralizing allegorical and didactic tradition in which female abstractions like Boethius's Lady Philosophy speak with authority and vigor." Teodolinda Barolini, "Notes toward a Gendered History of Italian Literature, with a Discussion of Dante's *Beatrix Loquax*," in *Dante and the Origins of Italian Literary Culture*, 360–378, 367.

2. I take here Rosenwein's definition of "emotional communities": "groups that share the same or very similar norms and values about emotional behavior and even about feelings themselves." Rosenwein, *Generations of Feeling*, 25.

3. Desmond, *Reading Dido*, 208.

4. "In building and populating her allegorical city," Judith L. Kellogg suggests, "Christine draws a powerful collective portrait of women that represents them as essential to the formation of the institutions and values of civilized life." Kellogg, "Transforming Ovid: The Metamorphosis of Female Authority," in *Christine de Pizan and the Categories of Difference*, ed. Marilynn Desmond (Minneapolis: University of Minnesota Press, 1998), 181–194, 189.

5. Desmond, *Reading Dido*, 223.

6. Kelley Harness, *Echoes of Women's Voices: Music, Art, and Female Patronage in Early Modern Florence* (Chicago: University of Chicago Press, 2006), 15.

7. Harness, *Echoes of Women's Voices*, 16.

8. For a history of Catherine's relationship with Ferdinando's father, Cosimo I, see esp. De Mar Jensen, "Catherine de' Medici and Her Florentine Friends," *Sixteenth Century Journal* 9, no. 2 (1978): 57–74.

9. Maria Galli Stampino, "A Regent and Her Court: Towards a Study of Maria Maddalena d'Austria's Patronage (Florence 1621–28)," *Forum Italicum* 40, no. 1 (2006): 22–35.

10. Galli Stampino, "Regent and Her Court," 24.

11. Angelo Solerti, *Musica, ballo e drammatica alla Corte Medicea dal 1600 al 1637* (Florence: Bemporad, 1905), 158. Quoted in Galli Stampino, "Regent and Her Court," 24. Translation my own.

12. Galli Stampino, "Regent and Her Court," 24. On anticlericalism in Counter-Reformation scholarship, see Amedeo Quondam, "Foreword," in *Innovation in the Italian Counter-Reformation*, ed. Shannon McHugh and Anna Wainwright (Newark: University of Delaware Press, 2020), xi–xxx.

13. In addition to Harness and Galli Stampino, see Jessica Goethals, *Margherita Costa, Diva of the Baroque Court* (Toronto: University of Toronto Press, 2023), 28–40.

14. Kelley Harness, "Judith, Music, and Female Patrons in Early Modern Italy," in Brine, Ciletti, and Lähnemann, *Sword of Judith*, 374.

15. Harness, "Judith, Music, and Female Patrons," 377.

16. Tylus, *Sacred Narratives*, 21.

17. Tylus, *Sacred Narratives*, 24–25.

18. Harness, "Judith, Music, and Female Patrons," 377.

19. Francesca Turina, "Poesie di Francesca Turina Bufalini in parte autografe, e di vari a lei," Inventario Azzi, busta 185, sec. 4, Archivio Bufalini, San Giustino. Translation my own.

20. Tylus, *Sacred Narratives*, 120.

Bibliography

Manuscript

Turina, Francesca. "Poesie di Francesca Turina Bufalini in parte autografe, e di vari a lei." Inventario Azzi, busta 185, sec. 4. Archivio Bufalini, San Giustino.

Primary Sources

Alighieri, Dante. *The Divine Comedy of Dante Alighieri*. 3 vols. Translated by Robert M. Durling with notes by Ronald L. Martinez. Oxford: Oxford University Press, 1996–2011.

———. *Vita nuova*. Edited by Michele Barbi. Florence: Bemporard, 1932.

Alle, Girolamo. *La vedova svecese cioe' la vita di santa Brigida*. Bologna: Carlo Zenero, 1648.

Ariosto, Ludovico. *Orlando furioso*. Edited by Lanfranco Caretti. Turin: Einaudi, 1992.

———. *Orlando furioso*. Translated by Guido Waldman. Oxford: Oxford University Press, 1998.

Augustine. *Letters*. Translated by Sister Wilfrid Parsons. Washington, DC: Catholic University of America Press, 1951.

Bembo, Pietro. *Prose della volgar lingua; Gli Asolani; Rime*. Edited by Carlo Dionisotti. Turin: TEA, 1997.

———. *Prose e rime*. Edited by Carlo Dionisotti. Turin: UTET, 1960.

Betussi, Giuseppe. *Libro di messer Gio. Boccaccio delle donne illustri, tradotto per m[esser] Giuseppe Betussi, con una additione fatta dal medesimo delle donne famose dal tempo di m[esser] Giovanni fino a i giorni nostri e alcune altre state per inanzi*. Venice: Comin di Trino di Monferrato, 1545.

Birgitta of Sweden. *The Revelations of St Birgitta of Sweden*. 4 vols. Translated by Denis Searby. Oxford: Oxford University Press, 2006–2015.

Boccaccio, Giovanni. *Corbaccio or the Labyrinth of Love*. Translated and edited by Anthony K. Cassell. Binghamton, NY: Medieval and Renaissance Texts and Studies, 1993.

———. *Decameron*. In *Tutte le opere*, 10 vols., edited by Vittore Branca et al. Milan: Mondadori, 1964–1994.

———. *The Decameron*. Translated by G. H. McWilliam. New York: Penguin, 1975.

———. *The Decameron*. Translated by Wayne A. Rebhorn. New York: Norton, 2013.

———. *De claris mulieribus*. Translated by Virginia Brown. Cambridge, MA: Harvard University Press, 2003.

———. *Filocolo*. Edited by E. Quaglio, in *Tutte le opere*, 10 vols., edited by Vittore Branca et al. Milan: Mondadori, 1964–1994.

———. *Il corbaccio*. Edited by P. G. Ricci. Turin: Einaudi, 1977.

Brantôme, Pierre de Bourdeilles, André de Bourdeille, Louis Lacour, and Prosper Mérimée. *Oeuvres complètes de Pierre de Bourdeilles, abbé et seigneur de Branthôme*. Nendeln, Liechtenstein: Kraus Repr, 1977.

Cabei, Giulio Cesare. *Ornamenti della gentil donna vedova: Opera del Signor Giulio Cesare Cabei. Nella quale ordinatamente si tratta di tutte le cose necessarie allo stato vedovile; onde potrà farsi adorno d'ogni habito virtuoso, & honorato*. Venice: Christoforo Zanetti, 1574.

Campanile, Iacopo. *Opera Nuova Nomata Vero Tempio d'amore*. Allife: Acillo, 1536.

Capasso, Giosuè. *Triumphem Novem Viduarem*. In *Le Farse; Il Trionfo; Il Lamento*, edited by Milena Montanile, 59–71. Naples: Istituto nazionale di Studi sul Rinascimento meridionale, 1990.

Castiglione, Baldassare. *Il libro del cortegiano*. Edited by Giulio Preti. Turin: Einaudi, 1965.

Colbertaldo, Antonio. *Storia di Caterina Corner regina di Cipro: La prima biografia*. Edited by Daria Perocco. Padova: Libro, 2012.

Colonna, Vittoria. *Poems of Widowhood*. Edited by Ramie Targoff. Translated by Ramie Targoff and Troy Tower. Toronto: Iter, 2021.

———. *Rime*. Edited by Alan Bullock. Rome: Laterza, 1975.

Dolce, Lodovico. *Dialogo della institutione delle donne*. Venice: Giolito de Ferrari, 1547.

Domenichi, Lodovico. *Vita di santa Brigida e santa Caterina di Svezia*. Edited by Enrico Garavelli. Manziana: Vecchiarelli, 2016.

Fonte, Moderata. *Il merito delle donne: ove chiaramente si scuopre quanto siano elle degne e più perfette de gli uomini*. Edited by Adriana Chemello. Mirano: Eidos, 1988.

———. *The Worth of Women: Wherein Is Clearly Revealed Their Nobility and Their Superiority to Men*. Edited and translated by Virginia Cox. Chicago: University of Chicago Press, 1997.

Fusco, Orazio. *La vedova del Fusco*. Rome: I Dorici, 1570.

Gambara, Veronica. *Complete Poems*. Edited by Molly M. Martin. Translated by Paola Ugolini and Molly M. Martin. Toronto: Iter, 2014.

Homer. *The Iliad of Homer*. Translated by Richmond Lattimore. Chicago: University of Chicago Press, 2011.

Hozier, Louis Pierre d', Antoine-Marie d'Hozier de Sérigny, and Gerald de Eynde. *Armorial general: ou, Registres de la noblesse de France*. Paris: Editions du Palais Royal, 1970.

Jerome. *The Sacred Writings of Saint Jerome*. Edited by Philipp Schaff. Altenmünster, Germany: Jazzybee Verlag, 2012.

Machiavelli, Niccolò. *Discorsi sopra la prima Deca di Tito Livio*. Edited by Mario Martelli. Florence: Sansoni, 1971.

Matraini, Chiara. *Selected Poetry and Prose: A Bilingual Edition*. Edited and translated by E. MacLachlan, introduction by Giovanna Rabitti. Chicago: University of Chicago Press, 2008.

Mattiotti, Giovanni. *Santa Francesca Romana. Edizione critica dei trattati latini di Giovanni Mattiotti.* Edited by Alessandra Bartolomei Romagnoli. Vatican City: Libreria Editrice Vaticana, 1994.

Narducci, Domenica. *Domenica da Paradiso. Scritti spirituali.* 2 vols. Edited by Gerardo Antignani. Poggibonsi: Edizioni Tipolito Arti Grafiche Nencini, 1984–1985.

———. *I sermoni di Domenica da Paradiso. Studi e testo critico.* Edited by Rita Librandi and Adriana Valerio. Florence: Sismel, 1999.

Ovid. *Metamorphoses.* Translated by Rolfe Humphries. Bloomington: Indiana University Press, 1960.

Paluzzi, Pier Mattei. *Vita della Beata Ludovica Albertoni.* Rome: Corvo, 1672.

Petrarch, Francesco. *Petrarch's Lyric Poems: The Rime Sparse and Other Lyrics.* Translated by Robert M. Durling. Cambridge, MA: Harvard University Press, 2005.

———. *Trionfi, Rime Estravaganti, Codice degli Abbozzi.* Edited by Vinicio Pacca and Laura Paolino. Milan: Mondadori, 1996.

Pizan, Christine de. *The Book of the Mutability of Fortune.* Edited and translated by Geri L. Smith. Tempe, AZ: Iter, 2017.

———. *Cent ballades.* In *Oeuvres poétiques de Christine de Pisan,* edited by Maurice Roy. 3 vols. Paris: Firmin Didot, 1886–1896.

———. *Le livre de la cité des dames.* Edited and translated by Éric Hicks and Thérèse Moreau. Paris: Stock/Moyen Âge, 1986.

———. *The Selected Writings of Christine de Pizan.* Edited by Renate Blumenfeld-Kosinski. New York: Norton, 1997.

Plutarch. *Plutarch's Moralia.* 16 vols. Edited by Frank Cole Babbitt. Cambridge, MA: Harvard University Press, 1969.

Romieu, Marie de. *Les premières oeuvres poétiques de Mademoiselle Marie de Romieu, Vivaroise: contenant un brief discours que l'excellence de la femme surpasse celle de l'homme, non moins recréatif que plein de beaux exemples. . . .* Paris: L. Breyer, 1581.

Savonarola, Girolamo. *A Guide to Righteous Living and Other Works.* Edited and translated by Konrad Eisenbichler. Toronto: University of Toronto Press, 2003.

Terracina, Laura. *Settime rime sovra tutte le donne vedove di questa nostra città di Napoli titolate et non titolate.* Naples: Mattio Cancer, 1561.

Tornabuoni, Lucrezia. *Lettere.* Edited by Patrizia Salvadori. Florence: Olschki, 1993.

Trissino, Giovanni Giorgio. *Epistola de la vita, che dee tenere una donna vedova.* Rome: Lodovico Vicentino, 1524.

Trotto, Bernardo. *Dialoghi del matrimonio e vita vedovile.* Turin: Francesco Dolce, 1578.

Turini Bufalini, Francesca. *Autobiographical Poems: A Bilingual Edition.* Edited by Natalia Costa-Zalessow. Translated by Joan E. Borrelli with Natalia Costa-Zalessow. New York: Bordighera Press, 2009.

Turrini Bufalini, Francesca. *Rime* (1628). Edited by Paolo Bà. In *Letteratura italiana antica* 11, 141–278. Pisa, Rome: Fabrizio Serra, 2010.

———. *Rime spirituali sopra i misteri del santissimo rosario* (1595). Edited by Paolo Bà. In *Letteratura italiana antica* 6, 153–220. Pisa, Rome: Fabrizio Serra, 2005.

Valier, Agostino. *Instituzione d'ogni stato lodevole delle donne cristiane* and *Ricordi di Monsignor Agostino Valier Vescovo di Verona lasciati alle monache nella sua visitazione fatta l'anno del santissimo giubileo 1575*. Edited by Francesco Lucioli. Cambridge: Modern Humanities Research Association, 2015.

Virgil. *The Aeneid*. Translated by Sarah Ruden. New Haven, CT: Yale University Press, 2008.

———. *The Aeneid of Virgil*. Translated by Allen Mandelbaum. New York: Bantam Books, 1971.

Vives, Juan Luis. *The Education of a Christian Woman: A Sixteenth-Century Manual*. Translated by Charles Fantazzi. Chicago: University of Chicago Press, 2007.

Voragine, Jacobus de. *The Golden Legend: Readings on the Saints*. Translated by William Granger Ryan. Princeton, NJ: Princeton University Press, 2012.

Secondary Sources

Acucella, Cristina. "Cambi Di Progetto: Vittoria Colonna, modello e antimodello nei proemi di Chiara Matraini." In *L'Italianistica oggi: ricerca e didattica*, edited by Beatrice Alfonzetti, Teresa Cancro, Valeria Di Iasio, and Ester Petrobon, 1–9. Rome: Adi Editore, 2017.

Adler, Sara M. "Vittoria Colonna: Michelangelo's Perfect Muse." *Italica* 92, no. 1 (2015): 5–32.

Alexiou, Margaret. *The Ritual Lament in Greek Tradition*. Cambridge, MA: Harvard University Press, 1974.

Alfie, Fabian. *Dante's Tenzone with Forese Donati: The Reprehension of Vice*. Toronto: University of Toronto Press, 2011.

Anderson, Benedict. *Imagined Communities: Reflections on the Origin and Spread of Nationalism*. New York: Verso, 1991.

Armstrong, Guyda. "Boccaccio and the Infernal Body: The Widow as Wilderness." In *Boccaccio and Feminist Criticism*, edited by Thomas C. Stillinger and Regina Psaki, 83–104. Chapel Hill, NC: Annali d'Italianistica, 2006.

Ascoli, Albert Russell. *A Local Habitation and a Name: Imagining Histories in the Italian Renaissance*. New York: Fordham University Press, 2011.

Bà, Paolo, and Giuseppe Milani. *I Bufalini di San Giustino: Origine e ascesa di una casata. Francesca Turina Bufalini, poetessa, 1553–1641: Una donna che ha dato lustro a una famiglia*. San Giustino: Comune di San Giustino, 1998.

Baernstein, P. Renée. "In Widow's Habit: Women between Convent and Family in Sixteenth-Century Milan." *Sixteenth Century Journal* 25, no. 4 (Winter 1994): 787–807.

Bardazzi, Giovanni. "Le rime spirituali di Vittoria Colonna e Bernardino Ochino." *Italique. Poésie italienne de la Renaissance*, no. 4 (December 1, 2001): 61–101.

Barolini, Teodolinda. "Boccaccio's Philosophy of Consolation: The Place of the Other in Life's Transactions." In *Boccaccio 1313–2013*, edited by Francesco Ciabattoni, Elsa Filosa, and Kristina Olson, 89–105. Ravenna: Longo Editore, 2013.

———. "Dante and Cavalcanti (On Making Distinctions in Matters of Love): *Inferno* V in Its Lyric Context." *Dante Studies* 116 (1998): 31–63.

———. "Dante and Francesca Da Rimini: Realpolitik, Romance, Gender." *Speculum* 75, no. 1 (2000): 1–28.

———. *Dante and the Origins of Italian Literary Culture*. New York: Fordham University Press, 2006.

———. *Dante's Lyric Poetry: Poems of Youth and of the "Vita nuova" (1283–1292)*. Translated by Richard Lansing and Andrew Frisardi. Toronto: University of Toronto Press, 2014.

———. "Errancy: A Brief History of Dante's Ferm Voler." In *The Oxford Handbook of Dante*, edited by Manuele Gragnolati, Elena Lombardi, and Francesca Southerden, 563–579. Oxford: Oxford University Press, 2021.

———. "The Scholar and the Widow: Corrupt Appetite and Moral Failure in Society's Intellectual Elite (VIII.7)." In *The Decameron Eighth Day in Perspective*, edited by William Robins, 148–189. Toronto: University of Toronto Press, 2020.

———. "'Sotto Benda': The Women of Dante's Canzone 'Doglia Mi Reca' in the Light of Cecco d'Ascoli." *Dante Studies* 123 (2005): 83–88.

Bartolomei Romagnoli, Alessandra. "Brigida di Svezia e la reinvenzione della Storia Sacra: il cammino la terra la visione." In *Predicatori, mercanti, pellegrini. L'Occidente medievale e lo sguardo letterario sull'Altro tra l'Europa e il Levante*, edited by Giuseppe Mascherpa and Giovanni Strinna, 189–217. Mantua: Universitas Studiorum, 2018.

Baskins, Cristelle Louise. *Cassone Painting, Humanism, and Gender in Early Modern Italy*. Cambridge: Cambridge University Press, 1998.

———. "Trecento Rome: The Poetics and Politics of Widowhood." In *Widowhood and Visual Culture in Early Modern Europe*, edited by Allison M. Levy, 197–209. London: Ashgate, 2003.

Baskins, Cristelle Louise, and Sherry Roush, eds. *The Medieval Marriage Scene: Prudence, Passion, Policy*. Tempe: Arizona Center for Medieval and Renaissance Studies, 2005.

Bell, Rudolph M. *How to Do It: Guides to Good Living for Renaissance Italians*. Chicago: University of Chicago Press, 2000.

Benson, Pamela Joseph. *The Invention of the Renaissance Woman: The Challenge of Female Independence in the Literature and Thought of Italy and England*. University Park: Pennsylvania State University Press, 1992.

Bernardo, Aldo. *Petrarch, Laura, and the Triumphs*. Albany: State University of New York Press, 1974.

Bertolotto, Claudio. "I ritratti marmorei dei Porporato e di Manfredo Solaro." In *Arte e devozione nella chiesa B. V. Maria del Monte Carmelo al Colletto presso Pinerolo. Gli ex voto ritrovati (secc. XVI–XVII)*, edited by M. Marchiando Pacchiola, 7–14. Pinerolo: Arti grafiche, 1994.

Bianco, Monica. "Per la datazione di un sonetto di Vittoria Colonna (e di un probabile ritratto della poetessa ad opera di Sebastiano del Piombo." *Italique* 11 (2008): 92–107.

Blanchfield, Lyn. "The Sincere Body: The Performance of Weeping and Emotion in Late Medieval Italian Sermons." *Quidditas* 20 (1999): 117–135.

Bloom, Harold. *The Anxiety of Influence: A Theory of Poetry*. Oxford: Oxford University Press, 1973.

Blumenfeld-Kosinski, Renate. *Poets, Saints, and Visionaries of the Great Schism, 1378–1417*. University Park: Pennsylvania State University Press, 2013.

Boanas, Guy, and Lyndal Roper. "Feminine Piety in 15th-Century Rome: Francesca Romana." In *Disciplines of Faith: Studies in Religion, Politics and Patriarchy*, edited by Jim Obelkevich and Lyndal Roper, 177–193. London: Routledge, 1987.

Bolzoni, Lina. *Il cuore di cristallo*. Turin: Giulio Einaudi, 2010.

Bolzoni, Lina, and Federica Pich. *Poesia e ritratto nel Rinascimento*. Rome: Laterza, 2008.

Bonfante, Giuliano. "Femmina e donna." In *Studia philologica et literaria in honorem L. Spitzer*, edited by A. G. Hatcher and C. L. Selig, 77–109. Bern: Francke Verlag, 1958.

Bornstein, Daniel Ethan, and Roberto Rusconi, eds. *Women and Religion in Medieval and Renaissance Italy*. Chicago: University of Chicago Press, 1996.

Bozzolo, Carla. "Il 'Decameron' come fonte del 'Livre de la cité des dames' di Christine de Pisan." In *Miscellanea di studi e ricerche sul Quattrocento francese*, edited by Simone Franco, 3–24. Turin: Giappichelli, 1967.

Bremmer, Jan, and Lourens Van Den Bosch. *Between Poverty and the Pyre: Moments in the History of Widowhood*. London: Routledge, 1995.

Brine, Kevin R., Elena Ciletti, and Henrike Lähnemann, eds. *The Sword of Judith: Judith Studies across the Disciplines*. Cambridge: Open Book, 2010.

Brisson, Luc. *Sexual Ambivalence: Androgyny and Hermaphroditism in Graeco-Roman Antiquity*. Berkeley: University of California Press, 2002.

Brown, Cynthia. "The Reconstruction of an Author in Print: Christine de Pizan in the 15th and 16th Centuries." In *Christine de Pizan and the Categories of Difference*, edited by Marilynn Desmond, 215–235. Minneapolis: University of Minnesota Press, 1998.

Brownlee, Kevin. "Christine de Pizan's Canonical Authors: The Special Case of Boccaccio." *Comparative Literature Studies* 32, no. 2 (1995): 244–261.

———. "Widowhood, Sexuality, and Gender in Christine de Pizan." *Romanic Review* 86, no. 2 (1995): 339–353.

Brundin, Abigail. *Vittoria Colonna and the Spiritual Poetics of the Italian Reformation*. Burlington, VT: Ashgate, 2008.

———. "Vittoria Colonna and the Virgin Mary." *Modern Language Review* 96 (2001): 61–81.

Burrus, Virginia. "'Equipped for Victory': Ambrose and the Gendering of Orthodoxy." *Journal of Early Christian Studies* 4, no. 4 (1996): 461–475.

Butcher, John, ed. *Francesca Turini Bufalini e la "Letteratura di Genere."* Città di Castello: Biblioteca del Centro Studi "Mario Pancrazi," 2018.

Callegari, Danielle. "Grey Partridge and Middle-Aged Mutton: The Social Value of Food in the Tenzone with Forese Donati." *Dante Studies* 133, no. 1 (2015): 177–190.

Calvi, Giulia. "Widows, the State, and the Guardianship of Children in Early Modern Tuscany." In *Widowhood in Medieval and Modern Europe*, edited by Sandra Cavallo and Lyndan Warner, 209–219. New York: Routledge, 1999.

Campbell, Erin J. "Prophets, Saints, and Matriarchs: Portraits of Old Women in Early Modern Italy." *Renaissance Quarterly* 63, no. 3 (Fall 2010): 807–849.

Canepuccia, Francesca. "How to Become a Prophetess: Strategies for Authorizing a Prophetic Mission in the Works of Francesca Romana." PhD dissertation, University of Oslo, 2022.

Cappuccilli, Eleonora. "The Semantics of Obedience. Birgittine Influences on Paola Antonia Negri's Letters." In *The Legacy of Birgitta of Sweden: Women, Politics and Reform in Renaissance Italy*, edited by Unn Falkeid and Anna Wainwright, 184–209. Leiden: Brill, 2023.

Carinci, Eleonora. "Canone, Gender, Genere Letterario: Il Merito Delle Donne Di Moderata Fonte." In *Dentro/fuori, sopra/sotto: critica femminista e canone letterario negli studi di italianistica*, edited by Alessia Ronchetti and Maria Serena Sapegno, 93–100. Ravenna: Longo Angolo, 2007.

———. "Una lettera autografa inedita di Moderata Fonte (al granduca di Toscana Francesco I)." *Critica del testo* 5, no. 3 (2007): 1–11.

Carlson, Cindy L., and Angela Jane Weisl, eds. *Constructions of Widowhood and Virginity in the Middle Ages*. New York: Palgrave Macmillan, 2000.

Castiglione, Caroline. "Why Political Theory Is Women's Work: How Moderata Fonte Reclaimed Liberty for Women Inside and Outside Marriage." In *Challenging Women's Agency and Activism in Early Modernity*, edited by Merry Wiesner-Hanks and Andrea Pearson, 141–162. Amsterdam: Amsterdam University Press, 2021.

Cavallo, Jo Ann. *The Romance Epics of Boiardo, Ariosto, and Tasso from Public Duty to Private Pleasure*. Toronto: University of Toronto Press, 2016.

Cavallo, Sandra. "Proprietà o possesso? Composizione e controllo dei beni delle donne a Torino (1650–1710)." *Ricchezze delle donne: diritti patrimoniali e poteri familiari in Italia* (sec. XIII–XIX), edited by Giulia Calvi and Isabelle Chabot, 187–208. Turin: Rosenberg & Sellier, 1998.

Cavallo, Sandra, and Lyndan Warner, eds. *Widowhood in Medieval and Early Modern Europe*. New York: Routledge, 1999.

Cestaro, Gary. "Rinaldo D'Asti: Drama of the Signifié." *Carte Italiane* 7, no. 1 (1986): 14–27.

Chabot, Isabelle. "Widowhood and Poverty in Late Medieval Florence." *Continuity and Change* 3, no. 2 (1988): 291–311.

Chemello, Adriana. "La donna, il modello, l'immaginario: Moderata Fonte e Lucrezia Marinella." In *Nel cerchio della luna: figure di donna in alcuni testi del XVI secolo*, edited by Marina Zancan, 59–170. Venice: Marsilio, 1983.

———. "Letteratura di condotta e vita delle donne nelle opere di Moderata Fonte e Lucrezia Marinelli." In *Conduct Literature for and about Women in Italy 1470–1900: Prescribing and Describing Life*, edited by Helena Sanson and Francesco Lucioli, 137–158. Paris: Classiques Garnier, 2016.

———. "Oltre il recinto." In *Oltrecanone: Per una cartografia della scrittura femminile*, edited by Annamaria Crispino, 34–50. Rome: Manifestolibri, 2003.

Chojnacka, Monica. *Working Women of Early Modern Venice*. Baltimore: Johns Hopkins University Press, 2001.

Chojnacki, Stanley. *Women and Men in Renaissance Venice: Twelve Essays on Patrician Society*. Baltimore: Johns Hopkins University Press, 2002.

Clark Walter, Katherine. *The Profession of Widowhood: Widows, Pastoral Care, and Medieval Models of Holiness*. Washington, DC: Catholic University of America Press, 2018.

———. "Purgatory, Punishment, and the Discourse of Holy Widowhood in the High and Later Middle Ages." *Journal of the History of Sexuality* 16, no. 2 (2007): 169–203.

Cockram, Sara. *Isabella d'Este and Francesco Gonzaga: Power Sharing at the Italian Renaissance Court*. Farnham: Ashgate, 2013.

Cornford, Benjamin. "Christine de Pizan's *Ditie de Jehanne d'Arc*: Poetry and Propaganda at the Court of Charles VII." *Parergon* 17, no. 2 (2000): 75–106.

Costa-Zalessow, Natalia. "Francesca Turini Bufalini's Encomiastic Poems for Lucrezia Tomacelli Colonna." *Italica* 90, no. 3 (2013): 365–377.

———. "The Personification of Italy from Dante through the Trecento." *Italica* 68, no. 3 (1991): 316–331.

Cox, Virginia. "The Exemplary Vittoria Colonna." In *A Companion to Vittoria Colonna*, edited by Abigail Brundin, Tatiana Crivelli, and Maria Serena Sapegno, 467–502. London: Brill, 2016.

———. "The Female Voice in Italian Renaissance Dialogue." *MLN* 128, no. 1 (2013): 53–78.

———. *Lyric Poetry by Women of the Italian Renaissance*. Baltimore: Johns Hopkins University Press, 2013.

———. *The Prodigious Muse: Women's Writing in Counter-Reformation Italy*. Baltimore: Johns Hopkins University Press, 2011.

———. *The Renaissance Dialogue: Literary Dialogue in Its Social and Political Contexts, Castiglione to Galileo*. Cambridge: Cambridge University Press, 1992.

———. "The Single Self: Feminist Thought and the Marriage Market in Early Modern Venice." *Renaissance Quarterly* 48, no. 3 (Autumn 1995): 513–581.

———. "Women Writers and the Canon in Sixteenth-Century Italy." In *Strong Voices, Weak History: Early Women Writers and Canons in England, France, and Italy*, edited by Pamela Jones Benson and Victoria Kirkham, 14–31. Ann Arbor: University of Michigan Press, 2005.

———. *Women's Writing in Italy, 1400–1650*. Baltimore: Johns Hopkins University Press, 2008.

Cox, Virginia, and Shannon McHugh, eds. *Vittoria Colonna: Poetry, Religion, Art, Impact*. Amsterdam: Amsterdam University Press, 2021.

Crabb, Ann. *The Strozzi of Florence: Widowhood and Family Solidarity in the Renaissance*. Ann Arbor: University of Michigan Press, 2000.

Crivelli, Tatiana. "The Print Tradition of Vittoria Colonna's *Rime*." In *A Companion to Vittoria Colonna*, edited by Abigail Brundin, Tatiana Crivelli, and Maria Serena Sapegno, 69–139. London: Brill, 2016.

Crum, Roger J. "Judith between the Private and Public Realms in Renaissance Florence." In *The Sword of Judith: Judith Studies across the Disciplines*, edited by Kevin R. Brine, Elena Ciletti, and Henrike Lähnemann, 291–306. Cambridge: Open Book, 2010.

———. "Severing the Neck of Pride: Donatello's Judith and Holofernes and the Recollection of Albizzi Shame in Medicean Florence." *Artibus et Historiae* 22 (2001): 23–29.

Cupperi, Walter. "Il nome fatale di Vittoria: note su due medaglie della Marchesa di Pescara." In *Lo sguardo archeologico: i normalisti per Paul Zanker*, edited by Francesco De Angelis, 239–253. Pisa: Scuola Normale Superiore, 2007.

D'Agostino, Alfonso. *La matrona d'Efeso e la vedova consolata: Il personaggio della vedova nella letteratura medievale*. Milano: CUEM, 2019.

Delmolino, Grace. "The Economics of Conjugal Debt from Gratian's *Decretum* to *Decameron* 2.10: Boccaccio, Canon Law, and the Loss of Interest in Sex." In *Reconsidering Boccaccio: Medieval Contexts and Global Intertexts*, edited by Olivia Holmes and Dana E. Stewart, 133–163. Toronto: University of Toronto Press, 2018.

De Maldé, Vania. "Appunti per la storia dell'elegia volgare in Italia tra Umanesimo e Barocco." *Studi Secenteschi* 37, no. 1 (1996): 109–134.

Desmond, Marilynn. *Christine de Pizan and the Categories of Difference*. Minneapolis: University of Minnesota Press, 1998.

———. *Reading Dido: Gender, Textuality, and the Medieval Aeneid*. Minneapolis: University of Minnesota Press, 1994.

DeVun, Leah. *The Shape of Sex: Nonbinary Gender from Genesis to the Renaissance*. New York: Columbia University Press, 2021.

Díaz, Sara E. "Authority and Misogamy in Boccaccio's *Trattatello in laude di Dante*." In *Reconsidering Boccaccio: Medieval Contexts and Global Intertexts*, edited by Olivia Holmes and Dana E. Stewart, 164–188. Toronto: University of Toronto Press, 2018.

———. "'Dietro a lo sposo, sì la sposa piace': Marriage in Dante's *Commedia*." PhD dissertation, New York University, 2012.

Diefendorf, Barbara B. "Widowhood and Remarriage in Sixteenth-Century Paris." *Journal of Family History* 7, no. 4 (1982): 379–395.

Dionisotti, Carlo. *Scritti sul Bembo*. Edited by Claudio Vela. Turin: Einaudi, 2002.

Ditchfield, Simon. "Thinking with Saints: Sanctity and Society in the Early Modern World." *Critical Inquiry* 35, no. 3 (2009): 552–584.

Doglio, Maria Luisa, and Mario Guglielminetti. "La letteratura a corte." In *Storia di Torino III: Dalla dominazione francese alla ricomposizione dello stato*, edited by Giuseppe Ricuperati, 599–672. Turin: Einaudi, 1998.

Douglas, Mary. *Purity and Danger: An Analysis of Concepts of Pollution and Taboo*. London: Routledge, 2015.

Durling, Robert M. "A Long Day in the Sun: *Decameron* 8.7." In *Shakespeare's "Rough Magic": Renaissance Essays in Honor of C. L. Barber*, edited by Peter Erickson, 269–275. Newark: University of Delaware Press, 1985.

Dutschke, Dennis. "Petrarch's Triumphal and Cheerful ('Allegra') Judith (Triumphys Cupidinis III, 52–57)." *Nuova Rivista Di Letteratura Italiana* 1, no. 1 (1998): 35–72.

Eckstein, Nicholas A. "The Widows' Might: Women's Identity and Devotion in the Brancacci Chapel." *Oxford Art Journal* 28, no. 1 (2005): 101–118.

Eisenbichler, Konrad. *The Sword and the Pen: Women, Politics, and Poetry in Sixteenth-Century Siena*. Notre Dame, IN: University of Notre Dame Press, 2012.

Elliott, Dyan. *Proving Woman: Female Spirituality and Inquisitional Culture in the Later Middle Ages*. Princeton, NJ: Princeton University Press, 2004.

Ellis, Roger H. "The Swedish Woman, the Widow, the Pilgrim and the Prophetess: Images of St. Bridget in the Canonization Sermon to Pope Boniface IX." In *Santa Brigida, profeta dei tempi nuovi*, 93–150. Rome: Libreria Editrice Vaticana, 1993.

Emmett, Kelin. "Resisting Marriage, Reclaiming Right: An (Early) Modern Critique of Marriage." *Journal of the American Philosophical Association* 8, no. 4 (2022): 721–740.

Esch, Arnold. *Tre sante ed il loro ambiente sociale a Roma: S. Francesca romana, S. Brigida di Svezia e S. Caterina da Siena*. Rome: Roma nel Rinscimento, 2001.

Esposito, Anna. "St. Francesca and the Female Religious Communities of Fifteenth-Century Rome." In *Women and Religion in Medieval and Renaissance Italy*, edited by Daniel Bornstein and Roberto Rusconi, translated by Margery J. Schneider, 197–218. Chicago: University of Chicago Press, 1996.

Evangelisti, Silvia. "Wives, Widows, and Brides of Christ: Marriage and the Convent in the Historiography of Early Modern Italy." *Historical Journal* 43, no. 1 (2000): 233–247.

Falkeid, Unn. *The Avignon Papacy Contested: An Intellectual History from Dante to Catherine of Siena*. Cambridge, MA: Harvard University Press, 2017.

Falkeid, Unn, and Anna Wainwright, eds. *The Legacy of Birgitta of Sweden: Women, Politics, and Reform in Renaissance Italy*. Leiden: Brill, 2023.

Ferm, Olle, Alessandra Perricciolí Saggese, and Marcello Rotili. *Santa Brigida, Napoli, l'Italia: atti del convegno di studi italo-svedese, Santa Maria Capua Vetere, 10–11 maggio 2006*. Naples: Arte tipografica, 2009.

ffolliott, Sheila. "Catherine de' Medici as Artemisia: Figuring the Powerful Widow." In *Rewriting the Renaissance: The Discourses of Sexual Difference in Early Modern Europe*, edited by Margaret Ferguson, Maureen Quilligan, and Nancy Vickers, 227–241. Chicago: University of Chicago Press, 1986.

Freccero, Carla. "Talking Commodities: Woman in a Renaissance Text." *Rethinking Marxism* 3, no. 4 (September 1990): 238–250.

Freccero, John. *In Dante's Wake*. Edited by Danielle Callegari and Melissa Swain. New York: Fordham University Press, 2015.

Friedrichs, Rhoda L. "The Remarriage of Elite Widows in the Later Middle Ages." *Florilegium* 23, no. 1 (2006): 69–83.

Galli Stampino, Maria. "A Regent and Her Court: Towards a Study of Maria Maddalena d'Austria's Patronage (Florence 1621–28)." *Forum Italicum* 40, no. 1 (2006): 22–35.

Garrard, Mary D. *Artemisia Gentileschi and Feminism in Early Modern Europe*. London: Reaktion Books, 2020.

Gilbert, Sandra M., and Susan Gubar. *The Madwoman in the Attic: The Woman Writer and the Nineteenth-Century Literary Imagination*. New Haven, CT: Yale University Press, 1978.

Giusti, Francesco. "Le circostanze del dolore. Il canzoniere di fine cinquecento di Francesca Turina Bufalini e i suoi modelli." *Rinascimento* 52 (2012): 251–290.

Goethals, Jessica. "The Flowers of Italian Literature: Language, Imitation and Gender Debates in Paolo Giovio's Dialogus de Viris et Foeminis Aetate Nostra Florentibus." *Renaissance Studies* 29, no. 5 (2015): 749–771.

———. *Margherita Costa, Diva of the Baroque Court*. Toronto: University of Toronto Press, 2023.

———. "Representing the Sack of Rome and Its Aftermath: 1527–1540." PhD dissertation, New York University, 2012.

Goethals, Jessica, and Anna Wainwright. "Ventriloquizing Birgitta: The Saint's Prophetic Voice During the Italian Wars." In *The Legacy of Birgitta of Sweden: Women, Politics and Reform in Renaissance Italy*, edited by Unn Falkeid and Anna Wainwright, 155–183. Leiden: Brill, 2023.

Gonzalez, Marta. "Pageantry and the Projection of Status: The Triumphal Entries of Catherine of Austria (1585) and Christine of France (1620) in Turin." *Mélanges de l'Ecole française de Rome. Italie et Méditerranée* 115, no. 1 (2003): 29–50.

Gouwens, Kenneth. "Female Virtue and the Embodiment of Beauty: Vittoria Colonna in Paolo Giovio's Notable Men and Women." *Renaissance Quarterly* 68, no. 1 (2015): 33–97.

Gragnolati, Manuele. *Experiencing the Afterlife: Soul and Body in Dante and Medieval Culture*. Notre Dame, IN: University of Notre Dame Press, 2008.

Greenfield, Matthew. "The Cultural Functions of Renaissance Elegy." *English Literary Renaissance* 28, no. 1 (Winter 1998): 75–94.

Griffin, Miranda. "Fortune's Touch: Reading Transformation in Christine de Pizan's *Mutacion de Fortune*." In *Ovidian Transversions: "Iphis and Ianthe," 1300–1650*, edited by Valerie Traub, Patricia Badir, and Peggy McCracken, 99–117. Edinburgh: Edinburgh University Press, 2019.

Grudin, M. P. "Making War on the Widow: Boccaccio's *Il Corbaccio* and Florentine Liberty." *Viator* 38, no. 2 (2007): 127–158.

Gutt, Blake. "Transgender Mutation and the Canon: Christine de Pizan's *Livre de La Mutacion de Fortune*." *Postmedieval* 11, no. 4 (2020): 451–458.

Hairston, Julia L. "Skirting the Issue: Machiavelli's Caterina Sforza." *Renaissance Quarterly* 53, no. 3 (2000): 687–712.

Hampton, Timothy. *Writing from History: The Rhetoric of Exemplarity in Renaissance Literature*. Ithaca, NY: Cornell University Press, 1990.

Harness, Kelley. *Echoes of Women's Voices: Music, Art, and Female Patronage in Early Modern Florence*. Chicago: University of Chicago Press, 2006.

Harris, Marguerite T., and Albert Tyle Kezel. *Birgitta of Sweden: Life and Selected Writings*. New York: Paulist Press, 1989.

Harris, Sarah. "Letting (H)Anna Speak: An Intertextual Reading of the New Testament Prophetess (Luke 2.36–38)." *Feminist Theology* 27, no. 1 (September 2018): 60–74.

Herlihy, David. *The Family in Renaissance Italy*. St. Charles, MO: Forum Press, 1974.

———. *Mapping Households in Medieval Italy*. Washington, DC: Catholic University of America Press, 1972.

Herlihy, David, and Christiane Klapisch-Zuber. *Tuscans and Their Families: A Study of the Florentine Catasto of 1427*. New Haven, CT: Yale University Press, 1985.

Herzig, Tamar. *Savonarola's Women: Visions and Reform in Renaissance Italy*. Chicago: University of Chicago Press, 2007.

Hoagland, Valerie. "Unstable Exemplarity: The Politics of Female Biography in Early Modern Italy." PhD dissertation, New York University, 2016.

Hollander, Robert. *Boccaccio's Last Fiction: "Il Corbaccio."* Philadelphia: University of Pennsylvania Press, 1988.

Holmes, Olivia. *Dante's Two Beloveds: Ethics and Erotics in the "Divine Comedy."* New Haven, CT: Yale University Press, 2008.

Hook, Judith. *The Sack of Rome: 1527*. 2nd ed. New York: Palgrave Macmillan, 2004.

Hughes, Diane Owen. "Mourning Rites, Memory, and Civilization in Premodern Italy." In *Riti e Rituali Nelle Società Medievali*, edited by Jacques Chiffoleau, Lauro Martines, and Agostino Paravicini Bagliani, 23–38. Spoleto: Centro Italiano di Studi sull'Alto Medioevo, 1994.

Hurlburt, Holly S. *Daughter of Venice: Caterina Corner, Queen of Cyprus and Woman of the Renaissance*. New Haven, CT: Yale University Press, 2015.

Jensen, De Mar. "Catherine de' Medici and Her Florentine Friends." *Sixteenth Century Journal* 9, no. 2 (1978): 57–74.

Jones, Ann Rosalind. *The Currency of Eros: Women's Love Lyric in Europe, 1540–1620*. Bloomington: Indiana University Press, 1990.

Jordan, Constance. *Renaissance Feminism: Literary Texts and Political Models*. Ithaca, NY: Cornell University Press, 1990.

Joyce, Paul. "Lamentations and the Grief Process: A Psychological Reading." *Biblical Interpretation* 1, no. 3 (1993): 304–320.

Kaiser, Barbara Bakke. "Poet as 'Female Impersonator': The Image of Daughter Zion as Speaker in Biblical Poems of Suffering." *Journal of Religion* 67, no. 2 (April 1987): 164–182.

Kay, Sarah. "The Didactic Space: The City in Christine de Pizan, Augustine, and Irigaray." In *Text und Kultur: Mittelalterliche Literatur 1150–1450*, edited by Ursula Peters, 438–466. Stuttgart: J.B. Metzler, 2001.

Kellogg, Judith L. "Transforming Ovid: The Metamorphosis of Female Authority." In *Christine de Pizan and the Categories of Difference*, edited by Marilynn Desmond, 181–194. Minneapolis: University of Minnesota Press, 1998.

King, Catherine E. *Renaissance Women Patrons: Wives and Widows in Italy c. 1300–c. 1550*. New York: Manchester University Press, 2004.

King, Margaret L. "Thwarted Ambitions: Six Learned Women of the Italian Renaissance." *Soundings: An Interdisciplinary Journal* 59, no. 3 (1976): 280–304.

Kirkham, Victoria. "Why Is Pampinea 28? Pythagoras Meets Aquinas in the *Decameron*." *Bibliotheca Dantesca: Journal of Dante Studies* 3 (2020): 26–70.

Klapisch-Zuber, Christiane. *Women, Family, and Ritual in Renaissance Italy*. Chicago: University of Chicago Press, 1985.

Kohl, Benjamin G., and Ronald Witt, eds. *The Earthly Republic: Italian Humanists on Government and Society*. Philadelphia: University of Pennsylvania Press, 1997.

Kolsky, Stephen. *The Ghost of Boccaccio: Writings on Famous Women in Renaissance Italy*. Turnhout: Brepols, 2005.

———. "Moderata Fonte, Lucrezia Marinella, Giuseppe Passi: An Early Seventeenth-Century Feminist Controversy." *MLN* 96, no. 4 (2001): 973–989.

Konstan, David. *The Emotions of the Ancient Greeks: Studies in Aristotle and Classical Literature*. Toronto: University of Toronto Press, 2006.

Kuehn, Thomas. *Law, Family, and Women: Toward a Legal Anthropology of Renaissance Italy*. Chicago: University of Chicago Press, 1994.

LaFleur, Greta, Masha Raskolnikov, and Anna Kłosowska, eds. *Trans Historical: Gender Plurality before the Modern*. Ithaca, NY: Cornell University Press, 2021.

Lancaster, Jordan. *In the Shadow of Vesuvius: A Cultural History of Naples*. London: I.B. Tauris, 2019.

Lansing, Carol. *Passion and Order: Restraint of Grief in the Medieval Italian Communes*. Ithaca, NY: Cornell University Press, 2008.

Larsen, Anne R. "Paradox and the Praise of Women: From Ortensio Lando and Charles Estienne to Marie de Romieu." *Sixteenth Century Journal* 28, no. 3 (1997): 759–774.

Le Goff, Jacques. *The Birth of Purgatory*. Chicago: University of Chicago Press, 1991.

Lester, Katherine, and Bess Viola Oerke. *Accessories of Dress: An Illustrated Encyclopedia*. North Chelmsford, MA: Courier, 2013.

Levy, Allison M. *Re-Membering Masculinity in Early Modern Florence: Widowed Bodies, Mourning, and Portraiture*. Burlington, VT: Ashgate, 2006.

———. *Widowhood and Visual Culture in Early Modern Europe*. Burlington, VT: Ashgate, 2003.

Lloyd, Karen J. "Baciccio's Beata Ludovica Albertoni Distributing Alms." *Getty Research Journal* 2 (2010): 1–18.

Lowe, K. J. P. "A Matter of Piety or of Family Tradition and Custom? The Religious Patronage of Piero de' Medici and Lucrezia Tornabuoni." In *Piero de' Medici "il Gottoso" (1416–1469): Kunst im Dienste der Mediceer*, edited by Andreas Beyer and Bruce Boucher, 55–69. Berlin: Akademie Verlag, 1993.

Luongo, Thomas. "God's Words, or Birgitta's? Birgitta of Sweden as Author." In *A Companion to Birgitta of Sweden*, edited by Maria H. Oen, 25–52. Leiden: Brill, 2019.

MacDonald, Joyce Green. *Women and Race in Early Modern Texts*. Cambridge: Cambridge University Press, 2002.

Magnanini, Suzanne. "Una Selva Luminosa: The Second Day of Moderata Fonte's *Il Merito delle donne*." *Modern Philology* 101, no. 2 (2003): 278–296.

Marcus, Millicent. "Misogyny as Misreading: A Gloss on Decameron VII.7." *Stanford Italian Review* 4, no. 1 (1984): 23–40.

Margolis, Nadia. "Christine De Pizan: The Poetess as Historian." *Journal of the History of Ideas* 47, no. 3 (1986): 361–375.

Martin, Molly M. "Critical Introduction." In *Veronica Gambara, Complete Poems: A Bilingual Edition*, edited and translated by Paola Ugolini and Molly M. Martin. Toronto: Iter, 2014.

———. "Veronica Gambara: Widowhood, Poetry, and Power in Italian Renaissance Court Culture." PhD dissertation, New York University, 2007.

Martinez, Ronald L. "Also Known as 'Prencipe Galeotto' (*Decameron*)." In *Boccaccio: A Critical Guide to the Complete Works*, edited by Victoria Kirkham, Michael Sherberg, and Janet Smarr, 23–40. Chicago: University of Chicago Press, 2013.

———. "Dante between Hope and Despair: The Tradition of Lamentations in the *Divine Comedy*." *Logos* 5, no. 3 (2002): 45–76.

———. "Mourning Beatrice: The Rhetoric of Threnody in the *Vita nuova*." *MLN* 113, no. 1 (1998): 1–29.

McClure, George W. *Sorrow and Consolation in Italian Humanism*. Princeton, NJ: Princeton University Press, 1990.

McHam, Sarah Blake. "Donatello's Bronze *David* and *Judith* as Metaphors of Medici Rule in Florence." *Art Bulletin* 83, no. 1 (2001): 32–47.

McHugh, Shannon. "A Guided Tour of Heaven and Hell: The Otherworldly Journey in Chiara Matraini and Lucrezia Marinella." *Early Modern Women* 9, no. 1 (2014): 25–46.

———. *Petrarch and the Making of Gender in Renaissance Italy.* Amsterdam: Amsterdam University Press, 2023.

———. "Rethinking Vittoria Colonna: Gender and Desire in the Rime Amorose." *The Italianist* 33, no. 3 (2013): 345–360.

McHugh, Shannon, and Anna Wainwright, eds. *Innovation in the Italian Counter-Reformation.* Newark: University of Delaware Press, 2020.

Medin, Antonio, and Ludovico Frati, eds. *Lamenti storici dei secoli XIV, XV, e XVI.* 3 vols. Bologna, 1887–1894.

Michel, Parisse. *Veuves et veuvage dans le Haut Moyen Age.* Paris: Picard, 1993.

Migiel, Marilyn. *A Rhetoric of the Decameron.* Toronto: University of Toronto Press, 2003.

Migiel, Marilyn, and Juliana Schiesari, eds. *Refiguring Woman: Perspectives on Gender and the Italian Renaissance.* Ithaca, NY: Cornell University Press, 1991.

Milligan, Gerry. "Masculinity and Machiavelli." In *Seeking Real Truths: Multidisciplinary Perspectives on Machiavelli*, edited by Patricia Vilches and Gerald Seaman, 149–172. Leiden: Brill, 2007.

———. *Moral Combat: Women, Gender, and War in Italian Renaissance Literature.* Toronto: University of Toronto Press, 2018.

———. "The Politics of Effeminacy in 'Il Cortegiano.'" *Italica* 83, no. 3/4 (2006): 345–366.

———. "Proving Masculinity before God and Women: Laura Terracina and Chiara Matraini Writing War in the Renaissance." In *The Poetics of Masculinity in Early Modern Italy and Spain*, edited by Gerry Milligan and Jane Tylus, 185–212. Toronto: University of Toronto Press, 2010.

———. "Unlikely Heroines in Lucrezia Tornabuoni's 'Judith' and 'Esther.'" *Italica* 88, no. 4 (2011): 538–564.

Mills, Robert. *Seeing Sodomy in the Middle Ages.* Chicago: University of Chicago Press, 2015.

Mirrer, Louise, ed. *Upon My Husband's Death: Widows in the Literature and Histories of Medieval Europe.* Ann Arbor: University of Michigan Press, 1992.

Monti, Simone. "Widows, Poetry, and Portraits: Livia Spinola and Francesca Turina on the Portraits of Their Dead Husbands." In *Petrarch and Sixteenth-Century Italian Portraiture*, edited by Ilaria Bernocchi, Niccolò Morelli, and Federica Pich, 43–61. Amsterdam: Amsterdam University Press, 2024.

Moore, Carey A. *Judith: A New Translation with Introduction and Commentary.* New York: Doubleday, 1985.

Moroni, Ornella. *Carlo Gualteruzzi, 1500–1577 e i corrispondenti.* Vatican City: Biblioteca apostolica vaticana, 1984.

Murphy, Caroline. *Lavinia Fontana: A Painter and Her Patrons in Sixteenth-Century Bologna.* New Haven, CT: Yale University Press, 2003.

Musto, Ronald G. *Apocalypse in Rome: Cola Di Rienzo and the Politics of the New Age.* Berkeley: University of California Press, 2003.

Muyo, Kristen Keach. "Boccaccio's Pisan Allegory of 'Death' in Petrarch's Triumphus Mortis." *California Italian Studies* 11, no. 1 (2022): 1–21.

Newman, Barbara. *From Virile Woman to WomanChrist: Studies in Medieval Religion and Literature.* Philadelphia: University of Pennsylvania Press, 1995.

———. "What Did It Mean to Say 'I Saw'? The Clash between Theory and Practice in Medieval Visionary Culture." *Speculum* 80, no. 1 (2005): 1–43.

Nurra, Fabrizio. *Chiara Maria della Passione, carmelitana scalza: un'eremita nel cuore di Trastevere.* Rome: OCD, 2012.

Oen, Maria H., ed. *A Companion to Birgitta of Sweden and Her Legacy in the Later Middle Ages.* Leiden: Brill, 2019.

Oen, Maria H., and Unn Falkeid, eds. *Sanctity and Female Authorship: Birgitta of Sweden and Catherine of Siena.* New York: Routledge, 2019.

Olson, Kristina. "Uncovering the Historical Body of Florence: Dante, Forese Donati, and Sumptuary Legislation." *Italian Culture* 33 (2015): 1–15.

Oort, Johannes van. *Jerusalem and Babylon: A Study into Augustine's* City of God *and the Sources of His Doctrine of the Two Cities.* New York: Brill, 2015.

Panizza, Letizia. "Plutarch's Camma: A Greek Literary Heroine's Adventures in Renaissance Italy." In *Italy and the Classical Tradition: Language, Thought and Poetry 1300–1600*, edited by Carlo Caruso and Andrew Laird, 101–117. London: Bloomsbury, 2013.

Papworth, Amelia. "Pressure to Publish: Laura Terracina and Her Editors." *Early Modern Women* 12, no. 1 (2017): 3–24.

Parker, Deborah. "Ideology and Cultural Practice: The Case of Dante's Treatment of Beatrice d'Este." *Dante Studies* 111 (1993): 131–147.

Perlove, Shelley Karen. *Bernini and the Idealization of Death: The Blessed Ludovica Albertoni and the Altieri Chapel.* University Park: Pennsylvania State University Press, 1995.

Perocco, Daria. "Caterina Cornaro: una corte, una regina e la creazione di un mito." *MLN* 129, no. 3 (2014): S35–S44.

Phillippy, Patricia. "Establishing Authority: Boccaccio's *De Claris Mulieribus* and Christine de Pizan's *Le Livre de La Cité des Dames.*" *Romanic Review* 77, no. 3 (1986): 167–194.

Planché, James Robinson. *A Cyclopaedia of Costume or Dictionary of Dress, Including Notices of Contemporaneous Fashions on the Continent: The Dictionary.* London: Chatto and Windus, 1876.

Psaki, Regina. "Women Make All Things Lose Their Power: Women's Knowledge, Men's Fear in the *Decameron* and the *Corbaccio.*" *Heliotropia* 1, no. 1 (2018): 1–13.

Pucci, Paolo. "Finalmente libera, ma non per molto: la vedova nella trattatistica italiana del XVI secolo." *Rivista Di Studi Italiani* 33, no. 1 (2015): 187–214.

———. *Tra ideale e reale. La vedova (in)dipendente nella trattatistica e nei carteggi italiani* (sec. XV–XVII). Rome: Edizioni di storia e letteratura, 2024.

Quondam, Amedeo. "Le cose (e le parole) del mondo." In Giovanni Boccaccio, *Decameron*, edited by Amedeo Quondam, Maurizio Fiorilla, and Giancarlo Alfano, 1669–1815. Milan: BUR Rizzoli, 2013.

Rabitti, Giovanna. "Vittoria Colonna as Role Model for Cinquecento Women Poets." In *Women in Italian Renaissance Culture and Society*, edited by Letizia Panizza, 478–497. Oxford: European Humanities Research Association, 2000.

———. "Vittoria Colonna, Bembo e Firenze: un caso di ricezione e qualche postilla." *Studi e problem di critica testuale* 44 (1992): 127–155.

Ray, Meredith K. "Scientific Culture and the Renaissance *Querelle des Femme*." In *Daughters of Alchemy: Women and Scientific Culture in Early Modern Italy*, 73–110. Cambridge, MA: Harvard University Press, 2015.

Reeves, Marjorie. *The Influence of Prophecy in the Later Middle Ages: A Study in Joachimism*. Notre Dame, IN: University of Notre Dame Press, 1994.

Refini, Eugenio. "Con Bel Parlar. Il Fascino Ambiguo Di Giuditta Figura Eloquentiae Tra Petrarca e Possevino." In *Le Donne Della Bibbia. La Bibbia Delle Donne. Teatro, Letteratura e Vita, Atti Del XV Convegno Internazionale Di Studio*, edited by Camos Gorris Rosanna, 275–286. Fasano: Schena Editore, 2012.

———. "Giuditta, Armida, e il velo della seduzione." *Italian Studies* 68 (2013): 78–98.

———. "'Parole Tronche et Imperfette': The Lament as a 'Mode' across Poetical and Musical Genres." *The Italianist* 40, no. 3 (2020): 441–462.

Regan, Lisa K. "Ariosto's Threshold Patron: Isabella d'Este in the 'Orlando Furioso.'" *MLN* 120, no. 1 (2005): 50–69.

Reid, Elizabeth. "Female Representation and Violence in the Ceremonial Entries of the Italian Wars." *Renaissance Studies* 36, no. 5 (2022): 750–768.

Richardson, Brian. "*Amore maritale*: Advice on Love and Marriage in the Second Half of the Cinquecento." In *Women in Italian Renaissance Culture and Society*, edited by Letizia Panizza, 194–208. Oxford: Oxford University Press, 2000.

Ricuperati, Giuseppe. *Storia di Torino III: Dalla dominazione francese alla ricomposizione dello Stato (1536–1630)*. Turin: Einaudi, 1997.

Riddle, Donald Wayne. "Early Christian Hospitality: A Factor in the Gospel Transmission." *Journal of Biblical Literature* 57, no. 2 (1938): 141–154.

Robin, Diana. "The Breasts of Vittoria Colonna." *California Italian Studies* 3, no. 1 (2012): 1–16.

———. *Publishing Women: Salons, the Presses, and the Counter-Reformation in Sixteenth-Century Italy*. Chicago: University of Chicago Press, 2007.

Rosenwein, Barbara H. *Generations of Feeling: A History of Emotions, 600–1700*. Cambridge: Cambridge University Press, 2016.

Ross, Sarah Gwyneth. *The Birth of Feminism: Woman as Intellect in Renaissance Italy and England*. Cambridge, MA: Harvard University Press, 2009.

Rossini, Ilaria. "La voce della vedova. Temi e motivi da Giovanni Boccaccio a Francesca Turini Bufalini." In *Francesca Turini Bufalini e La "Letteratura Di Genere,"* edited by John Butcher, 191–196. Città di Castello: Biblioteca del Centro Studi "Mario Pancrazi," 2018.

Russo, Vittorio. "Perorazioni d'amore da parte di 'donne' e 'femmine' nel *Decamerone*." In *Con le Muse in Parnaso*, 88–107. Naples: Bibliopolis, 1983.

Sahlin, Claire. *Birgitta of Sweden and the Voice of Prophecy*. Woodbridge: Boydell & Brewer, 2001.

Sanson, Helena. "Conduct for the Real Widow: Giulio Cesare Cabei's *Ornamenti Della Gentildonna Vedova* (1574)." In *Conduct Literature for and about Women in Italy, 1470–1900: Prescribing and Describing Life*, edited by Helena Sanson and Francesco Lucioli, 41–61. Paris: Classiques Garnier, 2016.

———. "Donne Che (Non) Ridono: Parola E Riso Nella Precettistica Femminile Del XVI Secolo in Italia." *Italian Studies* 60, no. 1 (Spring 2005): 6–21.

———. "Widowhood and Conduct in Late Sixteenth-Century Italy: The 'Unusual' Case of *La vedova del Fusco* (1570)." *The Italianist* 35, no. 1 (2015): 1–26.

Sanson, Helena, and Francesco Lucioli, eds. *Conduct Literature for and about Women in Italy, 1470–1900: Prescribing and Describing Life*. Paris: Classiques Garnier, 2016.

Sapegno, Maria Serena. *Al crocevia della storia: Poesia, religione e politica in Vittoria Colonna*. Rome: Viella, 2016.

———, ed. "La costruzione di un Io Lirico al femminile nella poesia di Vittoria Colonna." *Versants* 46 (2003): 15–37.

Scanlan, Suzanne M. *Divine and Demonic Imagery at Tor de'Specchi, 1400–1500: Religious Women and Art in Fifteenth-Century Rome*. Amsterdam: Amsterdam University Press, 2018.

Schiesari, Juliana. *The Gendering of Melancholia: Feminism, Psychoanalysis, and the Symbolics of Loss in Renaissance Literature*. Ithaca, NY: Cornell University Press, 1992.

Serrano, Andrés García. "Anna's Characterization in Luke 2:36–38: A Case of Conceptual Allusion?" *Catholic Biblical Quarterly* 76, no. 3 (2014): 464–480.

Shaw, Christine, and Michael Mallett. *The Italian Wars 1494–1559: War, State and Society in Early Modern Europe*. New York: Routledge, 2019.

Simpson, James. "Subjects of Triumph and Literary History: Dido and Petrarch in Petrarch's *Africa* and *Trionfi*." *Journal of Medieval and Early Modern Studies* 35, no. 3 (2005): 489–508.

Smarr, Janet Levarie. *Joining the Conversation: Dialogues by Renaissance Women*. Ann Arbor: University of Michigan Press, 2005.

Smith, Alison A. "Locating Power and Influence within the Provincial Elite of Verona: Aristocratic Wives and Widows." *Renaissance Studies* 8, no. 4 (2008): 439–448.

Smith, Graham. "Bronzino's 'Portrait of Laura Battiferri.'" *Source: Notes in the History of Art* 15, no. 4 (1996): 30–38.

Smith, Mary. "Marlowe and Italian Dido Drama." *Italica* 53, no. 2 (1976): 223–235.

Smith, William E. "Unintended Bigamies: Holy Widowhood, Marriage, and Sponsa Christi in Erasmus's *De Vidua Christiana*." *Harvard Theological Review* 110, no. 2 (April 2017): 241–264.

Solerti, Angelo. *Musica, ballo e drammatica alla Corte Medicea dal 1600 al 1637*. Florence: Bemporad, 1905.

Starn, Randolph. "Reinventing Heroes in Renaissance Italy." *Journal of Interdisciplinary History* 17, no. 1 (1986): 67–84.

Steinberg, Justin. *Law and Mimesis in Boccaccio's* Decameron: *Realism on Trial*. Cambridge: Cambridge University Press, 2023.

Stella, Clara. "A Lineage of Apocalyptic Queens: The Portrayal of Birgitta of Sweden in Domenica Narducci's Sermon to Caterina Cibo (1533)." In *The Legacy of Birgitta of Sweden: Women, Politics and Reform in Renaissance Italy*, edited by Unn Falkeid and Anna Wainwright, 107–128. Leiden: Brill, 2023.

Strocchia, Sharon T. *Death and Ritual in Renaissance Florence*. Baltimore: Johns Hopkins University Press, 1992.

———. "Funerals and the Politics of Gender in Early Renaissance Florence." In *Refiguring Woman: Perspectives on Gender and the Italian Renaissance*, edited by Marilyn Migiel and Juliana Schiesari, 155–168. Ithaca, NY: Cornell University Press, 1991.

———. "Remembering the Family: Women, Kin, and Commemorative Masses in Renaissance Florence." *Renaissance Quarterly* 42, no. 4 (1989): 635–654.

Sutherland, N. M. "Catherine de Medici: The Legend of the Wicked Italian Queen." *Sixteenth Century Journal* 9, no. 2 (July 1978): 45–56.

Swain, Melissa. "Spousal Sovereignty: The Ruling Couple and Its Representations in Quattrocento Italy with Special Reference to Federico de Montefeltro (1422–1482) and Battista Sforza (c. 1446–1472)." PhD dissertation, New York University, 2016.

Targoff, Ramie. *Renaissance Woman: The Life of Vittoria Colonna*. New York: Farrar, Straus & Giroux, 2018.

Terpstra, Nicholas. *Cultures of Charity: Women, Politics, and the Reform of Poor Relief in Renaissance Italy*. Cambridge, MA: Harvard University Press, 2013.

Todorovic, Jelena. *Dante and the Dynamics of Textual Exchange: Authorship, Manuscript Culture, and the Making of the "Vita Nova."* New York: Fordham University Press, 2016.

Tomas, Natalie. *The Medici Women: Gender and Power in Renaissance Florence*. Aldershot: Ashgate, 2003.

Torraca, Francesco. *Studi di storia letteraria napoletana*. Naples: Vigo, 1884.

Torrioli, Igea. *Francesca Turina Bufalini e la società colta tifernate nel sec. XVI*. Città di Castello: Grifani-Donati, 1940.

Trexler, Richard. *Dependence in Context in Renaissance Florence*. Binghamton, NY: Medieval and Renaissance Text and Studies, 1994.

———. *Public Life in Renaissance Florence*. Ithaca, NY: Cornell University Press, 1980.

Tylus, Jane. "'Su dunque, peregrino!': Pilgrimage and Female Spirituality in the Writings of Birgitta and Catherine." In *Sanctity and Female Authorship: Birgitta of Sweden and Catherine of Siena*, edited by Maria H. Oen and Unn Falkeid, 35–53. New York: Routledge, 2019.

———. *Reclaiming Catherine of Siena: Literacy, Literature, and the Signs of Others*. Chicago: University of Chicago Press, 2009.

———. *Sacred Narratives: Lucrezia Tornabuoni de' Medici*. Chicago: University of Chicago Press, 2001.

Valerio, Adriana. "Le lettere di Domenica da Paradiso tra Bibbia e Profezia." *Hagiographica* 6 (1999): 235–256.

Valone, Carolyn. "Roman Matrons as Patrons: Various Views of the Cloister Wall." In *The Crannied Wall: Women, Religion and the Arts in Early Modern Europe*, edited by Craig Monson, 49–72. Ann Arbor: University of Michigan Press, 1992.

———. "Women on the Quirinal Hill: Patronage in Rome, 1560–1630." *Art Bulletin* 76, no. 1 (1994): 129–146.

Vickers, Nancy. "Seeing Is Believing: Gregory, Trajan, and Dante's Art." *Dante Studies* 101 (1983): 67–85.

———. "Widowed Words: Dante, Petrarch, and the Metaphors of Mourning." In *Discourses of Authority in Medieval and Renaissance Literature*, edited by Kevin Brownlee and Walter Stephens, 97–108. Hanover, NH: University Press of New England, 1989.

Wainwright, Anna. "Outdoing Colonna: Widowhood Poetry in the Late Cinquecento." In *Vittoria Colonna: Poetry, Religion, Art, Impact*, edited by Virginia Cox and Shannon McHugh, 95–113. Amsterdam: Amsterdam University Press, 2021.

———. "Teaching Widowed Women, Community, and Devotion in Quattrocento Florence with Lucrezia Tornabuoni and Antonia Tanini Pulci." *Religions* 9, no. 3 (2018): 1–13.

———. "Widows, Lament, and Ottoman Anxieties in Quattrocento Florence." In *Gendering the Renaissance*, edited by Meredith K. Ray and Lynn Lara Westwater, 23–43. Newark: University of Delaware Press, 2023.

Wallace, David. *Giovanni Boccaccio, Decameron*. Cambridge: Cambridge University Press, 1991.

Waller, Marguerite R. *Petrarch's Poetics and Literary History*. Amherst: University of Massachusetts Press, 1980.

Walters, Lori. "The Figure of the Seulette in the Works of Christine de Pizan and Jean Gerson." In *Desireuse de plus avant enquerre*, edited by Liliane Dulac, Anne Paupert, Christine Reno, and Bernard Ribémont, 119–140. Paris: Champion, 2008.

Watkins, John. *The Specter of Dido: Spenser and Virgilian Epic*. New Haven, CT: Yale University Press, 1995.

Weaver, Elissa B. *Convent Theatre in Early Modern Italy: Spiritual Fun and Learning for Women*. Cambridge: Cambridge University Press, 2007.

———. "Dietro il vestito: La semiotica del vestire nel *Decameron*." In *La Novella Italiana: Atti Del Convegno Di Caprarola, 19–24 Settembre 1988*, vol. 2, 701–710. Rome: Salerno editrice, 1989.

———. "Fashion and Fortune in the Decameron." In *Boccaccio 1313–2013*, edited by Francesco Ciabattoni, Elsa Filosa, and Kristina Olson, 71–86. Ravenna: Longo Editore, 2015.

Weisl, Angela Jan, and Cindy L. Carlson, eds. *Constructions of Widowhood and Virginity in the Middle Ages*. New York: Palgrave, 2011.

West, Rebecca. "Decameron II, 2: A Dream Trip." *Italian Quarterly* 37, no. 143–146 (2000): 127–142.

Wheatley, Edward. "Rereading the Story of the Widow of Ephesus in the Middle Ages and the Renaissance." *Comparative Literature Studies* 51, no. 4 (2014): 627–643.

Wilczynski, Mimi. "I Nove Prodi Nella Divina Commedia." *Italica* 29, no. 1 (1952): 11–12.

Zak, Gur. "Boccaccio's Filocolo and the Polyphony of Consolation." *Mediaevalia* 42, no. 1 (2021): 187–225.

Zanini-Cordi, Irene. *Donne sciolte: abbandono ed identità femminile nella letteratura italiana*. Ravenna: Longo, 2008.

Zatti, Sergio. "Il mercante sulla ruota: la seconda giornata." In *Introduzione al Decameron*, edited by Michelangelo Picone and Margherita Mesirca, 79–98. Florence: Franco Cesati Editore, 2004.

Index

Note: Page numbers in italics refer to figures.

About the Author

ANNA WAINWRIGHT is an associate professor of Italian studies and core faculty in women's and gender studies at the University of New Hampshire. She is coeditor of the volumes *Innovation in the Italian Counter-Reformation* (University of Delaware Press, with Shannon McHugh), *Teaching Race in the European Renaissance: A Classroom Guide* (with Matthieu Chapman), and *The Legacy of Birgitta of Sweden: Women, Policy and Reform in Renaissance Italy* (with Unn Falkeid).